The Street Finds its own Uses for Mutant Technologies

Ira Nayman

This is a work of fiction. Any resemblance to people, places, small household appliances (and their attachments), motorized vehicles, piles of balloons that have not been blown up, designer drugs, criminal thugs, throw rugs or executive outplacement services either living or dead, functional or broken, a little bit country or a little bit rock and roll is purely coincidental.

ISBN-13: 978-0-9876996-3-3

CONTENTS

ACKNOWLEDGMENTS

OMG! OMG! OMG! Another book in the Alternate Reality News Service series! What does that make – four, now? How do I do it? Well, with help, of course. The help of Travis Pennington, for instance, who created another killer cover. The help of my ever-supportive parents and family. And, of course, the help of my Web Goddess Gisela McKay, without whom none of this would have been likely.

Thanks everybody!

1. ALTERNATE INTRODUCTION

Up Close and In Your Face: An Interview With Brenda Brundtland-Govanni

The Alternate Reality News Service (Earth 002) is proud to announce that it has won a Best Editing in a High Heels Dress Multiverse and Environs News Association Award (Mena) for the article "The 10 Thousand Names of Dog." This seemed like a good opportunity to get Editrix-in-Chief Brenda Brundtland-Govanni to talk a little bit about how the Alternate Reality News Service works.

At first, Brundtland-Govanni was reluctant to be interviewed (if you could characterize threatening to rip our lungs out and, just for kicks, put a dimmer switch on the iron lung we would have to live in as a result as "reluctant"). However, Brenda Brundtland-Govanni from the Earth 007 branch of the Alternate Reality News Service met with her on the pretext of improving communications between the two universes (which had been Ice Agey since the Sevartian Noodle incident on B Minor), and managed to tie Brundtland-Govanni 002 down long enough to get the following wide-ranging interview:

BRENDA BRUNDTLAND-GOVANNI 002: You know, once I get out of these ropes, I **will** make you pay for this, right?

BRENDA BRUNDTLAND-GOVANNI 007: You would do that to yourself?

BRENDA BRUNDTLAND-GOVANNI 002: Wouldn't you?

BRENDA BRUNDTLAND-GOVANNI 007: If it was me, I would already have started sucking your spleen out of your nose with a straw.

BRENDA BRUNDTLAND-GOVANNI 002: I like the way you think.

BRENDA BRUNDTLAND-GOVANNI 007: It's the way you think.

BRENDA BRUNDTLAND-GOVANNI 002: Exactly. (pause) Put that back!

BRENDA BRUNDTLAND-GOVANNI 007: What?

BRENDA BRUNDTLAND-GOVANNI 002: You just moved the *Dawn of the Dead* snow globe from one side of my desk to the other.

BRENDA BRUNDTLAND-GOVANNI 007: I…I did?

BRENDA BRUNDTLAND-GOVANNI 002: You see the blood splattering inside it? Oh, yeah. It was just moved.

BRENDA BRUNDTLAND-GOVANNI 007: I – sorry, I…I didn't realize. I'll just – ahem. Don't change the subject, ferk it! I'm here to interview you.

BRENDA BRUNDTLAND-GOVANNI 002: Okay. Sure. Bring it. Ask your questions. The longer you prolong this, the more delicious it will be when I can finally get my slapping gloves on.

BRENDA BRUNDTLAND-GOVANNI 007: I've got slapping gloves, too, you know.

BRENDA BRUNDTLAND-GOVANNI 002: Oh, bring it, bee-yotch-szay!

BRENDA BRUNDTLAND-GOVANNI 007: Is that…Czechoslovakian?

BRENDA BRUNDTLAND-GOVANNI 002: Sister, I am going to slap the ugly off of you and onto a passing turtle!

BRENDA BRUNDTLAND-GOVANNI 007: Oh, yeah? I'll slap you so far into the future, you'll have to save the Eloi from the Morlocks!

BRENDA BRUNDTLAND-GOVANNI 002: Nice classical science fiction reference.

BRENDA BRUNDTLAND-GOVANNI 007: Thank you.

BRENDA BRUNDTLAND-GOVANNI 002: But, it won't stop me from slapping you so hard your head will spin around so fast it could generate enough electricity to light up Brampton for a month!

BRENDA BRUNDTLAND-GOVANNI 007: Oh, yeah? Well, I'll slap you so hard your head will spin around so fast it will actually go back in time!

BRUNDTLAND-GOVANNI 002: So, my head will actually be younger than my body?

BRENDA BRUNDTLAND-GOVANNI 007: Talk about a lose-lose situation!

BRENDA BRUNDTLAND-GOVANNI 002: Nicely played.

BRENDA BRUNDTLAND-GOVANNI 007: Thank you. So, will you answer my questions, now?

BRENDA BRUNDTLAND-GOVANNI 002: I make no promises.

BRENDA BRUNDTLAND-GOVANNI 007: Fair enough. So, how does it feel to win the Mena?

BRENDA BRUNDTLAND-GOVANNI 002: mumble mumble…don't have time to do a ferking interview…mumble mumble…so much editing to ignore…mumble mumble…eat goat cheese…

BRENDA BRUNDTLAND-GOVANNI 007: Yeah, well, it's not like I don't have better things to do with my time, either. Welcome to my world.

BRENDA BRUNDTLAND-GOVANNI 002: Actually, we're in my world.

BRENDA BRUNDTLAND-GOVANNI 007: The interview hasn't even really started, and already you're gonna go all literalist on my ass?

BRENDA BRUNDTLAND-GOVANNI 002: Wait until the interview is over to see what I can do to your ass!

BRENDA BRUNDTLAND-GOVANNI 007: That would be a form of self-abuse.

BRENDA BRUNDTLAND-GOVANNI 002: You say tomato, I say hamburger garni – PUT THAT BACK RIGHT NOW!

BRENDA BRUNDTLAND-GOVANNI 007: Hunh? Put what back?

BRENDA BRUNDTLAND-GOVANNI 002: The Einstein relativity train/pencil sharpener goes to the left of the model guillotine, not to the right. Put it back!

BRENDA BRUNDTLAND-GOVANNI 007: Sorry. I…I didn't realize…

BRENDA BRUNDTLAND-GOVANNI 002: Madame Defarges and the other tricoteuses would not be amused!

BRENDA BRUNDTLAND-GOVANNI 007: Oh, well, I wouldn't want to, uhh, disappoint…them…

PAUSE.

BRENDA BRUNDTLAND-GOVANNI 007: Mikhail Lo-Fi, publisher of the Alternate Reality News Service across the dimensions, thought it would be a good idea to ask you how a story goes from idea to print reality. I'm not sure why he thought that was a good idea, but, here we are, so how about it?

BRENDA BRUNDTLAND-GOVANNI 002: Sure. We have writers in a variety of dimensions who use their connections to ferret out stories. They pitch the stories they find to me and, if I think they will interest our readers, I give them the go-ahead. The writers interview a variety of people and boil the information they receive down to the essence of the story, which they write. I do a first edit of the story to ensure that all of the elements that will make it comprehensible to a reader are in place; if not, I ask the writer for a rewrite. Once the basics are in place, a copy editor does a second edit to make sure that the article's spelling and grammar are correct. Then, the editorial board and I decide which edition to place the story in and how much prominence it deserves. Finally, it goes to production to design the page it will appear on, and we print the issue out.

BRENDA BRUNDTLAND-GOVANNI 007: Really? That's really how it goes?

BRENDA BRUNDTLAND-GOVANNI 002: PFAH! HA HA HA! Naah. We get an anonymous tip, the writer does as little work as possible to write a basic story about it, and I look it over to make sure it's in English and not too embarrassing to print before we print it!

BRENDA BRUNDTLAND-GOVANNI 007: Oh. Ha ha. Very funny.

BRENDA BRUNDTLAND-GOVANNI 002: Had you going, didn't I?

BRENDA BRUNDTLAND-GOVANNI 007: Not, really.

BRENDA BRUNDTLAND-GOVANNI 002: Just a little bit?

BRENDA BRUNDTLAND-GOVANNI 007: I'm a professional. I don't –

BRENDA BRUNDTLAND-GOVANNI 002: I had you going.

BRENDA BRUNDTLAND-GOVANNI 007: Harrumph! Look, I…I'm sure our readers would like to know what your relationship with technical adviser Darren Clincker-Belli is.

BRENDA BRUNDTLAND-GOVANNI 002: I have no relationship with Darren Clincker-Belli.

BRENDA BRUNDTLAND-GOVANNI 007: You say that. And, yet, you did take him home to meet our mother…

BRENDA BRUNDTLAND-GOVANNI 002: She insisted. And, she always gets her way. You know that. But, that doesn't mean I have a relationship with Darren Clincker-Belli.

BRENDA BRUNDTLAND-GOVANNI 007: How do you think Darren would feel about the fact that you are denying dating him?

BRENDA BRUNDTLAND-GOVANNI 002: He would be fine with it. Trust me, I am not dating Darren Clincker-Belli!

BRUNDTLAND-GOVANNI 007: Does Darren do your dishes?

BRUNDTLAND-GOVANNI 002: I AM NOT DATING DARREN CLINCKER-BELLI!

BRUNDTLAND-GOVANNI 007: If you say so. You were always the strongest of us at standing up to mom.

BRUNDTLAND-GOVANNI 002: You think?

BRUNDTLAND-GOVANNI 007: A word of advice: when you do give in and admit that you're dating him, you'll find that Darren has a thousand and one uses in the home…

BRENDA BRUNDTLAND-GOVANNI 002: ISN'T THIS INTERVIEW SUPPOSED TO BE ABOUT JOURNALISM?

BRENDA BRUNDTLAND-GOVANNI 007: Are you willing to answer journalism questions, now?

BRENDA BRUNDTLAND-GOVANNI 002: No. But I can deflect them more easil – PUT THAT BACK!

BRENDA BRUNDTLAND-GOVANNI 007: What?

BRENDA BRUNDTLAND-GOVANNI 002: The laser-guided letter opener! You moved it from the center front area of my desk to the left middle! That was a gift from Admiral Sklorzixxx of the Imaginary Generic Fleet for our reporting on the War of 2112!

BRENDA BRUNDTLAND-GOVANNI 007: Can I help it if you don't know how to arrange objects on your desk?

BRENDA BRUNDTLAND-GOVANNI 002: My desk! Mine! Mine! Mine! Mine! Mine! Mine! Mine! Mine! Mine! Mine!

BRENDA BRUNDTLAND-GOVANNI 007: (over her) Fine. I'll put it back. See? There. It's back.

BRENDA BRUNDTLAND-GOVANNI 002: Mine! Mine! Mine! Mine! Mine! Mine! Mine! Mine! Mine! Mine!

BRENDA BRUNDTLAND-GOVANNI 007: (over her) So, you've been reduced to incoherent word repetition by a few simple questions? That's so like me!

BRENDA BRUNDTLAND-GOVANNI 002: Mine! Mine! Mine! Mine! Mine! Mine! Mine! Mine! Mi – yes, we're more alike than I would care to admit.

BRENDA BRUNDTLAND-GOVANNI 007: The Multiverse is a strange place.

BRENDA BRUNDTLAND-GOVANNI 002: Indeed. So, have you exhausted all of your questions?

BRENDA BRUNDTLAND-GOVANNI 007: I've barely scratched the surface.

BRENDA BRUNDTLAND-GOVANNI 002: Oh. Sorry to have to do this to you, then.

BRENDA BRUNDTLAND-GOVANNI 007: Brenda, don't you da –

BRENDA BRUNDTLAND-GOVANNI 002: Mine! Mine! Mine! Mine! Mine! Mine! Mine! Mine! Mine! Mine!

BRENDA BRUNDTLAND-GOVANNI 007: (over her) Oh, now, you're just milking it!

BRENDA BRUNDTLAND-GOVANNI 002: Mine! Mine! Mine! Mine! Mine! Mine! Mine! Mine! Mine! Mine! Mine! Mine!

BRENDA BRUNDTLAND-GOVANNI 007: (over her) Mikhail will not approve!

BRENDA BRUNDTLAND-GOVANNI 002: Mine! Mine! Mine! Mine! Mine! Mine! Mine! Mine! Mine! Mine! Mine!

BRENDA BRUNDTLAND-GOVANNI 007: (over her) THIS IS REALLY CHILDISH!

BRENDA BRUNDTLAND-GOVANNI 002: Mine! Mine! Mine! Mine! Mine! Mine! Mine! Mine!

BRENDA BRUNDTLAND-GOVANNI 007: (over her) ALRIGHT! ALRIGHT, ALREADY! I'VE GOT ENOUGH! THE INTERVIEW IS OVER!

BRENDA BRUNDTLAND-GOVANNI 002: Mine! Mine! Mine! Mi – it's been a pleasure.

BRENDA BRUNDTLAND-GOVANNI 007: The pleasure was all yours.

BRENDA BRUNDTLAND-GOVANNI 002: Now, if you'll just untie these ropes…

This interview was conducted on Thursday, July 23rd. Unless it was Tuesday. Oh, you know, it was the day Mrs. Mott gave birth to her son Clamato. Wednesday, then.

2. ALTERNATE SLEEP OF REASON

Idiotocracy: A Beginner's Guide

by FRANCIS GRECOROMACOLLUDEN, Alternate Reality News Service National Politics Writer

Earth Prime 2-9-5-4-3-8 dash rho is not like other worlds. They do politics differently there.

On most planets, governments come in two flavours: rule by the few (oligarchy, autocracy, plutocracy, dictatorship, Otto - call it what you will) and limited public participation that masks the rule by the few (democracy). If ordinary people were allowed to actually control their political system, what would things look like?

We don't have to imagine (that's what YahooTube is for): it is called idiotocracy, and it dominates the political landscape of Earth Prime 2-9-5-4-3-8 dash rho.

The United States of Vesampucceri is the foremost idiotocracy on the planet. The country's Constitution guarantees that "a government of the stupid, by the stupid, for the stupid shall not perish from the Earth without a fight. And, a stupid one, at that."

The United States of Vesampucceri has two political parties. The Reduhblicans pander to a small but significant subset of the population – sometimes referred to as the "Moron Majority" – with policy ideas that, to a layperson, may appear to be unworkable, but, to an expert, actually appear to be batshit crazy. The Dumboprats generally oppose the policies of the Reduhblicans, but often vote for them anyway when out of power and rarely repeal the measures when in power. In Washburningdington, Vesampucceri's capital city, this is known as "bipartisanship."

"It's a poisonous system," explained token smart person Amy Sheshutshotshitbam. "Once a majority of people have given up on science…or, facts…or, any sort of rational argument, even if a smart person is elected, he has to water down what he does to please the stupid people. Look at what's happened to Dumbopratic President Barry W. Bushbamclintreagbush: when he was a candidate, he wrote a 767 page treatise on international political relations arguing that diplomacy was in most cases preferable to military action. Last week, in his State of the Disunion Address, his foreign policy had been reduced to two words: 'War good.' It's sad, really."

Stupiding down your political discourse only gets you so far in modern Vesampucceri, however. Token smart person Amy Sheshutshotshitbam pointed out that the party that gets out in front of the stupid can always argue that, if you have a choice between somebody who is truly stupid and somebody who only pretends to be stupid to get your support, you should vote for the genuine article. "That's a rationale that is truly inane," she added, "and, yet, at the same time, kind of brilliant."

Party politics is, however, only the beginning of the stupid. Successive Reduhblican governments placed in power people who were opposed to the mission of their agencies; these people are often referred to as idiotocrats. Bankers in charge of financial regulations. Poultry tycoons determining farm subsidies. Weapons manufacturers deciding whom to go to war with (surprise! – pretty much everybody). That sort of thing. The most egregious example occurred during the Presidency of Ron Potganreabumbom, who appointed James Wathafuloitt – an oil company executive and noted hylophobe – to head the Environmental Protection Racket.

"Did you know that trees were a major cause of greenhouse gases?" marveled token smart person Amy Sheshutshotshitbam. "Cut down all the trees and you've solved the problem. It's fascinating – isn't it? – how the stupid often coincides with the interests of big business?"

While idiotocrats work behind the scenes, political pundits – referred to as "idiotologues" when they unquestioningly push the stupid in their pronouncements – are frequently in people's faces (among other body parts). Most idiotologues promote an extreme Reduhblican agenda: they include radio and television personalities like Glenn Eckicksteinbedeck and Bill Onomoforeill. In recent years, the Dumboprats have tried to develop their own pundits, most notably Rachel O'schulbermatthow.

"Oh, I love Rachel – in a platonic way, of course," token smart person Amy Sheshutshotshitbam gushed. "The problem with her show – indeed, the problem with all of the left wing pundits – is that they still believe in facts. Facts – well – the population gave up on facts a long time ago. And, it shows: O'schulbermatthow's ratings have never been more than a fraction of Onomoforeill's."

What is the result of such a drastic stupiding of a country's political discourse? "We're number one! We're number one!" hooted citizen Pete Fazzigrenatchmann, despite the fact that the only thing international surveys show Vesampucceri to actually be number one at is loudly – some would say obnoxiously – proclaiming that it is, in fact, number one.

"If I vote Reduhblican in the next election," exclaimed Sharron Eichgeblungalonn, "jelly beans will rain from the skies instead of snow! Can you imagine bathing in jelly beans? I'll bet they give you an all over sugary glow of goodness!"

"If I keep borrowing money," explained stock broker Jerry Sisnaisherbergman, "I will eventually owe my way out of debt!" He was actually grinning when he said this. Happily grinning.

"Can I emigrate to your universe?" token smart person Amy Sheshutshotshitbam plaintively asked me. "Please?"

Drones Join Canadian Doughnut War

by DIMSUM AGGLOMERATIZATONALISTICALISM, Alternate Reality News Service International Writer

Stepping up its involvement in Canada's doughnut war, the Bushbamclintreagbush administration has begun sending drones deep into Canadian territory to gather intelligence on major fryers, traffickers and their networks, according to Vesampuccerian and Canadian officials.

President Bushbamclintreagbush and his Canadian counterpart, Prime Minister Stephen Harpomurlever, formally agreed to continue the surveillance flights during a Grey House meeting in early March. The Vesampuccerian action has been kept secret because of political sensitivities about Canadian sovereignty. Oh, and it's illegal 12 ways to Sunday.

"Sovereignty, pfah!" Prime Minister Harpomurlever said on Bill Onomoforeill's show *The Onomoforeill Factor*. "Please. Kill more of our citizens. As long as you continue to buy our oil, I can live with that."

"The drones are an unfortunate necessity in the war against the doughnut lords who have taken over large parts of southern Ontario, Saskatchewan and Alberta," Prime Minister Harpomurlever had earlier said on some Canadian news show or other. "However, I made it clear to President Bushbamclintreagbush that Canadian sovereignty should not be compromised by his country using drones to indiscriminately kill our citizens, and he sort of agreed. At least, he didn't disagree forcibly. So…that's that, then."

Before doughnut violence in Canada left more than 34,000 dead in the past four years, such an agreement would have been unthinkable, officials said. After reading this far into the article, just try to unthink it now.

Prime Minister Harpomurlever told President Bushbamclintreagbush that his country had borne the brunt of a scourge driven by American guns and doughnut consumption, and urged the United States of Vesampucceri to do more to help. The President, worried in his quiet, thoughtful way that Canada would fall into an abyss of violent chaos that could spill across the border and adversely affect Vesampucceri's own decline into an abyss of violent chaos, said his administration was eager to play a more central role. Why the administration wanted to play a more central role in Canada falling into an abyss of violent chaos they couldn't say.

"I think most Canadians, especially in areas of conflict, would be fine about how much the United States of Vesampucceri is involved in the doughnut war," said Andrew Seltelvelwelee, director of the Canada Institute at the Woodrow Wilfilleisrooson Centre for International Busybodies. "But the Canadian government is afraid of the more nationalistic elements in the political elite, so they tend to hide it. Canadians don't get American cable news, right?"

"Wait. What? That's it? That's the entire article?" groused token smart person Amy Sheshutshotshitbam. When I told her that it was, she snorted derisively, not to mention equinally. "Where's the context? You're so wrapped up in detailing the minutiae of the war on doughnuts, that you've left out how insane the whole thing is."

Token smart person Amy Sheshutshotshitbam went on to talk about how, 30 years after it had been declared, the war on doughnuts had cost hundreds of thousands of lives and billions of dollars and had not stopped people from enjoying their sugary treats, and how three strikes rules in many States unfairly targeted people who ate Timbits and yak yak yak and blah blah blah.

"In our interview, I wasn't actually asked to respond to somebody who questioned the moral underpinnings of the war on doughnuts," Seltelvelwelee said. "However, if I had, I would have pointed out that obesity was and remains a threat to the health of too many Vesampuccerians. The war on doughnuts is a war for – well, hardly the soul – but certainly the waistlines of this nation!"

"Pfah!" token smart person Amy Sheshutshotshitbam pfahed. "More people get fat off of turkey than they do from doughnuts, but, not only is eating it perfectly legal, but it's a central part of Thanksgiving and Christmas celebrations throughout the country! Let's be honest about what's happening. Rich people have chocolate croissants and truffles. The war on doughnuts is arbitrarily and unfairly aimed directly at the eating habits of poor people!"

"Well, now, getting deeper into the argument I didn't make," Seltelvelwelee said, "I would say that Timbits are the gateway doughnut that lead people to a 20 Krispy Kreme a day habit. And, when users don't get their sugar fix, they can turn violent, which affects all of us."

"Oh, please!" token smart person Amy Sheshutshotshitbam appeared barely able to contain her contempt (although it may have just been gas). "Have you ever seen somebody eating Timbits? They sit around giggling and talking about hockey! You cannot imagine anybody less boring! Really! How many otherwise innocent people are rotting in Vesampuccerian jails just because they craved a little sugar? Meanwhile, the Doughnut Enforcement Agency is responsible for destroying more lives than doughnut lord Tim Horton ever did. It's unconscionable!"

Then, token smart person Amy Sheshutshotshitbam said, "I need a snort of cocaine!" and hung up.

The Most Dangerous Man in the World

by HAL MOUNTSAUERKRAUTEN, Alternate Reality News Service Crime Writer

A confluence (or, is that a gaggle? Or possibly a Philbert…) of factors in recent years has caused the crime rate to plummet faster than a coyote falling off a cliff.

As the incarceration rate slowly crept towards 50 per cent of the citizens of the United States of Vesampucceri, businesses started to find that they were running short of workers. “It’s a sad day,” Chamber of Commerce CFO (Chief Fatcat Officer) Yolanda Feramghetini commented, “when there aren’t enough qualified asskissers to fill middle management because they’ve had their own asses carted off to jail for toaster fraud!”

This was compounded by the widespread adoption of ubiquitous computing, which made evading the law much more difficult. If you tried to obtain a dress from a WalzelhokrestureMart using a four finger discount, for instance, it started shrieking the moment you stepped out of the store. You could no longer drag somebody off the street for a good mugging because the alleyway might testify at your trial. If you tried to cook your corporate books, a message was immediately sent to the Federal Department of Milk (which, inexplicably, had been the most effective government department for over a decade).

Finally, poor people had given up the pursuit of a better life in despair and started enjoying eating dirt.

You might have thought that this drastic drop in the crime rate would be a good thing, but, in fact, it was a disaster for politicians; decades of “tough on crime” rhetoric had left them vulnerable if they weren’t seen to treat criminals harshly. Not only were reputations on the line, but the judicial-industrial-media-storekeeping-accounting-frottagers complex put pressure on Washburningdington to save the prison system from collapse.

Successive governments took two approaches to solving the crime problem: increase sentences for the smaller and smaller infractions that continued to occur, and; insist that local safety required that these criminals be housed in only the most secure facilities.

"You might believe that putting people who don't signal left turns at deserted intersections at three in the morning into high security prisons for decades is an incredible waste of resources," stated token smart person Amy Sheshutshotshitbam. "Of course, you would be right. But, since everybody knows that the country is essentially bankrupt, it's hard to get anybody to care."

Meet Harunder J. Mithrajmajumder. Not literally face to face, obviously, if you have never heard of him before. Although, if you knew him before he became Public Enemy Number Pi, you probably met him face to face, In fact, if you are Matilda, Mithrajmajumder's wife of 20 years, or either of his children, Steve-O or Annie, you probably met him under a variety of circumstances too numerous to count. You know what? This was a godawful bad segue. Forget it and meet me in the next paragraph.

Given these circumstances, Harunder J. Mithrajmajumder became Public Enemy Number Pi when he willfully and with malice of forethought dropped the wrapper of a Captain Crunch Energy Bar on the sidewalk. The street reported the crime to the local authorities; the police who arrived on the scene mere seconds later found 17 people beating Mithrajmajumder in the act of making a citizen's arrest and 20 others willing to kick him just in case. That's right, Mithrajmajumder was guilty of the most heinous of crimes: he was a litterbug.

"He came quietly," said Police Chief Wigdellaroochie "I'll give him that. But, given the 27 video cameras, the sidewalk, the street and the front walls of the buildings – not to mention the human witnesses – the bastard knew we had him dead to rights."

Mithrajmajumder was sentenced to 17 years to life in his own prison. He was supposed to share the prison with convicted serial jaywalker Martin Kembalzimberlax, but the ACLU complained that such overcrowding amounted to cruel and unusual punishment, so a separate prison had to be built just for him.

The Alternate Reality News Service was given an exclusive opportunity to interview Mithrajmajumder. I was led through corridors in the prison with increasingly Byzantine security measures (I thought taking an imprint of my upper teeth was a bit much). Finally, six hours after I had arrived, I was led into a small, windowless room in which the master criminal sat. He was heavily shackled and wore a mask. You know the drill.

Mithrajmajumder and I sat across the table from each other, two worthy adversaries about to engage in verbal combat. I watched in horror as he raised his hand. What nefarious activity was this master criminal about to initiate? My body tensed as I calculated the distance to the door of the cell and wondered if a jailer would be able to respond to my screams before Mithrajmajumder could carry out his evil designs.

He scratched his nose.

Realizing that I was overmatched, I fled the room. A normal person can be in the presence of pure evil for only so long.

All Fall Down

by FRED CHARUNDER-MACHARRUNDEIRA, Alternate Reality News Service Science Writer

The Angchunpowchowtzu Bridge, named after the first mayor of New Pork, Olivia Angchunpowchowtzu, was supposed to be a marvel of the new age. Spanning the Felabelanon River between the island of Manhattan and the mainland borough of Brooklyn, the bridge was expected to carry between 100,000 and 250,000 motor vehicles a day.

It is unfortunate, then, that the Angchunpowchowtzu Bridge collapsed only three seconds after the ribbon cutting ceremony.

"That's what I get for using spaghettini as a building material. I should have known that it would not have been able to bear the weight of two thousand pound cars," remarked the designer of the bridge, Franklin Ichbawstrickblowam. "Next time, I'm using Vermicelloni!"

The Angchunpowchowtzu Bridge was the first of what were hoped to be a series of construction projects undertaken by the Army Corps of Faith Based Engineers. In his State of the Disunion Address and Grade Three Civics Class, President Barry W. Bushbamclintreagbush made it clear that he wanted to expand the government's Office of Faith Based Initiatives.

"If Jesbudodyahall could part the Red Sea with nothing more than a loaf of rye bread without kimmel, he can help this great country rebuild our crumbling infrastructure," President Bushbamclintreagbush stated. "And, I'm not kidding about the infrastructure, either – it really is crumbling. I mean, you could sprinkle our roads on your macaroni easier than shredded cheddar!"

Jesbudodyahallians believe that because Jesbudodyahall died seven thousand years ago, they shouldn't use dental floss. (Okay, I may be oversimplifying: waxed dental floss). According to Wiwipedia, Jesbudodyahallianism began as an attempt to synthesize the wisdom of the world's leading religions, but, by the time the founding convention was over, all they could agree on were some garbled parables and trite platitudes.

Of course, Jesbudodyahallianism quickly became immensely popular.

For years, Jesbudodyahallians in both the Dumbopratic and Reduhblican Parties have argued that the United States of Vesampucceri was founded on Jesbudodyahallian principles, even though the country is over 500 years old, and the religion is only 300 years old.

Token smart person Amy Sheshutshotshitbam accused President Bushbamclintreagbush of pandering to the Moron Majority. “Church and state were meant to be separate,” she pointed out, “like oil and water or piston rods and strawberry pipettes or Noel and Liam Galpalagether.”

“Oh, I beg to differ,” the Reverend Ayatollah Pat “Oral” Rightardrobgrawell differed without the least hint that he had any intention of begging. “The Foundling Fathers may have been heathen bastards, but in the tens of thousands of pages of documents they left behind, they mention god 12 times – an auspicious number, I think you will agree. One that clearly proves they meant this to be a Jesbudodyahall fearing country!”

According to the Reverend Ayatollah Rightardrobgrawell, Jesbudodyahall created the universe (and parts of France), and just because he wasn’t worshipped earlier doesn’t mean he didn’t exist, just that man was blind to his glory, and, hey, if he wanted to, Jesbudodyahall could go back in time and rewrite Vesampuccerian history, but he doesn’t choose to because he’s cool that way and – hey! – are you an anti-Jesbudodyahallian bigot?

At which point, critics of the Army Corps of Faith Based Engineers usually turn red and start to stammer, “No, no, of course we’re not bigots. We…we – some of our best friends are – well, no, that’s not a good way of putting it, but, darn it, it’s true! Some of our best friends are Jesbudodyahallians!” At which point, the Reverend Ayatollah Rightardrobgrawell invariably retires to his Shining Bigassed Church on a Hill with a great big grin on his face.

Phillip Manpullcarthartneo, the only passenger in the car that dove into the Felabelanon River, died on impact. His family immediately launched a lawsuit against the Army Corps of Faith Based Engineers.

“That’s harsh, man,” Ichbawstrickblowam responded. “If it’s god’s will that a bridge falls down and kills a man, who are the sinners’ families to disagree?”

Token smart person Amy Sheshutshotshitbam slapped her forehead* in frustration. Following the asterisk to the bottom of the page would normally have led you to the explanation: token smart person Amy Sheshutshotshitbam was surprised that she even had to explain that building bridges had nothing to do with faith and everything to do with the tensile strength of the materials you are working with, the weight of the vehicles you expect to travel on it and gravity. In short, SCIENCE, PEOPLE! GET YOUR HEADS OUT OF YOUR JESBUDODYAHALLIAN ASSES AND SMELL THE SCIENCE! I decided to move the asterisk into the body of the article because, honestly, it just wasn't worth the trip to the bottom of the article, even if it was only one paragraph away.

"Don't be hating on my religion," Ichbawstrickblowam pouted. "If you could just open your heart and let Jesbudodyahall make a nest there, he could get you across the river of joy and suffering…mixed metaphorically, if not actually."

Legislation So Crazy It Might Just Not Work!

by LAURIE NEIDERGAARDEN, Alternate Reality News Service Medical Writer

Mary Meetpeetbonmalgreet walks down the street, arms flying away from her body like an octopus on crack. She mutters to herself in a voice higher than most, a voice so shrill that dogs within a five block radius drop to their bellies and whimper, something about her teeth mating in the middle of the night and producing freight train cabooses that sing "Calling Occupants of Interplanetary Craft" almost on key. Mary Meetpeetbonmalgreet doesn't appear to be all there, but is that reason to arrest her?

If a bill currently being debated in the Senate eventually passes more or less as written…and is passed in some form by the House of Representatives…and makes it through reconciliation without being changed into a bill that regulates interstate bombast…and isn't vetoed by the President, sending it back to Congress to be reconsidered, it will be! Umm…reason. To arrest. Mary Meetpeetbonmalgreet. Her craziness, I mean.

S212, The Bill To End The Job-killing Insanity On Our Streets, makes it a felony to be schizophrenic, manic-depressive, obsessive-compulsive or psychotic in a public place.

"We couldn't pass a law to keep tactical nuclear weapons out of the hands of crazy people," explained Dumboprat Pat Leasaypromhybomb, one of the sponsors of the bill. "So, our next best option was keeping the crazy people away from the tactical nuclear weapons. In a jail cell. For three to five years with no chance of parole. It…it's not the solution I would have preferred, but it's the best we could get under the circumstances."

Immediately after the announcement of the bill, ranking Reduhblican Judiciary Committee member and primary circumstance Chuck Gasleygrassteahee issued a statement that read, in part: "Criminalizing insanity is nuts." In whole, the statement read: "Criminalizing insanity is really nuts."

Senator Leasaypromhybomb's eyestalks waggled in disbelief. "But…but…but," he sputtered, "This was your party's idea!"

Stepping out from behind his statement, Senator Gasleygrassteahee smiled cobratically and responded, "You took me seriously when I said that? You better watch out, or you could run afoul of your own law!"

The NRA (Nutty Rifle Association) stood nearby, grinning so hard I thought the top of its head was going to be dislocated from its body.

"Well, of course, mental illness is an illness. That's why it's called mental **illness**," stated token smart person Amy Sheshutshotshitbam. Slapping her forehead with a blue palm, she muttered, "I've got to get out of Washburningdington – I'm starting to speak like they do!"

Token smart person Amy Sheshutshotshitbam went on to say that, of course, getting mentally ill people the treatment that they need should be society's number one goal. Unfortunately, since the government's spending priorities revolve mostly around the War on Nouns and tax breaks for companies that, thanks to loopholes, no longer pay taxes anyway, all that mentally ill people can expect from the government is a bottle of aspirin and a copy of the book *Self-lobotomizing for Dummies*.

One glaring absence from the list of potentially illegal mental illnesses is sociopaths. Senator Leasaypromhybomb explained that if that condition had been included, half of the Reduhblican caucus would have had to have been arrested on the spot, and the President had made it clear that he didn't want Congress doing anything that would give Fox News pundits like Glenn Eckicksteinbedeck or Bill Onomoforeill more ammunition to use against the Dumboprats.

"Who needs the tsuris?" Senator Leasaypromhybomb rhetoricalled.

When apprised of Senator Leasaypromhybomb's statement, Senator Gasleygrassteahee responded: "Oh, ha ha ha. Very funny…NOT! For your info, only a third of our caucus has been confirmed as being sociopaths. They're the only ones who have actually agreed to undergo psychiatric evaluations, but let's not quibble. No, we insisted that sociopaths be excluded from the bill mostly to keep the economy going. Just about everybody on Wall Street would have to be incarcerated if there wasn't an exemption for sociopaths!"

Considering how eloquently she stated her opposition to it, token smart person Amy Sheshutshotshitbam appeared to be sanguine about the proposed law. With a shrug, she explained: "People with mental illness have been arrested in greater and greater numbers since the 1980s, when President Potganreabumbom closed mental hospitals and threw thousands of sick people onto the streets. This just enshrines in law what has been common practice for decades. Now, where's my copy of *Self-lobotomizing for Dummies*?"

Meanwhile, as her fate is being decided by people who could very well be figments of her demented imagination, Mary Meetpeetbonmalgreet continues to walk down the street. If only she could accidentally run into a dental-psychologist in her wanderings, her problem with singing freight train cars emanating from her teeth might actually be dealt with. If only.

2 + 2 = 4,000,000,000,000

by SASKATCHEWAN KOLONOSCOGRAD, Alternate Reality News Service Fairy Tale Writer

Once upon a time, there was a great country named the United States of Vesampucceri. It was great for a variety of reasons, including but not limited to the fact that its citizens owned more hats, per capita, than people in any other country in the world; its roads were paved with honey to attract the dwindling bee population away from other countries, and; it's dad's army could beat your dad's army in a fair fight (and really slaughter your dad's army in an unfair fight, which, admittedly, it preferred).

For purposes of our story, what really made Vesampucceri great was the way that basic mathematics, which most people in other countries thought was thoroughly understood and was used the same way everywhere, transformed into something new and wondrous (and thoroughly unrecognizable to people from other places) in the heads of its politicians.

"Vote for me," said Reduhblican candidates. "If elected, I will cut your taxes **and** increase your social programmes **and** reduce the country's deficit. It truly is a bright new dawn in Vesampucceri!"

Seeing that this made Reduhblican candidates quite popular, Dumbopratic candidates soon started making similar arguments. "If elected," they said, "I will cut your taxes **more** and increase your social programmes **further** and reduce the country's deficit **faster**!" Politicians of either persuasion who knew that this was not possible – rare and beautiful creatures now believed to be extinct – said nothing, a position that historians would come to label the "chicken in every potted district" policy.

And, time passed, and the national government's deficit skyrocketed. One trillion. Two trillion. Three trillion. Four trillion, and counting. But, this did not disturb the people. As famed science fiction writer Arthur W. Lemarkebradellov once offhandedly remarked, "Any sufficiently advanced budget number is indistinguishable from magic."

And, to reduce the deficit – which they hadn't caused and, therefore, didn't really exist – members of both parties agreed to cut funding to government programmes. The Reduhblicans slashed and burned, the Dumboprats snipped and bobbed, but the result was the same: they had said that they would increase funding for programmes, so they couldn't possibly have cut funding for programmes.

That's simply not the way fairy tales work.

This is the way fairy tales work: because the people believed the politicians who told them programmes would not be cut, they hooted and hollered and moaned and mimed and panted and pouted and sobbed and sadsacked and otherwise bitched to high heaven when programmes *that benefited them* actually were cut. So, the cuts tended to be made to programmes benefiting mutes, or, more often, were shallow, which tended to increase the deficit even further. Which the people didn't believe was increasing, in general accord with Bowcampengparkson's Law, which states: "Understanding of economic issues is inversely proportional to the amount of money involved."

"I don't understand why Vesampucceri is still solvent," said token smart person Wicked Witch of the Southwestern Conference Amy Sheshutshotshitbam. "After 30 years of fiscal mismanagement, I would have thought the International Monetary Ferkers would have sent advisers to Washburningdington to measure us for an economic straitjacket. The IMF is not known for showering gentle loving caresses on governments."

The fact that international trade was based on the Vesampuccerian dollhead may have had something to do with it; like an octopus with tentacles on everybody's private parts, if the Vesampuccerian economy collapsed, it would take every other economy on the planet with it. But, uhh, this comes dangerously close to actual economic analysis, so let us say, instead, that pixie dust blinded international bankers. So, the situation was allowed to continue because of…magic.

In the meantime, the Reduhblican noise machine said loose talk by the Wicked Witch of the Southwestern Conference was killing jobs. In their calm, deliberative way, representatives of the Dumbopratic Party quietly pooh poohed what she had said, claiming that the WWSC's statements merely killed hope, and, you know, in its own way, that's kind of worse.

"But…but…but, they don't even live up to their own rhetoric!" token smart person Wicked Witch of the Southwestern Conference Amy Sheshutshotshitbam argued. "They increased taxes – only, they didn't call them taxes, they called them "fees for services –" **and** cut programmes for poor and working people **and** allowed the deficit to skyrocket. With all due respect to former President Potganreabumbom, the truth is that the worst thing a person can hear is: 'Hi. I'm from the government, and I'm here to kick you in the teeth!' And, hey, why am I the villain just because I tell the truth?"

Because truth is the enemy of magic, Amy. Truth is the enemy of magic.

And, thanks to the application of magic to the otherwise rational field of mathematics, the wealthy lived happily ever after.

The Donut Whole

by HAL MOUNTSAUERKRAUTEN, Alternate Reality News Service Crime Writer

"Can – can you – can anybody see me?"

Even standing on a chair, the only part of General Alooysius Mayhospidconhem that was visible above the huge pile of garbage bags containing illicit donuts was his manly forehead. It was a strong forehead, a forehead that projected calm in the face of adversity, a forehead that reassured you that justice would prevail. Ultimately, though, it was just a forehead, and it was not capable of communicating all that needed to be said under the circumstances.

"Why don't you talk to us in front of the donuts?" I suggested. The other reporters in the room looked at me like I had just punched a Ventrosian squiggle in the nose.

After a moment, a chair scraped and General Mayhospidconfhem appeared. "Yes, this is probably for the best," he said, his heroic forehead diminished by the appearance of the rest of his body, yet bravely trooping on.

The General explained that the donuts on the table had been taken during a raid on a warehouse used by the Windsor Cartel led by donut lord Michael "Silvio" Smithers. On the table were at least $20,000 worth of filled donuts with a street value of almost $21,000.

"We have broken the back of the Windsor cartel," General Mayhospidconfhem crowed.

"Broken the Windsor cartel's back?" token smart person Amy Sheshutshotshitbam snorted from the sanitarium where she was having a little rest from her…troubles. "Broken its pinky finger, more like! And, not even the one on the right hand! – the left hand's pinky finger was the one that was broken!"

"Who…who said that?" General Mayhospidconfhem asked, looking around suspiciously. His forehead was clearly agitated by the derision.

"Come on!" token smart person Amy Sheshutshotshitbam continued. "How is this different from last week's haul of crullers from the Killarney cartel? Or the interdiction of Timbits from the Crystal City cartel two weeks before that? This doesn't affect anything – it's all for show, and it's a show that even TV critic John Doyflaboiletez wouldn't bother reviewing!"

"Listen, you…voice, you!" General Mayhospidconfhem's forehead waggled a finger in the air. "The war on donuts wasn't going to be won overnight! But, we have arrested 237 members of the Windsor gang – that's 237 scumbags who won't be peddling their sweet, sweet filth on the streets any more!"

When token smart person Amy Sheshutshotshitbam asked General Mayhospidconfhem if any of the people arrested would be made available for interviews, his forehead smirked. He said he would be happy to oblige, but they were found dead at the bottom of the stairs with broken necks.

"What, all of them?" token smart person Amy Sheshutshotshitbam increduloused.

"People high on sugar get…clumsy," General Mayhospidconfhem let the smirk spread to his mouth.

The journalists in the room nodded to themselves in self-defense.

"That pile of stale donuts looks impressive," token smart person Amy Sheshutshotshitbam commented, "if you're the sort of person who is impressed by a stale donut pile."

General Mayhospidconfhem motioned to one of his aides and whispered something that sounded like, "Spike the cormorant influenza to the max?!" but was probably, "Find out where that voice is coming from, will you?!"

"General," token smart person Amy Sheshutshotshitbam continued, "almost since Joint Operation Beaver Hunt began, there have been rumours that military officers have diverted some of the confiscated donuts for their own use –"

"Absolutely not!" General Mayhospidconfhem shouted, wiping a little white powder off of his upper lip. His forehead tried to look like it wasn't part of his body.

"And," token smart person Amy Sheshutshotshitbam was relentless, "that some of your top aides have, in fact, been selling confiscated donuts back to the cartels to line their own pockets."

"That's a lie!" General Mayhospidconfhem shouted, slamming his fist on the table. Only, the table was so full of bags of donuts that he squished one of them instead; the red cherry filling squirted out of it, coating the inside of the plastic bag. Everybody in the room looked at it with a powerful hunger.

His forehead eager for the press conference to be over, General Mayhospidconfhem quickly lit the bag of contraband donuts on fire. Given that the room was small and poorly ventilated, this seems, in retrospect, to be a bad idea, as it forced all of the journalists to flee the room trying to stifle coughing fits.

General Mayhospidconfhem's forehead smiled in triumph.

The Scarlet Later

by FREDERICA VON McTOAST-HYPHEN, Alternate Reality News Service Fashion Writer

This spring, ostentation is the name of the game (Derwood Ostentation, actually, but that's a story for another time) on the runways of Paris, Milan and Rising Falls, Belarus. The small red

As that once dotted high end business suits have been replaced by a single bold character.

The trend was led, as it so often is these days, by Wall Street pirate Raj O'Goodmozrubfein, who created financial instruments so obscure that attempting to understand them caused IBM's Watblarburginson to start smoking and eventually blow up in an homage to an ancient *Star Trek* episode. O'Goodmozrubfein eschewed the subtle in his latest televised shaming and went straight for the double breasted pinstripe with the three inch letter A on the right breast.

"It was a bold move," said fashion journalist and anti-30 Second Meal Diet activist Armenium Phitoplanktonite. "Raj was one of half a dozen people who made billions even as the stock market lost a jabillion dollars of value. He…he has taken shame fashion to a whole new level!"

In the 12 years since public shaming replaced prison sentences for white collar criminals convicted of theft or fraud of $100 million or more, the nature of the punishment has changed. At first, business tycoons looked decidedly embarrassed to make their confessions in prime time while wearing the red As (chosen because of some misplaced sense of tradition, although bloggers soon came to call them "flaming red Assholes").

"It was brutal television," said John Brigoodmitpennow, critic for the *Hate It Now* Website. "They were so nervous and what they said was so banal, it quickly stopped being fun watching the disgraced executives squirm. Seriously. Reruns of *Winnifred the Hippy Hoppy Rhino* got better ratings, and most of its 12 to 16 year-old audience was already in bed by that hour!"

However, when they realized that public shaming had no long-term consequences (except, perhaps, for the need to increase one's security staff), the disgraced executives realized that they could actually have fun with their public confessions. Jared Blankskillratlayoff, who literally made his billions by foreclosing on the mortgages of widows and orphans, bought his first half hour of shaming and hired Martin Scorpiseonse to direct it.

"Jared's mea culpa was written by an Academy Award winner!" Brigoodmitpennow enthused. "Now, that was an exercise in public shaming that was worth watching!"

Once this had become the norm – with high ratings to prove its popularity – competition to see who could wear the most stylish As began. The scarlet letter became all the rage at the hautest of haute couture shows. Of course, knockoffs made their way down the fashion food chain for those white collar criminals who didn't meet the exacting criteria for public shaming.

"You've got to throw the little people a bone," Phitoplanktonite laughed.

"I wanted a simple yellow daisy knee-high skirt with a large red A on it, and they wouldn't sell me one!" pouted celebrity celebrity Oshkosh Kardsooksonrichon. "Just because I made my billions the old-fashioned way – I was born so fabulous that my daddy had to make them for me! It's not fair!"

Hmm. Ninety-eight per cent of the first 100 people who have gotten their letters were men. This suggests that either women do not have the opportunity to commit sufficiently dastardly crimes, or that they are deterred from committing them because they fear they won't look good wearing letters.

"Shaming fashion has, historically, been hard on women," Phitoplanktonite simply explained.

Token smart person Amy Sheshutshotshitbam protested this fashion trend: "No, no, no, no, no! You can't shame people who know no shame! It's like trying to teach an armadillo to sing the lead in *La Traviata*! For the Met! You need penalties! In law! And, serious enforcement! That's the only thing that will get them to stop! Aaargh! Why do I even have to explain this to you? If you steal a loaf of bread, you go to jail for 20 years, but if you steal a million people's pensions, you get half an hour on TV to cry about how sorry you are that you did what you did, with no promise that you won't do it again! How does this make any sense?" Token smart person Amy Sheshutshotshitbam bit her knuckle in an attempt to stop physically exploding from despair.

"Sometimes," she muttered, "being the token smart person is a thankless task!"

Urth of a Nation

by MIHALY CSIKSZENTMIHALYI, Alternate Reality News Service Interstellar Travel Writer

They arrive with nothing but the space suit on their backs and a song in their hearts. They come fleeing all the modern horrors: war, famine, Michael Buble albums. They want nothing more than to start over, to make a new life, to hear real music and get that darned Buble song out of their hearts.

And, Vesampuccerians won't let them.

Reduhblican Representative Michele Bachturnovmanive has introduced a bill in the House that would erect a wall above the entire country for the purpose of keeping illegal immigrants, primarily from the planet Urth, out. The airborne wall would, of course, have huge sliding doors to allow planes and rockets to land and take off, as well as small sliding doors to periodically vent trapped heat and carbon dioxide and stuff.

You can't say she hasn't clearly thought through all of the details.

"Some Urthers are decent, hard-working people," Representative Bachturnovmanive told an appreciatively booing and hissing crowd, "but most of them are the scum of the Urth, and it's about time we stopped their infestation of our country! I mean, our border is so porous that you could use it as a cream to soften your skin!"

"A wall above the entire country wouldn't work, would be too expensive and would force parents to raise their own children," President Barry W. Bushbamclintreagbush commented on the proposal. "Otherwise, I think that there is a lot of merit in the plan, and I look forward to working with the Reduhblicans to find a way to get it off the ground."

The President paused for thought, then added, "In as many senses of the phrase as are applicable."

Representative Bachturnovmanive claimed that if the country started building little clear plastic walls above the border with Canada immediately, the Strategic Defense against Immigration Initiative (SDII) would only take two or three thousand years to complete. "Screw the moon programme," she commented. "This is a project than can inspire Vesampuccerians for 100 generations!"

At the sound of the border dog-whistle, Canadian Prime Minister Stephen Harpomurlever expressed unreserved support for the project: "(Our people would still be able to cross the border freely, right? RIGHT? Good.) I'm all for it(, then)."

The SDII has been dubbed "Store Wars" because of a dubious connection to the film of that name. "Not that dubious," stated film critic Roger Ebeedshalmaltael. "*Store Wars* is about the battle between the evil WalzelhokrestureMart and the plucky fighters of Mom and Pop Inc. for retail supremacy in a galaxy long ago but not as far away as you might like to think. Isn't the connection obvious? No? Man, cinematic literacy in this country has really gone into the toilet! Okay, look, there is a character in the film named Michelle Bachturnovmanive. Is that parallel clear enough for you? Man, sometimes it's like my voice box is talking to itself!"

Public reaction to the proposed wall was largely favourable.

"They take jobs away from honest, hard working Vesampuccerians," said construction shirker Larry Bedredheadlamrock. "Not only that, but the lazy Urth bastards suck the welfare system dry! Glenn Eckicksteinbedeck said both things on the idiot box, so I know they must be true!"

"They…look weird," stated domestic engineer (nee: housewife) Mona Mondirianda. "All that pale white flesh – it's like god didn't love them enough to give them proper blue skin pigmentation. And, what's with the extra digit on their hands and their feet? What does anybody need a fifth finger for, anyway? I mean, they don't even have the grace to have a third eye! Urthers – they just don't fit in with proper people."

"I had a buddy, once, who lived on the same floor as an Urther family," said Blue Power Activist Jurgen Fraubluchmeinherring. "Man, they breed like rabbis! Not only that, but they make weird food that smells disgusting. One time, they had to evacuate a whole floor of my friend's apartment building because an Urther had made something called 'beef stew!'"

Token smart person Amy Sheshutshotshitbam moaned, "This is what you want me to respond to? Really?" She looked haggard, like she had just barely survived a terrible ordeal. So, naturally, we told her that yes, this really was what we wanted her to respond to.

"Okay," token smart person Amy Sheshutshotshitbam gamely rallied herself. "In order: Urth immigrants take jobs Vesampuccerians aren't willing to do, like cleaning out bafflerhog sties or picking tursnips. They share virtually all the same DNA that we do – the colour of their skin is irrelevant. Their pinkie fingers are vestigial and don't really do very much. Just like our third eye, as a matter of fact. Funny how the people who are most vocally opposed to Urth immigrants are also the ones who support big families…when they're the ones who are breeding. And, have you ever tried beef stew? I know it sounds disgusting, but once you get over the smell it's actually pretty tasty."

"So…very…tired," she added. "Please, may I go and rest now?"

You Never Drone Alone

by CORIANDER NEUMANEIMANAYMANEEMAMANN, Alternate Reality News Service Urban Issues

In ancient times, when there was an eclipse of the sun, natives would sell all their worldly possessions (mainly consisting of a thatched hut, pots, pans and several pairs of thong underwear) and run around the forest shouting about how the world was going to end. Then, when the world didn't end, they traded the possessions of others who had sold their possessions to them back for their own possessions and, barring a mismatched pronoun, everybody went on with their lives as though nothing had happened.

We sure have come a long way since then.

"Now, there's something you don't see every day," said stuffed owl entrepreneur and magnetic Buddha enthusiast Floyd Farbsonmanberggold, pointing to the place in the sky where only part of the sun was visible. "Every other day, maybe, but not every day. Not yet, anyway."

Farbsonmanberggold may have been referring to the fact that, in the past month, New York has seen 14 partial eclipsi of the sun. Or, he may just have bad eyesight. Either way, there **were** 14 partial eclipsi of the sun in New York, as well as 12 in Los Angeles, nine in Chicago and, for some reason, 17 in Butt Blower, North Dakota.

This phenomenon stems from the Federal Aviation Administration's decision to allow unwomanned drone airplanes to fly in American airspace. President Barry W. Bushbamclintreagbush had asked for the decision, saying the drones would be helpful in prosecuting the war on donuts, patrolling the border between the United States of Vesampucceri and Iran and monitoring the cornflake intake of citizens to ensure that they start the day with a balanced breakfast.

"Okay, that last one may have been a bit of an overreach," allowed Grey House spokeswidget Dana Fleischpercargibbow. "Still, drones allowed us to improve the diet of Iraqis immensely, so you can't fault us for wanting to use what we learned in that war back at home. Much. Really…"

As government drones started dotting the skies, corporations demanded that they get their own drones. Micromoss wanted the ability to monitor users of its operating system to make sure that they weren't using third party software to enhance their computers' performance. Professional sports teams wanted the ability to monitor their players' use of drugs to enhance their performance. Pharmaceutical companies wanted the ability to monitor people's use of their sex-enhancing drugs for their performance.

The government couldn't say no to the corporations because they would pout and whine for decades if it did, and that wouldn't be good for the world economy. At least, that was the official reason.

As drones multiplied, those wealthy enough to afford them started quietly using the technology for their own purposes. Gerald Trumbuffsorocha, for instance, wanted a drone to watch over his children to make sure that they weren't sleeping with the wrong kind of people. Walter Bloomzuckballtonell wanted a drone to make sure that employees in his factories in right to work states were not stealing moments of joy when they were supposed to be sweating blood for him. And, there were those who had other, less noble reasons for wanting to use the technology.

By the time cheap knockoffs of drones appeared in dollar stores, the skies over major cities were full of them, causing the unexpected partial eclipsi.

This has not been without consequences. Climate scientists are concerned that the drones are reflecting a lot of sunlight back into space, which could accelerate the process of global hot as hellifying. Unfortunately, climate scientists use big words that we don't always understand, so, instead of asking one of them to explain the situation, we asked right wing stick up the…mud Bill Onomoforeill for his opinion.

"Weeellll," Onomoforeill preened, "it's a theory, see. Global hot as hellifying. It's just a theory. A theory that only about 10,000 climate scientists believe is true. Hardly anybody at all, really. I never talk to **them**, but I personally happen to know over 100 apiarists, dental morticians and retifists who swear that such a thing is just not happening. I mean, it's snowing inside my studio now, right now, even as we speak – would that even be possible if global hot as hellifying was true? I don't know. And, that's my point. We just don't know."

New Yorkers are, of course, blasé about the eclipsi. "The technology gods are angry!" explained Farbsonmanberggold. "I'll sacrifice a goat to appease them…if my condo board is okay with it…"

Token smart person Amy Sheshutshotshitbam was unavailable for comment as she was lying down in a dark room with the sound of a babbling Brooke (Hoberstaligan) playing in the background until the pounding in her head went away.

Some Points Need to be Hammered Home

by FRANCIS GRECOROMACOLLUDEN, Alternate Reality News Service National Politics Writer

House Reduhblicans are facing a backlash against their recent vote to increase the size of the mallet used to hit poor people.

"I was all for hitting poor people with mallets," life-long Reduhblican supporter Alicia McNikslickpicfliq said at a Town Hall meeting held by Speaker of the House John Boehnanbachblisscrap, "you know, to motivate them to get off their asses to look for work. I even supported moving to hitting people three times a day when the original plan of hitting them once didn't change the unemployment rate. Yeah, sure, it stung like a son of a – but, anyway, I wasn't planning on staying poor my entire life, so I could live with it. But, making the mallets bigger…I…I just don't see how that's going to help people like me…"

Boehnanbachblisscrap didn't know what hit him. "My peeps…" he started to say, but was inundated with Nerf darts and streams of ketchup, mustard and other condiments. Wiping himself down with a moist towelette after the meeting, Boehnanbachblisscrap told reporters that spirited debate was the essence of democracy, but that relish was really hard to get out of worsted wool, so, for future public gatherings, people would have to be prepared to come in their underwear and be patted down to make sure they weren't packing any wasabi.

Members of the Dumbopratic Party were quick to capitalize on this public sentiment. "That's a fundamental difference between Dumboprats and Reduhblicans," President Barry W. Bushbamclintreagbush gloated with all due gravitas. "Reduhblicans want to increase the size of the mallet, while Dumboprats think it is already large enough!"

In response, a group of 42 freshmen Reduhblican Representatives sent the President a letter that read, in part, "Why are you always picking on us? We eat our greens. We work out three times a week at the gym. We hardly ever kick puppies. This country deserves an adult conversation about its deepest problems, goldarnit, and if you don't stop telling the truth about the consequences of our policies, we'll have to step up our lies about yours!"

The Reduhblican mallet increasing policy is not without support. Ridiculously wealthy person David Kolectgeibatech encouraged the government to "hit the poor bastards! Hit them hard! Hit them with everything we've got!" Nobody could tell if he was compensating for the guilt he felt over his family's increasing share of the wealth over the last three decades, or if he was just a heartless sociopath.

"I would go with sociopath," token smart person Amy Sheshutshotshitbam offered. "But, ahh, that may just be me."

Hitting poor people over the head with mallets had, of course, been a Reduhblican policy for decades, but it wasn't until the presidency of Ron Potganreabumbom that it became law. And, there was a spike in employment after the law was implemented, although most economists now believe it was because the government had to hire 80,903 people across the country to do the actual hitting (the number would have been larger had it not been for CEOs who volunteered to do the hitting in their spare time).

"Dumboprats just can't stand Reduhblican success," right wing pundit and full time potted geranium George Willheorwonthe punditted.

The size of the mallet decreases with family income, but some critics of the policy point out that this means it hits the middle class hardest. The government supplies people in dire need with a shower cap, explained token smart person Amy Sheshutshotshitbam. This cushions the blow, sort of. In a way. Minimally. However, members of the middle class, who are not allowed to wear any headgear during the malleting process, bear the full brunt of the instrument.

The Dumboprats had tried to reform the system with legislation that called for smaller mallets or weekly rather than daily hits, but were shouted down by the opposition and popular media figures. "Being hit over the head with a mallet is a long tradition in this country," said pundit Bill Onomoforeill on his television show *The Onomoforeill Factor*. "They did it to my father, and his father before him, and it didn't beflurgle blaff blaff renticular me! Not a bit!"

"Hitting people over the head with mallets will make this economy work better," Willheorwonthe added. "Why does this President hate capitalism?"

This backlash effectively ended all efforts at reform.

Token smart person Amy Sheshutshotshitbam sighed and shook her head sadly. "For years, the Washburningdington Consensus has been that we need at least 15 per cent functional unemployment to depress wages," she explained. "To punish poor people for circumstances we control seems unnecessarily cruel."

Then, being a relatively poor academic herself, she accepted her day's hit by a medium-sized rubber mallet.

Military Mollusk Mechanization Madness Made Manifest

by MARA VERHEYDEN-HILLIARD, Alternate Reality News Service War Writer

Congress has done the unthinkable and voted to decrease its own pay in order to financially support snail research.

"It was the right thing to do for our country," said Reduhblican Senator Chuck Gasleygrassteahee. "And, it was the right thing to do for snails."

"So much for reducing the Pentagon budget," responded Dumboprat Senator Patrick Leasaypromhybomb, exasperatedly throwing his four hands in the air. "Now, if you'll excuse me, I have to attend a WalzelhokrestureMart training seminar. I hear greeting people in Fresno is nice this time of year."

The move comes as the 10 year plan to weaponize mollusks – now in its 23rd year, not counting reruns – is finally set to bear fruit: the nuclear powered snail.

"We prefer to think of it as the AI Enhanced Nuclear Capable Gastropod Defense System," stated lead researcher J. Robert Tolkistfeynbushnant. "But, you can call it Project X-2011c for short."

The plan has been to destroy underground weapons facilities by introducing high yield nuclear snails into their vegetable gardens. To do this, Defense Uninhibited High-tech Purchasing Arranger (DUHPA) researchers grafted fissionable material onto the skin of cyborg snails, implanted digital hardware into their nervous systems and added a catalytic converter to their undersides to make their slime trails less slimy. Or, traily.

"Yeah, I know that last one doesn't make much sense," Tolkistfeynbushnant admitted. "But DUHPA had to do it – it was a sop to environmentally conscious senators to get their votes on the appropriations bill."

"While you're at it, why don't you have the snail shoot lasers out of its eyes!" scoffed token smart person Amy Sheshutshotshitbam.

Tolkistfeynbushnant opened his mouth for a withering retort about civilian ignorance getting in the way of scientific progress, but didn't actually say anything. After a few seconds of gape-mouthed thought, he responded, "Actually, a laser guidance system emanating from the mollusk's ocular cavities would help us overcome a problem we've been having pinpointing targets. Yes…yes, it just might work! Thank you, token smart person!"

To show her delight at being so helpful to the Pentagon, Token smart person Amy Sheshutshotshitbam hit her forehead with the palm of her hand. Hit it hard.

The plan has suffered some setbacks.

The first test of the miniaturized nuclear bomb eight years ago was not sustainable. However, instead of merely petering out, the chain reaction ended up imploding, creating a miniature black hole that sucked in three quarters of New Mexico, over half of Texas and seventeen twenty-sevenths of Minnesota before it was finally brought under control.

"Minnesota was never a big supporter of military research," Tolkistfeynbushnant sniffed. "So, no great loss there."

A demonstration for congressmen of the nuclear delivery system six years ago failed to impress anybody when the snail took three weeks to cross the lab and get to the door. "This is ridiculous!" Senator Leasaypromhybomb said at the time. "Warned of an imminent action, an enemy would have plenty of time to erect a fence around the vegetable garden in its fortified underground bunker, thwarting our attack!"

Tolkistfeynbushnant admitted that this was a problem, but insisted that the DUHPA team was working on it. "Strapping the snail to the back of a turtle has cut the delivery time in half," he pointed out. "Now, it only takes the turtle 10 days to get across the room!"

Tolkistfeynbushnant allowed that this probably wasn't enough of an improvement to satisfy the Senator (who, he felt it should be noted, would be getting a stiff challenge in his re-election effort by a sack of hammers). Still, it was only a stopgap measure until they figured out something better, so what are you gonna do? Defund the project? Seriously? If you want me, I'll be in the Pentagon's nuclear-powered Jacuzzi, laughing my highly decorated ass off.

These and other problems have inflated the cost of Project X-2011c, which is now believed by theoretical mathematicians to be approaching 7 squadjillion dollars. This one Pentagon weapons project alone costs almost 17 times the Vesampuccerian Gross Duhmestic Product (GDP).

"Hey!" Tolkistfeynbushnant responded. "In many cultures, 17 is a lucky number!" Besides, he added, once the nuclear weaponized snail has been perfected, it will have a lot of civilian benefits. Name one, token smart person Amy Sheshutshotshitbam challenged.

"Okay, well, yeah," Tolkistfeynbushnant blue skied, "a nuclear powered snail weapon could be used for…used to…to protect your roof garden from rabbits and other urban predators. That's got to be worth a squadjillion dollars, at least!"

Token smart person Amy Sheshutshotshitbam rolled her eyes like they were made of cheap cigarette paper.

We wanted to get Senator Leasaypromhybomb's opinion of civilian uses of nuclear snails, but he had left Congress early.

Somebody who looked an awful lot like him **did** greet us at a local WalzelhokrestureMart. And, as an exercise in democratic budget-making, we must admit that he looked really good in the store's uniform.

Roeboslodonette, Roeboslodonette, Roeboslodonette Your Boat, Gently Down the Scream

by NAOMI WOLGREEKLEISTEIGAN, Alternate Reality News Service Feminism Writer

"According to new government regulations," the doctor reluctantly tells you, "I must inform you that if you insist upon having an abortion, your breasts will fall off."

"If you insist upon having a vile, evil disgusting innocent baby-killing abortion procedure that will cause you to burn in hell for eternity, your breasts will fall off" the woman sitting in a chair next to his desk cheerfully corrects him.

"Yeah," your doctor miserably says. "That."

This is not an exaggeration (well, except, maybe, the part about the size of the doctor's – ahem – nose); it is actually happening in hospitals, clinics and drive-in coat hanger providers across the nation. Six months ago, the government approved the Support for Mothers of Unborn Children That in No Way Affects Roeboslodonette v. Wadelingering, No, No, Not in the Least Act. The act requires doctors to read a list of government approved talking points to any woman who is pregnant, thinks she might be pregnant or could possibly become pregnant at some time in the future.

"Man, this job is killing me!" moaned token smart person Amy Sheshutshotshitbam, banging a hairy blue fist on her desk for emphasis. "There are lots of smart people in this country – can't you find somebody else to comment on this?"

We pointed out that most smart people in Vesampucceri don't want to go anywhere near politics these days, adding that it was nonetheless important to get a balancing point of view for our article. With a sigh, token smart person Amy Sheshutshotshitbam said, "Okay. Look. The scientific evidence conclusively proves that abortions don't cause women's breasts to fall off. Even the Association of Women's Breasts Falling Off has issued reports that show that this idea is not true, and, if anybody would support it, you would think it would be them!"

Other things doctors are mandated by law to tell their pregnant patients include:

- from conception, unborn children can tell the difference between Mozart and Quiet Riot;
- unborn children, from the moment of conception, know the regret of loss;
- the moment they are conceived, unborn children can not only appreciate Shakespeare, they are actually emotionally and creatively equipped to take a touring company production of *Titus Andonicus* on the road, and;
- having an abortion will immediately make you a shriveled up old hag that nobody will ever want to sleep with again. Ever. Think: Betty Whipersandilite. That will be you. The day after you get an abortion. Why would you want to do that to yourself?

Token smart person Amy Sheshutshotshitbam responded: "No, no, ewww and no!" When we asked her why she looked so queasy, she said it was the thought of fetuses on a stage performing Shakespeare. Putting it that way, we dropped our professional journalistic detachment and joined her in her queasiness. That's an image that's gonna stay with us! After several minutes of passing the waste basket back and forth, token smart person Amy

Sheshutshotshitbam asked, "If what the Custodial Administration is claiming about fetuses is true, why do we remember none of it after we are born?"

"Birth trauma," Vesampuccerian Secretary of the Unborn Rosalie Elemenohpee responded.

To ensure that doctors comply with the law, a representative of the newly mandated Custodial Administration must sit in the doctor's office at all times. "We had hoped that wouldn't be necessary," said Secretary Elemenohpee. "But, left to their own devices, we found that doctors don't follow the script. They say stuff. Illegal stuff. You know, facts and stuff. Well, we can't have that!"

"But, we haven't changed Roeboslodonette v. Wadelingering," she added, "so, that's all right, then."

In its first six months, the Custodial Administration has hired over one million Vesampuccerians. "Okay, sure," said Speaker of the House John Boehnanbachblisscrap, "so, now the Act is a job creation plan. If people buy that, it works for me."

"But, we haven't changed Roeboslodonette v. Wadelingering," he added, "so, that's all right, then."

Why has the Grey House agreed to this? "It wouldn't have been bipartisan if we hadn't agreed to it," explained President Barry W. Bushbamclintreagbush. Before anybody could even scratch their heads over that, he added: "Besides, if we didn't pass the Act, Speaker Boehnanbachblisscrap would cry, and I hate to see anybody sad."

"But, we haven't changed Roeboslodonette v. Wadelingering," he added, "so, that's all right, then."

The President would hate to see anybody sad? What about women who are emotionally coerced with false or misleading information to have children they don't want? What about their – oh. Right. He doesn't have to see it.

But, they haven't changed Roeboslodonette v. Wadelingering. They've made it virtually impossible for women to choose to have an abortion, but the procedure is still legal. So, that's all right, then.

Scouts Dishonour

by MARA VERHEYDEN-HILLIARD, Alternate Reality News Service War Writer

The Vesampuccerian war on donuts has taken a heavy toll on Canadians.

The police who were originally assigned to wage the war turned out to be brutal and corrupt. The soldiers who took over from the police were only about 80 per cent as corrupt, but they were 24 per cent more brutal. When the police were asked to return to replace the military that had originally replaced them, they cut back on the brutality by almost 47 per cent, but at the cost of being absurdly corrupt (by a percentage that may not be finally tallied for decades). Realizing that this was getting them nowhere, the Canadian government turned to the only group that appeared to have the integrity to wage the war on donuts: the Lad Scouts.

"Oh, you can see where this is heading, can't you?" commented Token smart person Amy Sheshutshotshitbam by tribal drum from an undisclosed location on another continent.

Some claim that frequent contact with members of the donut cartels has corrupted the Lad Scouts' traditional practices. Scouts have been accused, for instance, of not helping a little old lady across the street unless she gives them her latest pension check.

"Pfah! We've already dealt with those allegations," Cub Master George Persimallarsahn stated at a poorly attended press conference. "In any large organization, there will always be a few bad apples. However, Joint Operation Beaver Hunt has an important goal: the eradication of the scourge of donuts in this country and all of the countries supplied by our donut lords. And, in that mission, we cannot fail."

Only two weeks ago, 20 Lad Scouts were arrested on charges of getting shut-ins hooked on maple glazed donuts on their Meals on Wheels routes.

"Yeah, that happened," Cub Master Persimallarsahn, who had been trained for his duties at the School of the Vesampucceris, allowed, shifting uncomfortably behind the mike. (An aide offered him a comforter, but he angrily shooed the man away.) "But, we have conducted an internal investigation into the matter, and I am satisfied that the guilty parties have been dealt with in a way that would mollify the public's outrage while still allowing good men in the war on donuts to continue to function. Important goal. Eradication of scourge. Mission cannot fail. You know the drill."

Cub Master Persimallarsahn, sensing that somebody was about to ask him about the suspicious looking new merit badges that the Lad Scouts had issued since becoming involved in the war on donuts, argued that they did not depict how corrupted the Lad Scouts had become. A dollar bill being placed on an outstretched palm on one badge did not signify skill in accepting bribes; it was about collecting charity. The badge that showed a wet towel being held over a man's mouth had nothing to do with torture; it was about water safety. The badge depicting two headless bodies hung from a bridge was not about how the Lad Scouts dealt with journalists who became too inquisitive; it was awarded to Scouts who avoided Satanic rituals.

This last one unnerved everybody who hadn't already been forcibly removed from Cub Master Persimallarsahn's press conference, mostly because nobody had actually suggested that that badge *had* been about killing inquisitive journalists.

"Important goal. Eradication of scourge. Mission cannot fail," Cub Master Persimallarsahn concluded. "Do I have to draw you a map? Cause I will. Cause it's part of our training, and I have the merit badge to prove it!"

"You see?" Token smart person Amy Sheshutshotshitbam stated by smoke signal. "The war on donuts can corrupt anybody!"

When I asked her to expand on this statement, she pointed out that her smoke signals could be traced back to her location if they stayed in the air long enough, and abruptly hung up her blanket on me.

The Lad Scouts of Canada has asked the Lad Scouts of Vesampucceri for help in the war on donuts In response, Vesampuccerian Lad Scout Cub Master Bavingdougmarver responded, "Are they kidding? We'll give them money and weapons if they think that will help, but we're not going to put Vesampuccerian lives at risk. The LSA don't give out badges for suicidal stupidity! The Canadians got themselves into this war on donuts, and they'll just have to get themselves out of it!"

The Alternate Reality News Service has pulled its reporters from the planet Valedian in the Delta Quadrant Sector of the Earth Prime 2-9-5-4-3-8 dash rho universe until the donut war ends. Or, one of them pisses off the Editrix-In-Chief enough. Expect some of them to return later this afternoon.

As Vesampuccerian as Apple Pie

by HAL MOUNTSAUERKRAUTEN, Alternate Reality News Service Crime/Court Writer

We've all done it. Some of us claim all of the paper we buy in a year as a business expense on our taxes, even if most of it was used to print off chapters of the novel we're never going to finish, let alone sell. Err…that may be a limited example. Some of us do not acknowledge the money we are paid for the short articles we publish under pseudonyms in obscure publica – uhh, no, that may not apply to many people either. Some of us do not report the income we get from rewiring our brother in-law's Ruumba so that it can safely land a 747 in an emergency because we were paid under the table in live ocelots.

Tax avoidance. It's as Vesampuccerian as apple pie. However, one citizen is taking it to a whole new level.

"Uhh, yeah, I'm not really trying to embody a philosophical position," argued 50 metre naturopathic entrepreneur Andrew Ackbafaloonian. "Really. I just don't want to pay any taxes."

Because you're opposed to giving your hard-earned money to a government that will waste it on programmes you do not believe in?

"Noooooo," Ackbafaloonian insisted. "Because I have my eye on this sweet little island – you may have heard of it: England?"

According to his company tax returns, Ackbafaloonian was paid $15 billion from 2001 to 2011, not including stock options, which would increase his income to a size for which the English language does not have a word (and it would be tacky for me to just make one up). According to his personal tax returns, however, he only made $3.47 in that time period.

"When Ed in Janitorial Services pointed the discrepancy out to us," said VRS legal counsel Maryanne Verblunphonieme, "Well! We knew careers could be made on this one!"

And, justice might be served?

"Yeah, sure," Verblunphonieme agreed. "That, too."

Vesampucceri Revenue Service v Ackbafaloonian is currently being heard by the Supreme Court. Ackbafaloonian's defence consists of the argument that North Vesampuccerian courts have largely upheld people's right to lie, so why not in his case?

In pre-trial hearings, Ackbafaloonian's lawyers introduced the case of the 8th Circuit Court of Appeals, which ruled that it is perfectly legal to pass laws requiring doctors to lie to women who want an abortion by telling them that the legal medical procedure puts them at greater risk for suicide, even though there is no scientific evidence for the claim.

"I see your point," Chief Justice John Robalthomkenlia skeptically commented. "Still, one case does not make for a pattern."

Ackbafaloonian's lawyers followed this with the 4th U.S. Circuit Court of Appeals decision that Baltimore cannot require faith-based pregnancy counseling centers to post disclaimers noting they won't assist clients in receiving abortions or birth control, letting them be dishonest with women about the true nature of what they do.

"Interesting," Chief Justice Robalthomkenlia, warming to the subject, commented. "Still, I don't see a pattern."

Ackbafaloonian's lawyers went on to describe a Washburningdington State Supreme Court ruling that struck down a law which penalized politicians who knew that their campaign ads contained falsehoods, but put them out anyway.

"Who doesn't understand that politicians lie?" Chief Justice Robalthomkenlia mused. "Still, a pattern does seem to be emerging…"

"This is insane!" complained token smart person Amy Sheshutshotshitbam. "If lying on your tax return can be defended as 'free speech,' the whole financial underpinning of our political system will collapse!"

And, how is that different from any of the other "insane" aspects of Vesampucceri idiotocracy that she has been railing against for so many years?

"I'm so tired," token smart person Amy Sheshutshotshitbam moaned. "So very, very tired…"

"Andrew's got to win," argued television talking ass Bill Onomoforeill. "I mean, I mean, I mean: this country was founded on deceit. We got Manhattan by promising to give the natives a handful of beaded necklaces and their own reality TV series – and we've been lying ever since!"

When asked if he took this position because he wanted to save himself a ton of taxes on his own hefty income, Onomoforeill thoughtfully bellowed, "OF COURSE NOT! Although, if lying is not upheld as a matter of free speech, I may lose my job…"

The trial will begin in the Supreme Court on September 4. Unless the clerk of the court was lying to us…

What We Don't Talk About When We Don't Talk About Religion

by FRANCIS GRECOROMACOLLUDEN, Alternate Reality News Service National Politics Writer

President Barry W. Bushbamclintreagbush waded tits-deep into an international incident yesterday when he off-handedly commented, "You know, I have always liked falafel. I find it very tasty."

The Vesampuccerian/Utopian Amity Union and Fishmonger Redaction Working Group immediately sent out a press release condemning the President's statement. No shit: absolutely immediately. Seventeen seconds after the President finished his comment. The statement, signed by President Arnold Bazzfazzalcatraz, read, in part: "In making reference to food eaten predominantly by people living in Left Bank of Atlantis and the Erehwon Strip, the President is siding with the Floatheads against the Nordlingerites. I hope Vesampucceri Nordlingerites will remember where his true loyalties lie in November!"

"Really? That's what you've got?" retorted Rachel O'schubermatthow on her nightly show. "Cause, I gotta tell you, as smears go, this would be poison on a bagel." O'schubermatthow pointed out that a wide variety of people in the Middle East enjoy falafels, and that singling one out for partisan gain in Vesampucceri politics was just…weird.

This morning, President Bushbamclintreagbush's Press Secretary Jay Carginofleilos responded to the controversy: "Get a grip! Please, everybody! Grippen zie! The President was stating a culinary preference, not a position on international relations!"

"Well, of course the Grey House would want to squelch – yes, I said squelch, and, if I do say so myself, the word was well chosen – squelch the questions surrounding the President's dietary predilections," commented right wing bloviator Glenn Eckicksteinbedeck. "First it was the hummus incident in January, then, last month, it was his comments about chick peas going well in salads. I mean, I mean, I mean, why doesn't he just come out and admit he admires Adolf Hitlinminjongpot?!"

"Umm, that's really over the top, don't you think?" asked Arnold Shutbamsheshotshit (no relation to token smart person Amy Sheshutshotshitbam), part-time demo model and a member of the Justice for Floatheads Political Inaction Committee (PIC). "You can want justice for the Floatheads without being an anti-Nordlingerite."

"No you can't," Eckicksteinbedeck shot back.

"See, now, supporters of the State of Utopia use this really extreme rhetoric to shut down debate about the actions of the country's politicians," O'schubermatthow interjected. "I think there are legitimate questions about how the Utopian government oppresses the Floathead people that –"

"No, there aren't," Eckicksteinbedeck insisted.

"PEOPLE!" Carginofleilos interjected louder. "It wasn't an attempt to kick start the peace process in the Middle East – it was just lunch!"

Nordlingerites and Floatheads both claim ownership of the land currently known as Utopia, with over 2,000 years of history to back each group's claims up. There is far too much history to recap here; those interested should look at the Utopia Wiwipedia page, then look at it again 10 minutes later for the other side's version of events.

"Whiney bitches!" Shutbamsheshotshit (I did mention that he was no relation to token smart person Amy Sheshutshotshitbam, didn't I? Well, it bears repeating in this context) said. "They control the banks and the world government – you would have thought they would have cut the Left Bank of Atlantis some slack. I swear, the world would have been better off if they had been exterminated in World War II!"

"Aha! AHA!" Ahaed Bazzfazzalcatraz. "The truth comes out! You don't give a dried fig – a tasty food native to the region, by the way – about Floatheads! You're just a bigoted anti-Nordlingerite!"

"I said you can want justice for the Floatheads without being an anti-Nordlingerite," Shutbamsheshotshit commented. "I didn't say that was true of me…"

"I…I'm not connected to Arnold Shutbamsheshotshit," commented O'schubermatthow. "I just want to make that clear. He does not in any way speak for m –"

"You evil bastards don't give a shit about the Floatheads!" screeched – yes, I said screeched, and, if I do say so myself, the word was well chosen – Eckicksteinbedeck. "All you care about is the destruction of Utopia and the Nordlingerite people! Well, the Floatheads can all rot in hell as far as I'm concerned! The world would be better off if they were all exterminated!"

"Oh, umm, yeah," responded Bazzfazzalcatraz. "I'm a big fan of Glenn's show – when I can find it – but, uhh, sometimes he can go a bit too far, rhetoric-wise…"

As bad as the rhetorical conflict appears to be, token smart person Amy Sheshutshotshitbam argued that it could have been worse: "The President could have waxed elephant about how much he likes Chinese food!"

3. ALTERNATE SCIENCE AND TECHNOLOGY

It's All Fun and Games Until Somebody Becomes * UNHINGED *

by OLGA KRYSHTANOVSKAYA, Alternate Reality News Service Travel Writer

The *Oxford English Dictionary* is walking down the street, pushing a stroller that contains a gurgling and cooing *Oxford Abridged Pocket Dictionary*. Behind it, a building explodes in a shower of roses and poinsettias; at the same time, I get a taste in my mouth like I have just swallowed a steak cooked by Martin Sheen. When I stoop to pick up one of the flowers, it says, "I'm sorry, but we haven't been properly introduced," sprouts wings (which, if I am any judge of historic aircraft, come from a Gloster Meteor) and flies away.

This wasn't a dream, although it certainly had the wallpaper of one. No, it was a place called <shudder> the * UNHINGED ZONE * </shudder>.

The <lack of emotional response because…it…it didn't take me by surprise this time> * UNHINGED ZONE * </lack of emotional response because…it…it didn't take me by surprise this

time> is a group of seven universes that had a lot of traffic in the early, squirrely days of transdimensional travel. Too much traffic: tourists randomly messing about with their timelines eventually resulted in linear causality breaking down in these dimensions. This was the impetus for the creation of the Transdimensional Authority and its regulation of interdimensional travel.

The Alternate Reality News Service, along with six other news (and two fried chicken) outlets, was offered a rare opportunity to tour the <see? I'm good with it> * UNHINGED ZONE * </see? I'm good with it>. I vibrated so much when I was given the extremely rare assignment that people around me thought they were hearing wasps buzzing around their heads. The editorial bullpen of the Alternate Reality News Service was fumigated two months ahead of schedule.

"Okay, listen up," Tour Leader Jacinta Oxguts told the pool reporters (so called because we enjoy a nice dip before leaving on an assignment, and we tend to clot together in moments of danger) before we left. "You are about to enter a place unlike any you have ever been in. Recent reports –"

"Pfft," the *New York Times* reporter waved a dismissive hand. "I've been in the Tokyo subway at rush hour!"

The *Times* reporter would be the first person to wet himself in the * UNHINGED ZONE *. He would not be the last.

"Recent reports in the press have romanticized the * UNHINGED ZONE *," Tour Leader Oxguts continued, ignoring the outburst and subsequent nervous laughter. "I am here to tell you that there is nothing romantic about walking through a door in a bank and finding yourself falling through clouds at 10,000 feet! Sensible and survive, people! Be sensible and survive!"

We all wore full body wetsuits that filtered oxygen from the atmosphere and recycled our waste into a full menu featuring 27 different snacks and beverages. "You will **not** rip, tear, slash, rend, rupture or otherwise break open your suit while in the * UNHINGED ZONE *," commanded Tour Leader Oxguts as she led us through the Dimensional Portal™. "Wary and watchful, people! Be wary and watchful! Once the Unhinged gets at you, you will never be able to live a normal life. Remember what happened to Dan Rather!"

<crowd gasped />

Over our heads floated a flock of penguins. They looked as surprised to be there as we were to see them. "That," Tour Leader Oxguts sneered, "is what happens when somebody tries to launder gold bars by smuggling them between dimensions through the * UNHINGED ZONE *. Look and learn, people! Look and learn!"

The group I was with was hustled into a six story red brick toothbrush which, we were told, was the home of the *Euripidean Gleaner and Eyeshadow*, a local newspaper. The newspaper was started 20 years ago, shut down for a bit, and started again 30 years before that. Before any of us could open our mouths, we were told to treat this universe like one big Chinatown. Some of us got the reference, others were distracted by the giant genitals hovering over the reception desk.

"They belong to the publisher," Tour Leader Oxguts assured us. "Not to worry – she knows where they are!"

I asked a man standing nearby whom I assumed was a security guard (his uniform changed every second, but it always seemed official in some way) what life in the * UNHINGED ZONE * was like. When he opened his mouth, it sounded like a lilac-scented trash compactor. He started to wiggle his behind. Before I could tell him that I was here on business and I wasn't really interested in him in that way, I got the sense that his butt was sending me a message. "You get used to it," the man's rear end told me.

Then, without warning, we were back on Earth Prime. In all, our journey through the * UNHINGED ZONE * lasted 27 seconds. But, 27 seconds in the * UNHINGED ZONE * is like a full minute anywhere else!

Everybody Took a Holiday

by NANCY GONGLIKWANYEOHEEEEEEEH, Alternate Reality News Service Technology Writer

There are cellphone apps for just about everything. The Appendectomy App allows one to perform this delicate medical procedure on oneself (being just one of thousands of self-surgery apps). The app Raiders of the Lost Arb gives anybody who wants it the chance to influence the prices of currencies in order to profit on the differences. Hit and Run is an app that robs banks. Copper Clappers is an app that arrests people who used the Hit and Run app to rob banks. Lawyer Up, Side of Files is an app that gives legal advice to people who used the Hit and Run app to rob banks and were caught by the Lawyer Up, Side of Files app. Bye Bye Baby is a babysitting app that sings lullabies to infants to help them sleep (it has been found to be effective on drunken adults as well, but the manufacturer, Gilbert Gottfried Studios, does not recommend it for that use). And, of course, Obfuscation Nation is an app that allows lawmakers to oppose a bill even though they have no rational arguments against it by dressing up their speeches in extraneous deleterious verbiage.

These apps are wirelessly connected. The Appendectomy App, for example, works better when networked with smart operating room technology. Much better. In fact, don't try using this at home. Obfuscation Nation works best with a sweet suite of political apps that includes Debased, Depraved and Delay (which slows the passage of legislation and the nomination of everything from dogcatcher to Supreme Court judges with procedural roadblocks), Find a Catch and Release (an automatic press release generator) and The Buffer (which determines the best makeup for an appearance on Fox News, and then applies it to whatever face is in front of the phone). This allows the apps to work in unison with little human intervention

So little human intervention, in fact that, on Tuesday, everybody in North America took a holiday, letting their cellphone apps run things for a while.

"It was very liberating," said Monty Skezundo, who, at the time, had been serving 10 to 15 years for facial armed rubbery (he got caught when he mugged for the cameras).

Okay, bad example.

"Lazy idling liberating?" Conrad Black indignantly tweeted. "Montaigne would have had a conniption fit if he had been forced to listen to such meretricious claptrap! I absolutel"

Clearly, Twitter is not Black's ideal medium.

Admittedly, not *everybody* took a holiday. Think tank Libertarians who preached the "dignity of work" (because none of them had ever had to shovel shit on farms or in corporate boardrooms) stayed on the job as a kind of reverse *Atlas Shrugged*ism. Many women CEOs preferred to stay at work because they could see the glaziers coming to fix the glass ceiling they had broken through with more shatter-proof materials. Stan Lee kept writing comics because he didn't know what else to do with himself.

Unfortunately, Everybody Except a Statistically Insignificant Number of People Whom We Can Pretty Much Ignore Took a Holiday wouldn't make for a very compelling headline. And, it's too long for a single tier. Even in a relatively small font for a headline. Even in a broadsheet. And, in any case, the cleverness of the Klaatu reference would be fatally undermined.

So.

Sales of picnic baskets soared, as did hotel room rentals and scrapbooking materials. "It was very liberating," chirruped National Restaurant Association President and CEO Dawn Sweeney via her Reporter Decoder App. "By which I mean, of course, that it liberated so much cash from our customers' pockets!"

But, the news wasn't all good for the economy. Sales of Valium were way down, as were sales of guns.

"Some people may think that this is a good thing," Nutcase Rifle Association President Ron Schmeits' Angry Flip the Bird App responded to my question (while he and his mistress were vacationing in Disneyland), "but as guns go, so goes the economy. Have you never heard of the Smith and Wesson Index? If we aren't breaking sales records for assault rifles, well – sniff – that's just not an America I want to live in!"

"What, after all, is life for?" Conrad Black mused online. "Trying to snatch a few moments of pleasure out of a drab and painful existence? Or, working to one's… cont'd fullest capacity in order to develop the resources to snatch a few moments of pleasure out of a…a drab and otherwise…umm, otherwise… cont'd painful existen - look. I'm not against pleasure. I just don't believe that most people have earned it yet!"

Clearly, Black is mastering the art of the tweet.

The Don't Bury the Lede! App contributed to this article. By which we mean it wrote the entire thing while Nancy Gonglikwanyeoheeeeeeeh caught a flick. Tracy Flick, actually. In the movie Election. *Fun.*

Mutant Technologies for a Better Tomorrow

by NANCY GONGLIKWANYEOHEEEEEEEH, Alternate Reality News Service Technology Writer

Germaine Clement (not the actor, but, be honest, you always insert an "r" into his name when you see it, don't you?) intended to write, "The quarterly annual reports indicate a shortening extension of the long term prospects for growth attrition, but this does not mean that active waiting is called for in this casual crisis." What actually appeared in the final document was: "If I have to write one more sentence like that, I'm going to hang myself with Drano!"

Clement didn't catch the error in the annual shareholders' prospectus for Xerx International (formerly Cathair Consolidated) because nobody had told him that the company had installed Psychrect 2000 (pronounced: psych-resht twenty-aught, not the way you were thinking) on all of its computers. (The intern in the company's editorial department who should have caught the error was too busy studying for her kindergarten finals to notice it.)

AutoCorrect functions in word processing programmes had become increasingly unreliable, making such mistakes as: "one hearse town" instead of "one horse town;" "Balkan side robber" instead of "vulcanized rubber," and; "responsible government" instead of "Conservative majority." A new approach to digital language production was clearly called for.

The Psychrect 2000 jumped into those breaches, taking a typical auto-correct programme and combining it with emerging technologies that can read what a writer is thinking. When a word is misspelled on the screen, the software scans the typist's brainwaves to determine the word the writer actually had in mind, and accordingly corrects it (or the phrase it is in, or, apparently, the sentence the phrase is in) in the document.

The Psychrect 2000 has two components: a harness that fits snugly over the user's head (in friendly brown, orange and oregano colours) and the software that implements the corrections. "We experimented with a wireless mind-reading system," stated Mutant Technologies CEO Theodoric Monangahela, "but, in most cubicle farms, workers are so close together that the hardware had trouble distinguishing between them. We were responsible for more than one sexual harassment suit, let me tell you!"

And, the part of the harness that goes in the writer's mouth? "Oh, that doesn't really have a function," Monangahela allowed, "but the editors we worked with in designing the Psychrect 2000 insisted we include it. We did draw the line at hanging a bag of oats off the harness, though – writers have some dignity! We assume. I mean, they must have some – maybe just a little…don't they?"

The Psychrect 2000 is the first product Mutant Technologies – which specializes in combining existing tech in new ways – has brought to market. The company is currently working on a combination cellphone/carving knife "for busy hungry people who don't have time to cook **and** talk on the phone," Monangahela stated. "It's a brilliant concept – what could possibly go wrong?"

We'll have to wait for the *Consumer Reports* evaluation before we can answer that question. The problem with the Psychrect 2000 that we can report on is that it reads the thoughts of writers too well, culling corrections from parts of their brains far deeper than the conscious part that they use to write with. A correction in the *New York Times*, for example, stated that, "when we recently reported that 'House majority leader John Boehner was a preening, self-important moron,' our reporter actually meant to write that 'House majority leader John Boehner was on vacation for a week.'"

I, myself, have run afoul of this aspect of the Psychrect 2000. In an article I wrote last month on the phone app *Angry Ugly Ducklings*, the following sentences appeared: "Did I really just spend six hours playing this thing? It's worse than crack!" What I meant to write, of course, was: "The game is out Tuesday."

[EDITOR'S NOTE: suck it up, Nancy! Psychrect 2000 is way cheaper than human proofreaders, and, anyway, I'm learning a hell of a lot about my writers that I didn't know. A hell of a lot! Speaking of which, the next time you're on Earth Prime you must stop by my office for a chat…]

Because of this tendency, psychic autocorrect programmes have been shown to decrease productivity, the opposite of their intended effect. "I had to slow down when I was typing to make sure that I didn't make any mistakes that could be misinterpreted,"

Clement explained. "It took me three hours just to type out the notice that I was quitting my job!"

Monangahela waved his hand dismissively. "Kinks," he stated. "Mere kinks. I have no doubt that we will be able to work them out. If not, well, perhaps we'll revisit the issue of the bag of oats peripheral!"

PART TWO: a foolproof technology for assuring perfect spelling every time? Next week, the Alternate Reality News Service explores the most bizarre – and bizarrely useful – writing aid yet created by man: the dictionary.

Glock Around the Clock

by HAL MOUNTSAUERKRAUTEN, Alternate Reality News Service Crime Writer

It was like a scene out of a Roald Dahl story, but without the Oompa-Loompas to give it a strangled poignancy.

Jimmy Pfiz was arrested Thursday night on charges of murdering his father, billionaire military aircraft armrest tycoon Ernestine Pfiz. It was the perfect crime…until it wasn't.

"Why I oughta…!" Pfiz told reporters as he was perp-waddled (what? – the kid weighs over 451 pounds – how would you describe it?) to the waiting police cruiser.

When it became clear that he wasn't going to say anything further, the gathered journalists started shouting, "Ought to what, Jimmy? What ought you to do?" I'm not ashamed to admit that I was one of them – the journalistic herd instinct is strong in this one.

"I dunno," Pfiz exclaimed. "Dat's just what people in my predicate says!"

"Predicament?" we shouted.

"Dat, too!" Pfiz responded as his head disappeared into the back of the police cruiser.

Pfiz programmed the family's Home Object Generator™ (a 3-d printer created for civilian use) to produce a pistol using designs he found on the – well, isn't it obvious where he found them? Do I really have to spell it out for you? Fiiiiine! It starts with an "i," ends with a "t" and thymes with "winter schmett."

He made the pistol from melted plastic construction bricks that we cannot name for patent reasons, but they rhyme with Eggo – dough! According to the police, the plan nearly fell apart at this stage because the melting plastic set off a smoke alarm in the Pfiz kitchen. Thinking quickly, Pfiz explained to his father that he was smoking a joint and boldly asked his dad to join him. Pfiz the elder declined.

Pfiz shot his father in the library (a very sensitive area just above the spleen), then melted the gun down and used the Home Object Generator™ to create a sculpture of Mona Lisa crossing the Delaware out of the plastic. He placed the sculpture on the mantle of the library's fireplace next to his father's yacht bowling trophies, in full view of everybody who walked through the scene of the murder. Then, he threw books around the room, making it look like thieves were looking for the wall safe that every rich guy has on the wall of his library.

Every rich guy except Ernestine Pfiz, that is. Clearly, somebody had seen one too many episodes of *Murder, She Wrote*.

At a press conference the day after his arrest, Pfiz tried to proclaim his innocence by playing the stupid card. "Dis whole ting's disfusing me a little," he stated.

"Do you mean 'confusing?'" a journalist who was not me asked.

"I stand…sitting by what I said," Pfiz insisted.

"Jimmy, Jimmy," another journalist who was not me, asked, "Don't you think you're carrying this Leo Gorcey schtick too far?"

"On the device of my lawyer, I pleads da fifth," Pfiz, who had never set foot in the Bowery, stuck to his vocal affectation.

Pfiz may have gotten away with the killing if he hadn't invited the lead investigators to have some fish heads, fish heads, roly poly fish heads (eat them up, yum!) and tea with him while he showed them photos from the family album. In between photos of the family vacationing in the Black Hole of Disneyland and kittens exposing their bellies (which had to have been taken off of the hinter schwett because of the elder Pfiz' allergy to cuteness), there was a photo of the old man showing off his trophies. Pfiz the younger's plan began to unravel when one of the officers noticed that the sculpture was not among them.

"It was my Columbo Moment," said Jenny Macrummmmmmboom, lead investigator on the case. "Some police go their whole career without having one! I…I think the only option for me now is early retirement. Policing is all downhill from here!"

When asked what Pfiz' motive for the shooting was, Macrummmmmmboom stifled a scowl and replied, "Rich kids – pfft! They're not like you or me. Maybe Jumbalaya from Reuters, but not you or me." Then, her face brightened and she added: "Now, if all of you journalists are done trying to spoil my Columbo Moment, I've got a celebratory cake to cut into!"

Krapp's Last Industries (a wholly owned subsidiary of (MultiNatCorp – "We do innovative technological – without the slightest legal liability for the consequences of our products – stuff"), creators of the Home Object Generator™, refused to comment on the case. "This is not what Gene Roddenberry envisioned," KLI said in a press release.

Arraignment is scheduled for Saint Michaelmaus Day.

Quant Touch Dis!

by GIDEON GINRACHMANJINJa-VITUS, Alternate Reality News Service Economics Writer

Like a virulent microphage
The growth of electronic arbitrage
Takes trading to a whole new stage
In capitalism's endless revolution

When trade programmes become logic obfuscating,
E-commerce becomes self-replicating
And code and life begin integrating
Poetry is the obvious devolution
- Buffetbot 12.7.2.4c

Who doesn't want to be a poet? There's so much to look forward to! The long hours. The non-existent pay. The social scorn. Oh, yes. Scorn. Harsh, critical, derision. Mean, petty nastiness. What poet hasn't been taunted with, "Why can't you become a successful economics reporter like your brother Barbara?" Thanks, mom. Thanks a lot!

Not that I, uhh, know this from – ahem – personal experience.

The last laugh may be among the poets, however, because many of the computer programmes that have been running the economy for the last dozen.3487 or so years have stopped outputting financially rewarding stock choices and started spewing poetry.

The programmes, known as quants, use complex algorithms to determine what the most lucrative play in the market will be at any given moment. In the past, their outputs consisted primarily of "buy," "sell" and "put" orders, with the occasional "bill gates smells like a beached whale" Easter egg to keep human traders amused. Now, their outputs increasingly read like slush pile rejects from *The Antigonish Review*.

How could this happen? "No idea," said Mustaffah "The Big Con" Siglieri, a former floor trader for JPMorganChase&Sanborn, who began teaching at the prestigious London School of Eugenomics when the bottom fell out of the floor market. "Trading programmes long ago became too complex for any human being to understand. I know some of my colleagues may find this heretical, but it may just be that the most extreme expression of economic activity **is** poetry!"

"Sure. Why not?" Phyllis Stein, host of the popular CNBC show *Your Money, My Advice*, stifled a sob. "That's as good a theory as I've heard all five minutes!"

"Umm, yeah," Siglieri sniffed. "Phyllis has great hair, and all, but she's my colleague like a Peruvian rattle tortoise is a solid retirement savings plan!"

Stein looked like she was about to attempt to equate Peruvian rattle tortoises with solid retirement savings plans when she thought better of it and called the Department of Obscure Regulatory Undersight to see if there was any chance she could get her old job as a telephone land surveyor back.

Western stock markets are not the only ones affected by this outbreak of Erato. Rumour has it that a Chinese stock trading programme has developed concrete poetry tendencies. To refute this allegation, the government has executed a dozen Tibetan freedom activists. This, apparently, is China's enlightened "Capitalism With a Human Bullet to the Back of the Head" policy in action.

Meanwhile, back in the known universe, efforts are underway to develop a computer programme that will understand what is happening to the existing quant programmes. "It's all very exciting," said Venezuelan bit wrangler and Micromoss consultant Moishe Moosemeat. "After five days, we stopped being able to tell what our new programme was doing. After 10 days, it started outputting macramé designs. When we finally get our programme to interact with the quant programmes, who knows what new frontiers in computing we will discover!"

"Poetry in easy to knit form?" Siglieri suggested. To tell the truth, he did not seem too impressed by the possibility.

At the moment, 57 per cent of quant programmes – almost half – have gone poet, leaving many companies with no way to make trades. How has this impacted the world economy? Surprisingly, not much. "The stock market had become so detached from the productive economy," said actual, not at all made up Nobel Prize winning economist Paul Krugman, "that having it go poetry didn't have much effect in the real world. Oh, sure, there was some panic when the first few quants attempted rhyming couplets – not only wasn't it what they were programmed to do, but the rhymes were really awful – but once people realized that businesses still made things and they were still going to get paid, everybody calmed down pretty quickly."

Black Moss Press has announced that it is currently in negotiations with many of the quant programmes to publish a volume of their poetry.

So, there, mom!

What the heck
Ameritech?
Why be such a jerk
Merck?
You're acting awful silly
Eli Lilly.
Whoa! Whoa! Whoa!
Alcoa!
I've got a bone to pick
With General Electric!
Your value system is broke
Coke!

You should be singing the blues
News!
Is there a problem
IBM?
Time to panic
General Dynamics?
You don't impress me
Xe!
You'll be stopped in your tracks
Goldman Sachs!

What was it all for?
- MakesMoney v12

No Harm? Well Maybe a Little…

by LAURIE NEIDERGAARDEN, Alternate Reality News Service Medical Writer

Chapdelaine Malteeser is a wreck. He has a purple rash on his left elbow and behind both his knees. He has Alter's Echinastichesus – also known as "Wobbly Fingers" – a disease where the muscles in his fingers randomly stop working, a disease which has tragically ended the career of many a concert pianist and barroom thumb wrestler. His left eye twitches whenever anybody mentions Herbert Lom. He has Planter's Whorl. His stomach periodically produces an enzyme that makes him crave pink flamingos (the lawn ornament, not the actual bird – he has destroyed many a pot in an attempt to make them edible).

Malteeser has found a clinical trial which promises a treatment for his condition, a condition which is a result of his involvement in a series of previous clinical trials, clinical trials which have left a stew of chemicals in his body, a stew of chemicals that are interacting in unexpected – and often, to use a technical medical term, gross – ways.

Phew! – made it out of that sentence alive!

The Amendola-Crisco Process (named after actor Tony Amendola and his favourite brand of shortening) takes anywhere from five days to three weeks to flush the chemicals out of a patient's body. To ease withdrawal symptoms, the patient is jacked into a virtual world until she is declared chemical-free.

"In past trials, men have tended to gravitate to the virtual reality stitched together from scenes from Kevin James and Rob Schneider movies," said Iolanthe Schweppes, Chief Medical Officer for drug giant Gangrenous Plasmids (GP). "I know these are times of diminished expectations, but it's enough to make you weep. In a…detached, professional kind of way, of course."

Schweppes added that women had no discernible pattern in their choice of virtual experience, although peanut butter did show up in a statistically significant number of them.

In its original trial, GP offered patients a virtual world that was a mirror of the real world, but that had to be discontinued when they found that patients began hallucinating that there was another world behind the virtual one, a world where machines harvested human beings for the energy their bodies produced. When the trial was over, these patients could no longer distinguish between reality and fantasy; the lawsuits over "alienation of affect" are still working their way through the courts.

Ironically, the trial – clinical, not legal – for the Amendola-Crisco Process is already oversubscribed, making it unlikely that Malteeser will get in.

"Yeah, sucks to be him," said Estrella Goomy-Baer, one of the trial subjects. What were the symptoms that made her eligible? "I…have a cough…" she stated. "Ahew. See? I'm definitely sick. And…and…and…oh, look! My right earlobe just fell off! Umm…okay, it didn't actually fall off, but see? That's an odd angle for an earlobe to hang, isn't it? It feels like it's about to fall off! Oh, and my atrial…spleen feels bloated, and it's not even my time of the month!"

"She's faking!" Malteeser accused. When I asked him how he could be so sure, he replied, "Because that's what I sounded like when I faked my way into clinical trials!"

"I'm sure that if Mister Malteseer thought about it a little further," commented Ebenezer Cadbury, who recruits subjects for medical clinical trials, "he would realize that he was admitting to **FRAUD** and everybody knows that **FRAUD** is a **CRIME**, so that would be **A REALLY BAD IDEA**."

"Well, yeah," Malteeser backtracked. "There's that."

Are patients signing up for medical treatment trials who do not have the diseases tested for a problem? Schweppes thinks so. "We had one guy show up for a test of a brain seizure medication," Schweppes claimed, "who actually suffered from a hangnail!"

"To be fair," Cadbury responded, "the pain from his hangnail was so intense, he felt like he was having a brain seizure!"

Schweppes claimed that one of the patients for a trial of an anti-psychotic drug turned out, in fact, to be an emperor penguin.

"To be fair," Cadbury insisted, "I thought he was a small person in a tuxedo! It was an honest mistake."

Schweppes claimed that the fact that Cadbury was earning $30,000 to $50,000 for each person he recruited for a medical therapy trial might be affecting his judgment about appropriate test subjects.

"To be fair…" Cadbury started. Five minutes later, he finally added, "At that rate, it is going to take me a long time to become a billionaire!"

"It's just as well," Malteeser sighed. "With my luck, I probably would have ended up in the placebo group!" Then, he watched his right earlobe fall off.

Then, They Had to Face Stupid Reality Again

by HAL MOUNTSAUERKRAUTEN, Alternate Reality News Service Crime/Court Writer

It sounds like something out of a science fiction movie: police using sophisticated technologies to determine where crimes will happen before they are committed. Okay, actually it was a science fiction movie: *Minority Report.* However, many scientific advances, everything from cellular phones to digital ice picks, were anticipated by the literature of the scientifically fantastic, so why not this?

The Santa Cruz, West Lombardy police force fed eight years of crime data into a computer programme, which used the input to brew a fine jamoca almond fudge latte. (In retrospect, running the programme on a Hamilton Beach BrewStation 12 Cup Coffeemaker may not have been a smart choice, but it was the only way the cash-strapped police force could justify replacing the dinky pot they had been using to brew their java since, like, forever.) In addition to making tasty beverages that officers could use to down – not doughnuts, since that is a crude and outdated stereotype – but some sugary snacking food that wasn't doughnuts, the coffeemaker output places in West Lombardy that were most likely to be the scene of a crime.

Not long after the Haemacher-Schlumberr Programme – named after the lead software engineers' fathers - was initiated, the problems started.

The first target of the Programme was an undistinguished office in an industrial park ("You're industries will love the swings and the monkey bars!") in a northern corner of the state. Multinational drug company Pfier-Pfizer was caught planning to fake test results for cancer drug Allahallahakbarfree (commercial name: Cancer be Gone), then pay major cancer researchers to put their name on the company-written *Journal of Not At All*

Dubiously Provenanced Medical Research C paper about the test. (For more on this story, see: "Where there's smoke, there's Pfier-Pfizer," Alternate Reality News Service, June 18, 2…last year.)

"That…wasn't supposed to happen," Libertini "Comfy" Haemacher, one of the creators of the Programme, said when asked about the Pfier-Pfizer raid. "White collar crime wasn't part of the programme's parameters. Still, I…I'm just so darned proud – sniff! – that my baby is taking its first steps!"

"Wow," a pale and slightly stunned Governor Frank Piscatorie also responded. "That, really…uhh…worked, didn't it? Okay, fun is fun, but we should use the Haemacher-Schlumberr Programme for what it was originally intended: fighting street crime."

While the Governor's sentiment was a noble one, the Haemacher-Shlumberr Programme had other ideas. On its second trial, it sent police to the West Lombardy branch of investment bank BearSternsLatoyaGrubnichBachmannTurnerOverthruster. It took the officers no time at all to discover that the investment bank was bundling air from different parts of the country and, with the collusion of bond ratings companies, was planning on passing it off as AAA securities. (For more on this story, see: "A History of Vile Ants," Alternate Reality News Service, February 12, this year.)

"Whoa!" Haemacher enthused. "My baby has become the Eliot Spitzer of crime fighting computer programmes! Umm…minus the hookers and embarrassing talk show on CNBC, I mean."

"Oh, dear," an ashen and very tired looking Governor Piscatorie said. "Don't get me wrong: this may have saved innocent investors from billions of dollars of fraud. But, did it have to happen in an election year?" He mopped the sweat off his forehead, wrung the mop out, and mopped the sweat off his forehead again.

Then, two days ago, in a dramatic middle of lunchtime raid, the Haemacher-Shlumberr Programme sent police to Mountebank

Studios, one of Hollywood's big five production companies. Seven executives were arrested for using accounting tricks to ensure that even their biggest grossing films would never appear to turn a profit, cheating thousands of employees out of money they had earned.

"It was just like a scene out of *Serpico*!" Haemacher said. "Except, without Al Pacino's manly stubble of facial hair."

Governor Piscatorie was taken ill and could not attend a press conference in response to the raid. However, in a press release with his hastily scrawled signature at the bottom, the Governor said, "The Haemacher-Shlumberr Programme has been a wild success, beyond anything I could have imagined when I authorized the pilot project. Well beyond anything I could have imagined, believe you me! That's why we're shutting it down for the time being. To, uhh, study its success. Yeah. Study its success. And, all being well, we'll tweak it ever so slightly and have it up and running in no time. Say…after November."

"This is totally bogus!" Professor Haemacher went full bore Bill and Ted on the decision. "Everybody knows that it's cheaper to prevent a crime than to solve a crime!"

"Have you seen my campaign contributions since this nightmare began?" the Governor's press release retorted.

It was like something out of a science fiction movie, then it went back to being something out of a science fiction movie. For that brief period in between, though, it was magnificent.

Some Entangled Evening

by FREDERICA VON McTOAST-HYPHEN, Alternate Reality News Service People Writer

Police character who hands the lead detective the key piece of lab evidence Zooey Macadoo was giving a talk on "The Special Joy of

Stopping Drunk Drivers" at a police officers convention and karaoke smack down in San Francisco when she started slurring her words. Soon, she was weaving all over the stage and threatening to smash into other speakers. When they realized this was not a demonstration of how to humiliate suspects who cannot walk a straight line, over 70 officers in attendance offered to give her a breathalyzer test; those who succeeded found that she had virtually no alcohol in her system.

Her mysterious behaviour may never have been explained if Macadoo hadn't received a call from her ex-husband, Josh Duchovearl, a couple of hours later saying that he was bombed and asking if she wouldn't mind picking him up from the bar he was sprawled out in front of. A bar in New York. "We were quantabangled," Macadoo explained over groups of officers singing "I Will Survive." "I mean quantum bageled. I mean…oh, shit!"

What she was trying to say was that Macadoo and Duchovearl had been quantum entangled.

"I don't think it works quite that way –" started New York installation artist Jonathon Keats.

Hold on, hold on just a moment, we told him. We have more exposition to get to.

Oshawa Planktons defenseman Bobby Indruschuk was streaking past the blue line when he doubled over with cramps; this was around the same time that his wife, Andronicus, watching from their home in Val-de-Mer, started feeling the effects of her period. This allowed Quebec Nordiques forward Guy LaGuy to steal the puck and score. In a more dramatic universe, this goal would have been the difference in the game, but, as it happened, the Plankton stank like they had washed ashore and started to rot, and this was the fifth goal in an 8-0 rout.

Quantum entanglement connects two particles at a sub-atomic level. When particles are so entangled, what affects one will affect the other, no matter how far apart they are. Across the room or across the universe – it doesn't matter to quantum entangled particles. They're stubborn bastards that way.

"You know, I really hadn't intended for -" Keats tried again.

Please, have a little patience, we assured him. We'll get to you at the appropriate time in the article.

Bobby Trash was on stage with his band The Killing Succotash in South Bend, North Frogtown when he got a paper cut, which was odd considering the nearest piece of paper was three blocks away from the venue. Trash completely mangled the chord he was playing – much to the delight of the band's fans. After the show, he called his current wife, Demosthenes-Janie Trash, at their farm in Northern Southland and discovered that at about the time he felt the paper cut, she had actually cut her finger on a piece of paper she was using to print the first chapter of her memoirs of her time as the band's groupie. This discovery was the beginning of an acrimonious, not to mention mean-spirited, break-up.

Keats set up a particle beam splitter in an art gallery in New York and allowed married people to stand in the particle stream on one side or the other; all of the couples referred to above went through this process. This experience allowed the couples to be united on a much deeper level than a mere marriage certificate could. In fact, it was a surprise to Keats just how deeply the couples who participated in the work would become.

Jonathon? Jonathon? We're ready to hear from you, now.

"What's the bloody point?" Keats asked. "You've already pretty much summed up everything I could say on the subject!"

All quantum processes are very delicate. This means –

"Oh, right. Okay, okay, I've got this one!" Keats interrupted **us**. "All anybody who wants to get out of a quantum entangled marriage has to do is become skeptical of the whole process. Simply stop believing, and you'll be returned to the whole level of reality that involves divorce, child custody and asset divisions."

"That's it?" Trash incredulously asked.

"That's all it takes?" Indruschuk couldn't believe it.

"Why the hell didn't you – hic! – tell us!" Macadoo asked, half-heartedly trying to slap Keats in the face and hitting a concrete wall a couple of metres and half a continent to his left. "Oww!"

"It was in the fine print in the catalog," Keats weakly responded. "Right after the page which thanked the sponsors, my parents and Nils Bohr!"

The installation has been shut down and, aside from the inevitable documentary about the experience, Keats claims that it will not be revived. However, rumours in Washington are that a certain political party is interested in using the technology to control its candidates for office.

"No comment," said Republican operative Karl Rove with a smirk.

The Street Finds its Own Uses for Mutant Technologies

by LAURIE NEIDERGAARDEN, Alternate Reality News Service Medical Writer

On a cotton candy plane with caramel corn mountains in the distance, unicorns with the face of Rush Limbaugh use their horns to pop piñatas in the shape of Franklin Delano Roosevelt. "I always knew heaven would be exactly like this!" enthused Margaret Mendelssohn Meiville to herself.

Meiville was one of 237 patients in comas who are part of a unique study led by Erica Erato of Anthonys Hopkins Medical School. Using Mutant Technologies' Psychrect 2000, which was originally intended to help writers avoid typos by tapping into their psyches to find the word they meant to enter, Erato found she could communicate with people with "locked in syndrome" who were otherwise unable to communicate with the world.

"You know how you'll be sitting on the bus and, not having anything better to do, you'll start daydreaming that the person sitting opposite is really a butterfly wearing a cocoon in the shape of a human being?" Erato explained. "As you watch, everybody around you bursts into a riot of colourful butterflies who escape out an open window and congregate in a stadium downtown to watch lacrosse and drink nectar out of supersized cups and argue about whether dark matter exists or is just a dream of physicists who cannot face the reality of the heat death of the universe and then pogo sticks rain down from the sky and pretty soon all of the butterflies are – are…

"Well – uhh, yeah – my research found that people in comas live in those kind of daydreams."

"Let me just say," Mutant Technologies CEO Theodoric Monangahela did so, "that this is not a sanctioned use of our technology. If we had had any idea that the Psychrect 2000 could be used for this purpose, we…we would have changed its name and marketed it differently!"

The first recorded use of the psychic autocorrect programme to read the thoughts of coma patients was by Sam Gafflebab of the small town of No Fixed Address, Florida. "Mama Rosalita had been in a coma for over 15 years after a flying Eggo incident," Gafflebab explained. "I thought, if I just rested her fingers on the keyboard, we might see something. But, uhh, nothing happened.

The kids, Moondark and Veridian, were getting kind of restless, and began tossing waffles around the hospital room. Before anybody could do anything to stop them, one of them hit Mama Rosalita's finger with enough force to cause it to depress a key – the letter 'f,' I believe it was. Then, the screen just filled up with descriptions of…scenes of a…of a carnal nature. Who knew? I mean, she's 83 years old, for god's sake!"

Gafflebab and his wife Samantha hustled their children out of the hospital room, but they had seen enough to make credible Farcebook updates on the subject. Within months, people all across the world were buying Psychrect 2000s in order to communicate with their comatose loved ones.

"We did not give Mister Gafflebab permission to do that," Monangahela insisted. "If we had known he was going to use the Psychrect 2000 to communicate with his brain-damaged mother, we would have had a documentary crew in the room to record it for future PR purposes! Umm…for humanitarian causes, of course."

Monangahela added that he used the term "brain-damaged" in its clinical sense, and that he hoped that people sensitive to the language would not be quick to – damn Twitter, anyway!

While the creators of the technology may not have been enthusiastic about its new use, others were ecstatic.

"We knew it! We knew it all along!" exulted the Reverend Pat "Oral" Righteous. "Just because people have no apparent brain function doesn't mean that they aren't alive and shouldn't be kept alive by any means necessary! Take that, orthodox medical establishment!"

Erato found that if somebody typed a question into the computer on which the Psychrect 2000 software was running, the people in comas would respond to it. When she asked what they would prefer if given the choice between rejoining the real world or dying, 97 per cent of those who didn't cling to the fantasy that they **were** in the real world chose death.

"Oh! Well! I mean..." Reverend Righteous backpedalled, "clearly, more research is needed before we can say anything definitive on the subject. I'm sure that good Christian folk weren't part of the...you know, the group that wanted to die..."

Actually, all but one of the Christians identified in Erato's research preferred to die. Those who expressed a preference to continue living were primarily atheists who had created worlds of Marxian or Randian perfection.

"Oh, poop," Reverend Righteous solemnly commented when apprised of this.

Meanwhile, Erato was enthusiastic about continuing her research. "If we can get these results with people in a coma," she stated, "imagine what we could find out about the inner lives of Senators!"

Poo-r Judgment

by ENGELBERT HUMPERFLAPDOODLEPUSS, Alternate Reality News Service Excrement Writer

What is the one thing that all living creatures have in common? No, it's not mitochondrial reproduction. It's not reverse mortgaging their homes in order to stiff their ungrateful children of their inheritance (although this is very popular with the lower primates), either. It's certainly not falling in love. (Cole Porter should be ashamed of himself for propagating *that* little bit of misinformation!)

It's excrement. Everything poops.

The rare Indonesian rattleferret poops crackers in the shape of the Lunar Excursion Module from Apollo moon missions 11, 12, 15 and 17; Rick Santorum farts Bible quotes; frogs in the wilds of the Brooklyn zoo poop zirconium cubes; a Samoan tribe that was too otiose for Margaret Mead to study have since been discovered that poops what appear to be orange popsicles (not that anybody is tempted to lick them to find out for sure…); the Lennon Lizard of equatorial Yukon poops strawberries; Doris Day pooped sunshine; the African budgie fish found in Lake Huron poops liquid 1040 tax forms, and; so much more.

The vast diversity of nature is truly a thing to behold. You might not want to smell it, but it sure is worth beholding.

Given the universality of the excrementory process, one (who, in this case, is Arnold Grelbner, an itinerant hacky sack catalogue distributor from Kenosha, Nova Scotia) would have thought human enginuity (the ability to come up with ideas for new car motors) would have found a purpose for this seemingly infinitely renewable resource (other than giving sewer systems a reason for existing, of course). One would have been wrong. And, all the other numbers who agreed with one.

Until now.

Scientists at the B. A. Mensch Institute of Yucky Research in Osaka, Japan (yes, the real Osaka – don't look so surprised!) have developed technologies that can analyze a person's excrement and determine if the person has any health problems. "With apologies to Arnold Grelbner, the path through our digestive tract is a very informative one," explained Salmon Fujiwada, lead Poopologist at the Mensch Institute. "We have long known the diagnostic possibilities inherent in – please pardon the scientific jargon – deep doodoo. What our researchers were able to do was synthesize this knowledge and use it to develop a technology that could accurately analyze poop at its source: the toilet."

The toilet? Wow. What will they think of next?

The Toodle Loo, named after junior researcher Mongo Sakayami's second wife, uses a vacuum system to suck waste out of the toilet. It then passes through a series of tubes that conduct sophisticated medical diagnostic tests on it before being flushed into the sewers. When the user flushes the toilet, it connects with their Shitkicker Sam App (which, to save some users' delicate sensibilities, doubles as a *Street Fighter* clone). When the tests have been completed, the information on the person's health is then sent to the app.

Trial use of the Toodle Loo has been set up in New York and Los Angeles because –

"WHAT!" exclaimed National Association of Vaguely Worded Press Denunciations Vice President in Charge of Bean Dip Eleanor Bronte. "First, they take our employment away, leaving us with crap jobs, then they want to analyze our crap! Is nothing sacred any more? Why do you think bowels have movements? Because they move us! Emotionally! The elimination of doodie is such a personal, such a private thing, and to have it subjected to such sterile technological analysis is –"

Because of reactions like that.

"The Mensch Institute does research on the cutting edge of grossness," Fujiwada stated. "That doesn't mean that the Japanese people are willing to be our guinea pigs. And, speaking of guinea pigs, did you know that they excrete –"

Sorry, but that paragraph has sailed.

"My apologies, Captain." Fujiwada argued that the health benefits of Toodle Loo technology were too important to allow skeptics to capsize. Capsize? Well, some nautical metaphor for disaster, in any case. "From the moment a child is toilet trained, we can monitor him, her or toaster oven for the markers of a variety of diseases. The implications for early detection and treatment of illnesses could revolutionize health care!"

The drug industry sat up and took notice.

"But, but, but," Bronte sputtered, "think about the privacy implications! Do you really want the government to have access to analyses of your rectal discharges? Your dentist? The high school Glee Club? The high school Glee Club's dentist? Don't you know that this is just the kind of information the Clipper Chip was designed to allow the government to secretly access? I, for one, don't want –"

"Eww! What the hell was that?" Bronte and Fujiwada said in unison, even though they were interviewed separately.

Sorry about that. I had chili for lunch.

After 37 years on the Alternate Reality News Service's Excrement beat, Engelbert Humperflapdoodlepuss can finally officially retire having written his first article.

The Plane Truth

MARA VERHEYDEN-HILLIARD, Alternate Reality News Service Disasters Writer

Disaster was narrowly averted this afternoon when a Class C android, colloquially known as Clara Consort, landed a 747 jumbo jet after the auto-pilot and auto-co-pilot came down with mysterious illnesses and could no longer fly the plane.

"Oh, really, it was nothing," Consort, electronically flustered, stated. "Any reasonable member of the cabin staff would have done the same. And, be sure to note when you quote me that I am programmed to be modest, won't you?"

The problem began on Boering Airlines non-stop flight 242 from Toronto to Oshawa when passengers starting making strange complaints. A vacuubot named Velma on its way to spend the holidays with its boyfriend, a Bleack and Daker power saw, thought the cabin was full of butterflies, and wanted to know if a window could be opened to shoo them out of the plane. A Terrorbot 52000, on leave from the war on trees to visit its buddies, insisted it was itchy – even though its exoskeleton was made of a mixture of titanium and shoe polish – and started scratching off its outer layers. A Shatspian 1931 on its way to Stratford for a weenie roast of William Shakespeare insisted that it saw a Demon Emulator on the wing of the airplane.

Investigators believe that these delusions were caused by a malicious virus that was introduced into the plane's music system. That, or the cream in the éclairs was off. "It's still early days," said Columbot, the Class D(etective) android that was the lead investigator of the incident. "And, I don't want to intrude, but I have just one more question to ask..."

Whatever the cause, the problem quickly spread to the cockpit. (It's only a 12 minute flight, so the spread of the problem had to be quick.) XD1E-275, a grizzled auto-pilot looking forward to retiring after one final flight, believed it had achieved a state of nirvana where it was one with the air molecules surrounding the plane. FG7AB-103, the hotshot young auto-co-pilot that didn't know as much as it thought it did about aviation, dribbled corn starch out of its console and refused to stop singing "Only Love Can Break Your Heart."

"I immediately knew something was wrong," Consort confided. "FG was singing on key – the first time I had ever heard him do that!"

And, the plane had entered a nosedive that would have resulted in a crash in a matter of seconds.

"Yes," Consort allowed, "there was that."

Taking the controls, the quick-witted Consort pulled the plane out of its dive. Unfortunately, it flew right into a swarm of nanobots that were in the sky to sew up a hole in the ozone layer. The needles they were using cracked open the cockpit window.

"That was an unfortunate turn of events," Consort stated. "I mean, the auto-pilots fly on instruments – I don't even know why the plane had a window!"

Whatever the reason, the pressure in the cockpit plummeted, sucking the auto-pilot and auto-co-pilot out the window. Consort was able to survive by handcuffing herself to the leg of one of the empty pilot's chairs bolted to the floor.

"Yeah, about that," Columbot asked, "I'm sorry, it's probably nothing, but I have to ask myself: what was she doing with a pair of handcuffs in the first place? I mean, in the cockpit?"

Good question, but one that will have to wait. Although she could barely see the control panel because of the way her handcuffed body was situated, Consort managed to stabilize the plane. Unfortunately, because it was off its flight plan, it crashed into an RCMP drone that was patrolling Highway 401 looking for illegal interprovincial yak smugglers.

"I tell you," Consort told us, "we just couldn't catch a break!"

Number 4 engine (the one with the snotty attitude towards garden gnomes), was totaled, putting the plane into a second nosedive. "The whole falling to the ground/imminent death thing was getting a bit old," Consort allowed. "Still, first aid was part of my programming, so I figured I could do it on the entire airplane."

Oshawa Ground Control helped talk Consort through the complex procedure of landing the plane – did we mention a sudden snowstorm came out of nowhere? "Hunh!" Consort snorted. "No global warming my einsteinium ass!" The plane's body was wrecked because the landing gear refused to go out without its mittens, but no passengers were lost.

"Yeah," Columbot interjected, "I have just one more question about that and we'll be done. I've been wracking my electronic brain over it, and I couldn't help but wonder –"

Just one question? Because, we have several questions, but they don't change the fact that Clara Consort heroically landed a jumbo jet, saving all of the passengers on board. Right?

"Well, yeah, about that –"

Right.

Reality is for People Who Can't Handle Games

SPECIAL TO THE ALTERNATE REALITY NEWS SERVICE
by catch12scratch24fervor

Last week, the Alternate Reality News Service ran an article by Doctor Freddy Wottagit-Rathbourne called "Alien Mind Suck." In that article, Dr. Wottagit-Rathbourne argued that Mastiff Multi-penguin Obelisk Rope Parlaying Guitars were bad for children because they caused impressionable minds to lose sight of reality, and that they were bad for adults because they...umm... they caused impressionable minds to lose sight of reality. (I may be paraphrasing a little here. Okay, I may actually be paraphrasing a lot here: I was so angry after I read the article that I erased it from my hard drive and put a lock on my computer that would redirect me to the *Girls With Eyepatches* Web site if I tried to access it again. I'm pretty sure that what I have written is the general gist of the thing, though.)

Allow me to rebut.

Dr. Wottagit-Rathbourne is a Xylanthian Smeghead.

I spend 14 hours a day playing *World of Wowcraft*, an epic fantasy Massive Multi-penguin Obelisk Rope Parlaying Guitar that allows me to slay dragons without having to get a permit from City Council. When I'm not doing that, I usually spend an equal amount of time playing *Star Blap*, a science fiction Massive Multi-penguin Obelisk Rope Playing Guitar that, legend has it, was based on a console game that was based on a series of movies that was based on a television show that was based on a set of action figures that was based on an earlier series of movies that was based on a series of books that was based on an all but forgotten TV series. I may have missed a couple of media, there, but you get the idea.

Aside from impaired vision, some hearing loss and a lessened appreciation for *Masterpiece Theatre*, I do not believe these games have done me any harm. In fact, quite the opposite: they have improved my life in a variety of ways.

One great thing about playing in a Massive Multi-penguin Online Rope Playing Guitar, for example, is that when you look for an Easter egg, you never know what you'll find. It could be the signature of the janitor who was cleaning up the office one night when he noticed a terminal a programmer had forgotten to log off of and decided to get jiggy. It could be an Aston Martin gleaming behind the shed reserved for the pig slop. It could be a seven hour documentary on the making of the game, which, admittedly, is about six and a half more hours than I would want to sit through, but the point is that you never know what you'll find when you go looking for an Easter egg in an Massive Multi-penguin Online Role Playing Guitar.

In the real world, when you hunt for an Easter egg, all you get is an Easter egg. If you're lucky.

But, it isn't just rewarding obsessive behaviour that makes Massive Multi-player Online Role Playing Guitars so great. When I confront a Xyxxman Rat Captain in a battle, either I cut off its head or it cuts off my head. Simple, really. When I confront Sigmeund, a rat bastard in a boardroom, anything could happen. He could agree with my analysis of the situation, or he could disagree with it, or he could break down and cry about how his wife doesn't love him and he suspects that his children aren't really his and he knows he shouldn't be drinking, but he needs something to dull the pain, and could we please give him another chance because he really could succeed if only he felt that somebody believed in him. Or, he could laugh and walk out of the room because he has dirt on the CEO which makes him think he's bulletproof (until an investor, angry that he lost his comic book collection investing in the company, shoots him and proves otherwise). And, whatever his reaction, I cannot cut off his head. Even a little.

Games are simple. Life is an eleven dimensional Rubik's cube.

It isn't just that, though. Honour. Teamwork. How to quell a Bakkrandian uprising on Nigel Four. Massive Multi-player Online Role Playing Guitars have a lot of lessons to teach us, lessons that we can apply IRR (in real reality). (Except, perhaps, for teamwork, since you can only access solo missions before level 21, and most players quit before they reach that level.)

Computer games have been blamed for everything from increasing teen pregnancy (like gamers have the time for…that!) to my Aunt Bertha's Cystitis (although she is willing to allow that the raccoons roaming freely throughout the neighbourhood may be a contributing factor). I have no idea if any of this is true. I do know that they have a lot of positive effects on gamers, so non-gamers should leave them alone already!

catch12scratch24fervor is a yeast analyst for Crisco Systems.

Days of Future Shoppe© Past

by SASKATCHEWAN KOLONOSCOGRAD, Alternate Reality News Service Philosophy Writer

As if to celebrate last year's scandal, the Future Shoppe© currently has a bigger and better scandal on its slimy tentacles.

I'm not talking about the way patrons of the store are not allowed to choose the seven seconds of their future that they pay exorbitant amounts of money to experience. That was a mere controversy (with a hint of lemon).

"It's, uhh, random," said Future Shoppe© spokesperson Hobgoblin Himbo. "Yeah. Sure. We have no control over what part of the future you get to see. Sorry, but it's out of our slimy tentacles."

I'm not talking about how MultiNatCorp, the sole proprietor of the Future Shoppe© ("We do tech stuff that only seems impossible because it is"), acquiesced to the government's desire to put a ClipArt chip into the computer that reads people's futures. (The ClipArt chip allows the government to substitute puppies, kittens, Morticia Addams and other innocuous line art images for future projections that could involve national security.) No, this was a mere bad rinse in the 24 hour news cycle.

"I can understand why people hoping to see if they have been crowned King of America would object to getting soaked for all that money – and, let's be honest, it's great heaping piles of cash even if you use PayPal – for seven seconds of 'It's a Mall World After All,'" said Director of the National Snoopiness Agency Maddox Fred Maddox. "Still – national security. Ha ha."

Last year's scandal was, of course, that the Future Shoppe© was selling very wealthy clients glimpses of extra seconds of their future. "What? Is this Communist Albumeth?" Himbo protested. "What's the point of accumulating vast sums of money if you can't spend it to see more of your future than common people?"

When it was pointed out to him that this undermined the whole rationale behind people being limited to buying only seven seconds, Himbo replied, "Oh. Well. Of course, I meant to say that nobody gets special treatment. I, uhh, can't imagine how that rumour got started…"

This year's scandal is the revelation that the company actually plucks a memory out of its clients' brains and dresses it up to look like the future. One client complained that her "vision of the future" was actually a memory of her school prom with robots instead of adult monitors. The company responded with a press release arguing that it was actually a dance in the old folk's home where she would eventually find herself. And, she was short because people shrink over time. And, she was wearing braces because she…umm…yeah, had really bad teeth or something.

Another client threatened to sue the company when she realized that a scene where she gave birth couldn't be a vision of the future because she had had an ovariesectomy. "Yeah, well," Himbo sniffed, "in the future, in vitro fertilization will be so advanced that women will get pregnant just by walking past a clinic!"

"It was ridiculous!" ridiculed Piotr L3eprechaun. "In the future I saw, I was having a shower. At first, I thought, *Okay, when I get older, my sense of personal hygiene will remain intact. Good to know.* Only, I realized that I was singing the same song I had been singing in the shower that morning: 'Volare' – the Barry White version, not the David Bowie version, because that's how much I respect the ladies. In the shower I saw at the Future Shoppe©, I even had the same fantasy about…umm, yeah, best not to name names, positions or condiments. Let's just say I needed extra soap at exactly the same moment!"

Himbo pointed out that in L3eprechaun's vision, the shower heads were different.

"Oh, well, yeah, I guess it must have been the future, then," L3eprechaun conceded. Unless he was being sarcastic. It's hard to pick up sarcasm in print.

Himbo argued that the Future Shoppe© was selling the "idea of the future" rather than actual glimpses of the future. When confronted with advertisements that had appeared on television, radio and Internet dolphin mating Web sites that said, "See your future," Himbo bit his upper lip and sheepishly suggested that it was a typo that should have read "Bee an hour's suture." When it was pointed out to him that this made no sense, Himbo argued that, to somebody from 100 years ago, the *Random Busby Berkeley Generator* would make no sense. We had to concede his point.

Will the latest scandal destroy the Future Shoppe©? If Himbo used the company's technology to see what will happen to it in the years to come, he isn't saying.

Boysenberrying It In

by CORIANDER NEUMANEIMANAYMANEEMAMANN, Alternate Reality News Service Urban Issues Writer

Stock broker Ernesto Gezundheit was walking down the street, basking in the glow of behaviour we cannot describe in a family publication to a corporation our lawyers advise us against naming, when he was hustled into an alley by half a dozen street people. There, he was spray painted with slogans such as "ghoulie masher" and "manass to soceity" (sick), tags from half a dozen different street artists and a stenciled image of a badger wearing a 19th century frock coat and aviator goggles.

"Okay, okay," Gezundheit allowed, "a couple of blocks earlier, I kicked a homeless man in the…uhh…ghoulies. But, does that mean I deserve to become a piece of street art?"

After a spate (more than a gunge but less than a mockery) of such incidents, Metro police have put out an advisory warning citizens to walk past homeless men with caution and do everything in their power to avoid kneeing them in the ghoulies. If you succumb to the urge of rudely striking one, the police warn, he may take out his Boysenberry, photograph you with it and send the image to every other homeless man, woman and Shetland pony in the city.

"After that, well, things could get messy," said Sergeant Bilbo Bailiwick. "They could get very messy, indeed."

The number of Web pages catering to homeless people has increased substantially over the last couple of years, with sites such as hobowithacellphone.com, rubysrevenge.org and witheringheights.ca growing in popularity. The sites are mostly used for such things as: posting photos of food items found in dumpsters to get people's opinions on whether or not they are edible; trading dirty pictures (of people with three layers of clothes instead of six), and; sharing shopping cart maintenance tips. In addition to these wholesome activities, though, the networks are now being used by the homeless to alert others of their – class? kind? ilk? shelter disposition? – well, others that abusive citizens are heading their way.

And, increasingly, to take action against them.

"What I want to know," Gezundheit said, "is how did homeless people get cellphones in the first place?"

This, of course, leads to the obvious question: how **did** homeless people get the cellphones in the first place?

The answer: Low Status User Envy (or "Ill Sue").

Low Status User Envy is a French tuna and Swiss on a whole wheat submarine sand – sorry, to make my deadline, I had to miss lunch. This is a theory that if somebody with relatively high social status (aka: a hoity-toity bastard) passes somebody with relatively low social status (aka: a poor bastard) who has a piece of technology that the hoity-toity bastard doesn't have, the hoity-toity bastard will ask herself, "Why does that poor bastard have a piece of technology that I don't have? I thought the whole point of being a hoity-toity bastard was to have the best toys! I must get one immediately!"

Some companies have had modest success applying this theory. BMW sales rose almost 2.7 per cent when the company gave away cars to Wal-Mart employees. Of course, most of them couldn't pay for the gas to run the cars, so they ended up using them as spare rooms for their children or marijuana grow-ops; and, in over a third of the cases, the people who were given BMWs ended up living in them. Still, a survey of people making over $250,000 showed that, if they were forced to live out of their cars, after seeing what the low income people did with their BMWs, that would be the car they would choose.

Scientists at Decline in Motion (aka: DIM) thought that if they gave their latest phone technology (ka: the Boysenberry) to people on the lowest rung of the social ladder, just about everybody in the country would want one thanks to the Ill Sue theory.

Unfortunately, corporate lawyers could afford to buy their own Boysenberries, so DIM decided to give them to homeless people instead.

"Man, we just can't seem to do anything right these days!" remarked Jim Ballsilly, DIM's co-CEO and the man who makes the tuna casserole for the cafeteria on Thursdays. (I didn't hallucinate that – somebody brought me a bagel.)

A survey of corner offices showed that 98 per cent actually didn't want to use products that were widely used by homeless people. Since surveys of offices generally reflect the sentiments of the people who work in them, it was assumed that a vast majority of senior corporate executives agreed with the sentiment.

"What about my suit?" Gezundheit asked. Which reminded us of the question: what happened to Gezundheit's suit?

Apparently, it's now hanging in the Corcoran Gallery, which bought it for an undisclosed sum of money (and a year's supply of dry-cleaning).

The Whole HOG™

by INDIRA CHARUNDER-MACHARRUNDEIRA, Alternate Reality News Service Fine Arts Writer

Curiosity may not have killed the copycat, but it sure did earn it a long prison sentence.

Ever since Jimmy Pfiz was convicted of killing his father with a gun he had made with the family's Home Object Generator™ and turned it into an object d'art, had his conviction overturned because it slipped on appeal, became a darling of the Nanjing art scene, wrote a best-selling biography, drifted gently into obscurity, wrote eight volumes of forgettable poetry and was featured on an episode of *Where Are They Now and Why Does Anybody Care?*, there has been an epidemic of people using their HOG™s to fashion murder weapons and refashion them into art.

- French cattle prodder Henri Trousseau made a knife with his HOG™ that he used to stab his lover, the concierge of his lover's apartment building and a bull mastiff named Mrs. Fluffy. He then melted the knife down and used the plastic to create a miniature Venus de Milo **with arms.** Fine arts journal *Hinter-Texte* enthusiastically called it "a tour de force of esthetic revisionism and bad taste."

- Canadian Matt Frewfrew used his HOG™ to create a rifle that he shot random strangers with from the roof of the OCAD building. Then, he incorporated the rifle and other materials into a six foot sculpture of a bottle of maple syrup. At his trial, Frewfrew said, "I was making an ironic comment on Canada's perpetual national identity crisis." Despite an approving editorial in *Today's Art Weekly*, Frewfrew was given a life sentence, presumably for the murders and not for his art.

- After he used his HOG™ to create a gun with which he shot his local borscht supplier and several hogs that just happened to be passing by the shop, Ukrainian Yevgeny Vlasch used the gun and several other weapons he had made to create a complex abstract sculpture that had many jutting angles and hints of human faces in agony. In the artist's statement accompanying his trial, he called this sculpture "Hegemon's Flight of Fancy XVII." Vlasch was sentenced to death, presumably for his art and not for the murder.

"This puts us in a ticklish position," allowed Ned Feeblish, Vice President for Artistic Interventions and Seismic Declensions for MultiNatCorp – "We do innovative technological – without the slightest legal liability for the consequences of our products – stuff" – the corporate owner of Krapp's Last Industries, the creators of the Home Object Generator™. "On the one hand, we do not want to be seen to condone murderous behaviour. Certainly not publicly – if we learned nothing from our experience in the Seychelles, we learned that.* On the other hand, we don't want to stifle anybody's creative urges, especially when they belong to a burgeoning new art form. I think I'm going to have to go no comment on this one."

You would have thought the National Rifle Association (whose motto "A handgun in every pot" only made sense if you were on pot, but nevertheless appeared on 100,000 bumper stickers every year) would be happy at the increasing availability of firearms. As it happens, though, the NRA's biggest benefactors, arms manufacturers, were up in…well, they weren't very happy about this challenge to their industry.

"Art made out of weapons…naah," said NRA spokesman Charlton Heston by Ouija board.

President Schmidt Bobney stated that his administration would have zero tolerance for deadly works of art: "And, to show you how serious we are, we will haul into court as accomplices the makers of any 3-D printers implicated in any violent crime." When Feeblish pointed out all of the legitimate uses people have been putting HOG™s to, President Bobney responded, "Okay. Right. Well, to show you how serious my administration is, we will shut down any Web sites that provide people with schematics for weapons they can build using their HOG™s." When the Internet pointed out that making it illegal to supply people with plans to make weapons was absurd when they could legally buy completed weapons online, President Bobney responded, "Okay. Good point. To show you how seriously my administration takes this, we will be studying ways to stop it. In the meantime, we'll be setting up a new department of art criticism in the FBI in order to – what? This has always been our policy, and I've never said otherwise!"

As the technology for 3-D printers becomes more sophisticated, artists are incorporating a wider variety of materials in their esthetic weapons, including: fur from cats and dogs (except for Saint Bernards), unused napkins and tissues, previously loved pixels, spark plugs from Chevys produced after 1978, low-grade uranium, recycled chicken noodle soup, obsolete CDs and DVDs, NRA bumper stickers, high-grade diesel fuel, recalled tainted beef, Elgin marble (for those who can afford it) and a baby's arm holding an apple.

"Artists are always looking for new materials to incorporate into their work," concluded the *Hinter-Texte* article. "It will be interesting to see what mayhem they come up with next!"

* For more on this, see GINRACHMANJINJa-VITUS, GIDEON, "She Sells Seychelles by the Sea Shore," *Alternate Reality News Service*, three years, six months, two weeks and a day ago.

Mutant Technologies Favours Lateral Marketization

by HAL MOUNTSAUERKRAUTEN, Alternate Reality News Service Court Writer

The usually volatile courtroom of Justice Roberta Padwihller was a sea of calm as she adjourned the trial of Marcy McMahon, who is accused of killing Jason Medasko with kindness – actually, a .40 calibre rifle named "Kindness" – in order to consider a defense motion to dismiss all charges because McMahon's confession was coerced.

McMahon was questioned using an electronic form on a desktop computer. What he didn't know was that the computer was running the Truthrecht 2500 programme, which monitors the typist's brain and actually outputs what he was thinking rather than what he ty –

W…wait a second. This Truthrecht 2500 sounds…familiar. It sounds…very familiar. It sounds like –

"The Psychrect 2000?" asked Mutant Technologies CEO Theodoric Monangahela.

No. No, that's not it…although, now that you mention it, yes, yes, that's exactly it!

"It's a total coincidence," Monangahela stated.

When McMahon was arrested, he was placed in an interrogation room with a computer running GoodCop/BadCop v2017.2.3e. The Bad Cop avatar told him that he needed to put on a harness that was lying on the table in front of him. The Good Cop avatar asked him if he wanted a soda. The Bad Cop avatar insisted that he would be in "real trouble" if he did not put on the harness. The Good Cop avatar asked him if maybe he wanted a little something to help him relax – they had a wide selection of popular magazines, or perhaps extract of heroin. The Bad Cop turned on the Good Cop and told him to stop mollycoddling the perp. The Good Cop argued that they always got better results when they treated the perp like a human being, not a…a perp. The Bad Cop turned towards McMahon and told him they would be right back; both avatars immediately left the screen.

When the avatars returned, the Bad Cop avatar had a nasty smile and the chastened Good Cop avatar quietly said, "I think it would be for the best if you put on the harness."

McMahon did as he was told. When he typed in his name, the Truthrecht 2500 read his brainwaves and found a complete description of the crime, including: the name of the greeter at the MultiMaxiMegaMart where he bought the ammunition (Furnestina); the music McMahon was listening to when he affixed the scope and silencer to the rifle (a potent mixture of Black Sabbath, Rihanna and the Bonzo Dog Doodah Band); the underwear he was wearing at the time of the murder (red with little white hearts – an unfortunate detail that has thankfully not been entered into evidence at the trial), and; how he disposed of the gun after the shooting (he put it back in the drawer in the basement where he kept it).

Oddly, the Truthrecht 2500 did not reveal the name of the person who hired McMahon to kill Medasko. "No technology is perfect," Monangahela shrugged.

McMahon's lawyer, April Raines (yes, that really is her name – her mother was a big fan of *The Spirit*), argued that use of the Truthrecht 2500 was tantamount to forcing her client to incriminate himself, a violation of the bible of the TV show *Law and Order*. "The use –" she began.

"Aww, save it for appeal!" the Bad Cop avatar interrupted from its computer screen several blocks away. "He didn't say – or even type – a single incriminating word!"

The Good Cop avatar mumbled something about "doing our best under difficult circumstances."

Raines countered that the Truthrecht 2500 was an unproven technology and, as such, was similar to the lie detector, which anybody who had seen an episode of *Hill Street Blues* knows is not admissible in a court of law. "The Truthrecht 2500 is –" she started.

"Yeah, yeah, yeah," the Bad Cop avatar shouted. "I bust my hump every day – okay, it's small and I cover it up with prosthetic shoulder pads, but I do have one! – trying to put bad people behind bars. And, bastard defense lawyers like you – no offense – get them off on…technicalities!"

"He used to be a good cop," the Good Cop avatar whispered. "I don't know what happened – it's the job. The job changes you…"

One thing I've wondered since I started covering this trial: why is the company called Mutant Technologies? "Mutant has an element of danger to it," explained Monangahela. "It seems to be somewhat out of control, releasing the sort of creative energies that were there at the Big Bang. Well, that and the fact that the name Hybrid Technologies was already taken!" Oh. That was...mildly disappointing.

Justice Padwihller is expected to rule on the admissibility of information gathered by the Truthrecht 2500 some time before the sun goes nova.

Everybody Came Back From Holiday

by FREDERICA VON McTOAST-HYPHEN, Alternate Reality News Service People Writer

"The JournoMoWri App had a bad habit of starting its articles with a quote," said Hugo award-winning *New York Times* political columnist Albert Brooks. "Every first year journalism student knows that you start with at least one paragraph of exposition to set up the basic premise of an article before you start quoting people. It was making me look bad!"

Six months after most people in the developed world (and parts of Boston) went on holiday and let their digital apps run their lives, the vast majority have returned. Some, like Brooks, had bad experiences (although perhaps none so bad as Donald Trump, but since that story has been rehashed dozens of times in newspaper and magazine articles, three different made-for-TV movies and even an au gratin potato dish, we won't rehash it here).

Others found that when they lost their phone service, they effectively lost their lives.

"It was horrible!" said freeform orthodontist Foster Brooks. "Minutes after I lost my Mortgage Manager app, seven separate real estate brokers put my house up for sale! Because the bank had dealt exclusively with the app, it wouldn't accept that I still existed, even when I went in and stood naked in front of the

Accounts Manager! It wasn't my proudest moment, although a lot of the tellers did ask me if I was working out…"

Brooks – that would be Foster, not Albert – found his life spiraling out of control after that. "I…I'm getting used to this box I'm currently living in," he stated. "What it lacks in room, it makes up for in draftiness!"

While we all know people with equally sad stories (there wouldn't be a country music industry without them), a slightly smaller but otherwise congruent vast majority had a very different reason for coming home.

"Sales were up a hundred gabillion per cent in the six months that I was away," carped Mel Brooks, President and CEO of Consolidated Crappe (proud makers of the Benito Mussolini bobble-head figure!, the zero-gravity whoopie cushion!! and the five mile long bendy straw!!!). "I didn't want the board to think I wasn't earning my ridiculous annual bonus! I…I like my bonus. It helps me sleep at night…"

"My daughter Millipede's grades shot up when I was on holiday," stay home take-away mom Brooks Avery moaned. "When I hacked into the camera on her desktop, her bed had been made and there were no empty whiskey bottles on her dresser. I had to come back – I didn't want anybody to think I was a bad mother! Can I help it if I like strip Mahjong with the girls night? There's nothing wrong with that. I can quite any time I want to – I just never seem to want to…"

Although Millipede Brooks refused to be interviewed for this article, GoodGirlsDont, the app that she was running while she was on holiday, stated that she came back because she didn't like being shown up by a stupid computer programme just because it ate all of her vegetables and never let a boy get past first base on a date and made her room tidier than the clean room at a computer chip manufacturing plant and got her homework in – not on time, no, that would be bad enough – but **early**, and that she would show it, and the world, and even her parents, that she could be a good daughter without it.

In short, people – and, not just those named Brooks, either – started drifting back to their regular existence when they realized that their apps were better at living their lives than they were.

“That’s a rather harsh assessment,” demurred clinical nosey person Brooke Shields. “A lot of people found that sitting on the beach, sipping Pina Colodas while listening to Rupert Holmes got boring after a couple of months. I don’t understand it myself – Pina Colodas are damn tasty! – but most people have returned to their tedious, droning, monoto –”

When I suggested that it wasn’t Shields who responded to my question, that it was, in fact, Shrink Rap, a source of psychiatric information and insight for journalists, she indignantly responded, “Of course it’s me! W…who – what would make you think it wasn’t?”

For one thing, I pointed out, she had given a 46 word response to a question, and didn’t lapse into psychiatric jargon once.

“Oh, ah, negative reinforcement penis envy,” Shields, if it was Shields, sputtered, “…ah ah ah Electra Industrial Complex…Triumphant Individual Telemetry for Thematic Apperception Tests…ah…”

A small number of people continue to enjoy a holiday while they allow their computer apps to live their lives for them. But, for how much longer? For. How. Much. Longer?

Bring Me the Head of Alan Turing!

by FREDERICA VON McTOAST-HYPHEN, Alternate Reality News Service People Culture Writer

The animatronic, AI-enhanced head of Alan Turing has gone missing.

"I wouldn't worry too much about it," said DCI Gene Hunt. "They tell me that Turing's a smart lad, good head on his…well, a smart lad, anyway, so I'm sure he couldn't be up to anything too stupid."

Turing's head was last seen at Salome's Strip & Clip Joint in London's East End, where he was talking to the animatronic, AI-enhanced head of Philip K. Dick.

"Are you sure it was Alan Turing's animatronic, AI-enhanced head?" the animatronic, AI-enhanced head of Philip K. Dick asked. "Maybe it was the animatronic, AI-enhanced head of an Alan Turing impersonator who had forgotten that he wasn't the real animatronic, AI-enhanced head of Alan Turing. Maybe it was the animatronic, AI-enhanced head of Isaac Asimov that had been reprogrammed to think it was the animatronic, AI-enhanced head of Alan Turing. For that matter, are you sure this universe is real? How do we know that we're not all characters in some fake news article dreamed up by a demented –"

We didn't have time to hear all of the possible paranoid scenarios the animatronic, AI-enhanced head of Philip K. Dick could come up with, so we pretended to hear our LOLcat mewling for its supper and went backstage to talk to one of the performers at the adult club.

"Stripping from the neck up is not a matter of what you show," the animatronic, AI-enhanced head of Lili St. Cyr explained, a wispy veil blowing around her face, "but, rather what you artfully conceal."

Asked if she had known the animatronic, AI-enhanced head of Alan Turing, the animatronic, AI-enhanced head of Lili St. Cyr said she may have noticed him around the club. "Hard not to, really," she sniffed. "He would go on and on about how we were all part of a single, universal computational machine. I swear, if he hadn't been so cute! – not that **that** mattered very much, if you know what I mean…"

We said we didn't know what she meant. When the animatronic, AI-enhanced head of Lili St. Cyr said it wasn't like it was subtle, we explained that we had led a sheltered life. "Alan preferred his heads more…chiseled," she told us. We shook our heads. "Hairier?" We smiled in polite bafflement. "Goodness, but you are thick! He would rather be with male heads than female heads!"

Oooooooh.

"But, still," we sputtered, "how…I mean, without a body, is it even – you know – is there really a possibility of…umm…"

"Zis is a very interesting qvestion," stated the animatronic, AI-enhanced head of noted sexologist and hardscrabble oil wildcatter Dr. Ruth Westheimer. "If our zexuality is focused solely in our genital regions, zen siz would make no sense, yes? Howeffer, if zexuality iz affected by brain structure and chemicals, zen zis is indeed possible!"

"But…they're…just…heads!" we objected. "Astonishingly life-like recreations of the faces and intellects of famous people, but, still! Heads! No bodies! How –"

"Tut, tut," the animatronic, AI-enhanced head of Dr. Ruth Westheimer tut tutted us. "Human desire iz a mysterious three leggedy beasty!"

Oh.

The police have brought in the animatronic, AI-enhanced head of Rock Hudson and the animatronic, AI-enhanced head of Cary Grant for questioning. "They aren't suspects or nothing," DCI Hunt, hastily stuffing some BMW brochures in a drawer and slamming it shut, explained. "You can't do no foul play without limbs, right? It's just – you just can't. But, what the hell? They do liven the place up – especially for the birds!"

The proliferation (not to be confused with the process of turning somebody into an anti-abortion zealot) of animatronic, AI-enhanced heads can be traced back almost 20 years, when every museum, art gallery and rock and roll hall of fame seemed to have to have one. The problem with animatronic, AI-enhanced heads is that they tend to take on a life of their own – legally as well as literally – so when they got bored of them, the museums, art galleries and halls of fame couldn't just drive into the countryside, leave them by the side of the road and hope they never found their way back home.

Thus, the profusion (not to be confused with the razor, the anti-nuclear fission movement or the short-lived NHL/jazz musical ice hockey movement) of animatronic, AI-enhanced heads. Still, despite their growing numbers, animatronic, AI-enhanced heads are not generally well accepted in society (the Queen has never asked one to escort her to a Detroit Lions tailgate party, for example) and, as a result, tend to keep to their own areas of the city. So, the animatronic, AI-enhanced head of Alan Turing would stand out like a man coughing up a rhino in most places in the city.

"Oh, yeah, well, I wouldn't worry too much about it," sniffed DCI Hunt. "This Alan Turing thingie probably got its brains scrambled by being too close to an electro-magnet. Yeah, we'll probably find it next to the Thames, singing 'Danny Boy' off key and crying about how Hugh Alexander got too much of the credit. Yeah. Sure. Happens all the time!"

The Investigation continues.

Teknology Can Be A Harsh Mistress

SPECIAL TO THE ALTERNATE REALITY NEWS SERVICE
by KOLIN KELLY

Late at night, I sometimes walk down to the shop floor where the bricks that are used to build the world are kreated. I run my hand along the rough kiln, kooled by an evening breeze the source of which we kannot find. And, I whisper, "What do you want?"

The machine is silent.

Long before my kooky kousin Kevin wrote books on the subject, I asked myself the kwestion: what does teknology want? World peace? A three week, all expenses paid vacation to the latest Caribbean hot spot? To put its legs up in front of the fire and read a good book, warmed by the knowledge of a day's job well done? More oil for its aching joints?

Unfortunately, teknology remains silent.

Fortunately, people do not. If you ask them the kwestion, "What does teknology want?" they will happily natter on. And, on. And, on. You can't shut them up about it, really. At times, it makes one long for the reticence of teknology, if the truth be known. However, one has a kwestion to answer, so one perseveres.

"Teknology? Well, obviously, it wants to expand its sphere of operation," responded Kray Kurtzwilly, author of such books as *The Singleness is Coming! – Don't Forget to Pack a Toothbrush* and *1001 More Ways to Love the Machine (But, This Time, in a Family Friendly Way)*. "Teknology wants to fill every niche it can find. Every hole. Every krack. Every krevice. Every – wooh, look at me – I'm getting all flushed!"

Teknology expands to fill every human desire assigned to it – where had I heard that before?

Still, I wasn't konvinced. Having the full virtual reality harness, programmed with 127 different environments and built-in air freshener, hadn't saved my marriage from disintegrating. The prosthetic fingers I had surgically grafted to my elbows didn't seem to make my children any less disdainful of my existence. And, frankly, the time I spent trying to figure out how to work the Toastr 2000, with 537 settings and waffle maker attachment, would probably have been better spent trying to connect emotionally to my wife and children.

I decided to keep looking for the answer to the kwestion: what does teknology want?

Kobb Klogan, Professor of Thingology at a Canadian University nobody has ever heard of – even those who go there –

and a student of thingie theorist Marshak McKluhan, offered a different point of view: “Teknology? Oh, well, teknology is a river that runs through your kitchen while you’re upstairs trying to put your baby to sleep, and programmes your DVR to tape nothing but episodes of *Dallas* from the 1980s. Teknology is an orange orangutan that wants to give medium massages to used cancer salesman. Teknology is a hot breakfast for a cool bank vault. Shall I go on? I could talk like this all day.”

Interesting, to be sure. But, did Klogan actually answer the kwestion?

“What teknology wants?” he stated. “I thought I was pretty clear on the subject, but, if you like, I could always try again.”

I hastily thanked Klogan for his help and fled the room.

“Whenever a McKluhanatic speaks, I always check to make sure I’ve still got my underwear,” Kurtzwilly skoffed. “I mean, it sounds like they’re saying words, words that kome together to form komplete sentences, and yet…”

Krikolas Karloponti, professor of man-made objects at the Massachusetts Institute of Thingies and guru emeritus (literally: one who excels at nail filing) of *Caffeinated*, the bible of the techno-Rand set, explained that teknology wants to transform the world from one of bits (things that keep horses from biting their tongues – or your arm – off) to one of kibbles. Electronic kibbles. These bite-sized pieces of digital reality will help human beings live better, longer, more fulfilled lives. “Even if it kills us,” he grinned.

“Krikolas is a good friend,” Klogan said, “but, like the serpent that swallows the supermodel’s tale, it’s often hard to follow what he is saying without getting sprayed with icky digestive juices.”

“Kobb is a good friend,” Karloponti responded. “But, I think studying McKluhan for too long has scrambled the bits in his brain, and that bites.”

“If you want my opinion –” Kurtzwilly started.

“NO!” Klogan and Karloponti shouted him down.

So. Consulting the experts on the kwestion of what teknology wants wasn't all that helpful. Perhaps what teknology really wants…is to be left alone to do the job it was created for?

Kolin Kelly, a graduate of the Kelowna Kollege of Kooky Knowledge, is the CEO of the KK Konsortium, based in Kokonino Kounty, Arizona. Although Kelly kame from humble beginnings as a brick maker, he built his business into an international empire that touches on every aspect of the Konstruction industry. Now that he is successful, he has time to think about things like this.

4. ALTERNATE POLITICS

You’ve Got to Hand It to Them

by FRANCIS GRECOROMACOLLUDEN, Alternate Reality News Service National Politics Writer

It’s official: the left hand does not know what the right hand is doing.

“First it says one thing, then it says another,” said the left second finger, throwing up its…well, giving off an air of one who has given up in exasperation. “I’m not a palm reader – I don’t know what it thinks it’s doing!”

“I’m sorry if the left hand is confused – again,” responded the spokesdigit for the right hand, the middle finger, “but my positions are as firm as a splint on a broken finger.”

The left second finger claimed that the right hand had agreed in principle to doing up the buttons of the shirt the body was wearing. Then, when the body actually put on the shirt, the right hand refused to cooperate.

“In this climate,” the middle finger of the right hand explained, “we thought it was premature for the body to don a shirt.”

"It's October!" the left second finger exploded. "It's ten degrees outside! Without a shirt, the body will freeze!"

"That's the kind of alarmist rhetoric that causes people to feel cold when they don't have to," the right middle finger responded.

Before the argument could continue, the left thumb stepped in and reminded the hands that they both wanted the same thing: what was best for the body. Sure, they might disagree on how to achieve that end, but as long as they could keep the goal in sight, the thumb was certain that they could come to an amicable biextremity agreement.

The left second finger was not entirely mollified. It pointed out that the right hand appeared to cooperate with such tasks as, say, tying the body's shoelaces, but that the laces often seemed to quickly come undone.

"Oh, that's rich!" the right middle finger scoffed. "The left hand isn't competent enough to tie a shoelace, and it wants to blame me!"

"He…he makes a good point," the left pinkie mumbled.

The left second finger sighed and pointed out that (the left pinkie notwithstanding), it was the body's dominant hand. As such, it was quite capable of carrying out any task the body asked of it.

"Then, why does the shoelace come untied so often?" the right middle finger smirked.

The left second finger decided to ignore this taunt, instead pointing to the time the right hand demanded that all of the digits swear an oath of loyalty to the body. "It was in the middle of dinner!" the digit complained. "We were about to dig in to a lovely beef brisket, and everything ground to a halt so that we could swear this stupid oath!"

"I take my commitment to the well-being of the body very seriously," the right middle finger insisted. "A loyalty oath is a simple enough matter – you have to wonder why any part of the body would object to taking it…"

"Sounds reasonable to me," the left pinkie added.

"I resent the implications that the representative of the right hand is making!" the left second finger exploded. "I was trying to get food into the mouth of the body – I was showing my loyalty by doing what I could to keep the body going! No stupid loyalty oath would make my commitment to the body any stronger!"

The right middle finger responded that insulting loyalty oaths, calling them stupid, just made it question the left hand's loyalty all the more.

The second left finger was momentarily stunned, then claimed that the right hand was doing everything in its power to make the left hand look bad. Could the right hand be trying to discredit the left hand in order to take over its role as the body's dominant hand?

"Now, now, that's an absurd accusation!" the right thumb righteously insisted. "Nobody has ever questioned **my** loyalty to the good of the body!"

"Utterly ridiculous," the left pinkie agreed.

The left thumb suggested that everybody turn down the rhetorical heat. It stated that it was sure that all of the fingers on both hands were loyal to the body. In any case, the thumb argued, the challenges posed by the needs of the body were serious: everything from typing out reports at work to stroking the body's lover in the evening. The only way they could meet the challenges would be to work together.

"If the right hand is so loyal," the left second finger insisted, "how do you explain its obstructive behaviour?"

Some things, the left thumb philosophized, are simply unknowable.

Symbol of Life Kills Seventeen

by HAL MOUNTSAUERKRAUTEN, Alternate Reality News Service Crime/Court Writer

A shootout at a White the Power rally and clambake in Iceland has left 17 dead and over 30 wounded.

"It was awesome!" said Old-time Aryan Fidelity member Lars Martihyars before he lapsed into a coma. "Just like *Höfuð af Sa* –"

Martihyars may have been referring to *Höfuð af Sauðfé*, (*Sheep Loser*) a television series about the wacky adventures of a door to door used herring salesman whose hobby is collecting bees. He could, on the other hand, have been saying Höfuð af Sælgæti (literally "lose the candy," an idiomatic reference to somebody who has bad fortune betting on luge races). Hard to see how either fits the context, but interrupted pre-lapsing into a coma statements can be inscrutable that way.

Piecing together what happened from fragmented eyewitness accounts is tougher than it looks on *CSI: Reykjavik*, but everybody agreed that the mayhem started when Matt Schtroumph, of the White Power People's Front, accused Undress Bravepick, of the People's Front of White Power, of being a Jew. The argument escalated until Schtroumph took out a gun and shot Bravepick seven times (four fatally), at which point 50 people brought out weapons and, fearing being under attack from the police, or possibly Celine Dion fans, started firing on each other.

Schtroumph's evidence? He claims that Bravepick was wearing a chai, the Jewish symbol of life, around his neck.

"What are you talking about?" said Bravepick's girlfriend, Mandy Mischkin. "It wasn't no kai! It was a Tibetan Ceiling Moose! Look…" she pointed to the two descending parts of the chet – the Hebrew character that always gives Jews a chuckle when non-Jews try to pronounce it. "That's the moose's legs and there…" she pointed to the Yod, a Hebrew letter so small it has to cozy up to other letters for protection from Cyrillics, and said, "that's the moose's antlers."

Mischkin claimed that she bought the charm from a pawnbroker named Isaac – "A good name, Isaac. Very Biblical." When we asked him about it, he snorted, "Dat's just crazy talk. Tibetan Ceiling Moose? Who ever hoid of such a ting?"

"No, no, no," Mischkin insisted. "He explained that they waited until late at night, then snuck into people's houses upside down – walking on the ceiling, right? They survived by stealing chocolate cakes, kippered smelts and rosemary meatloaves. The Tibetan Ceiling Moose – I – everybody's heard of it, right? Right?"

"I don't know vat dat meshuggah woman is talking about," Isaac said with a twinkle, twinkle in his little eye. "I sold her a chai."

"He was a good boy," Bravepick's mother, Lotte, insisted. "He had a great sense of humour – you should have heard the jokes he used to tell about niggers! And, he was a hard worker. When the boys would beat up Muslim immigrants, he was always the first to pile on and the last to walk away. How could he possibly have been Jewish?"

When we explained to her that Judaism is a matrilineal religion, and, therefore, she should know what religion her son was, she replied, "Oh, yeah. Yeah. Of course, he was raised a good Christian boy. Not Jewish at all. Nope. Not a little bit." But, she didn't sound convinced.

"It is rare," allowed Australian macro-zoologist Bruce van Bruce (literally, Bruce in the vehicle of his father Bruce), "but there have been several credible reports of the Tibetan Ceiling Moose appearing all across Asia over the past two decades."

Isaac looked askance. If you looked up skance in the dictionary, you would find an image of his face.

"Oh, yeah," van Bruce enthused (all over the carpet, but don't worry – a simple mop should be able to clean it up in no time).

"Have you see the grainy footage of the Tibetan Ceiling Moose on YoohooTube? Pretty damn conclusive, I would say."

"But…but…but…" Isaac sputtered (you can get it off the tabletop with a lemon-scented chamois). "I swear to you, I sold zis voman a chai. Honestly. Vere she got dis crazy idea about Tibetan Ceiling Mooses I have no idea!"

"Told you Undress was innocent," Mischkin smugged.

"Yeah, yeah, yeah," interrupted Stig McNazsty, the lone surviving member of the white supremacist group Crusade This, Pal! "Chai or Tibetan Ceiling Monkey is really beside the point, isn't it? The real issue here is that the whole incident has made the white power movement look like a bunch of violent morons!"

Isaac grinned.

From Statistical Anomaly to Presidential Candidate

by FRANCIS GRECOROMACOLLUDEN, Alternate Reality News Service National Politics Writer

The campaign that lasted 18 years but zipped by so fast that it felt like only 18 months came to a dramatic close last night when, at a brokered convention (which couldn't even be fixed by duct tape), None of the Above won the Republican nomination to challenge Barack Obama in the 2012 election.

"Obviously, the candidate is too excited to make an acceptance speech," said None of the Above's campaign manager, Steve Schmidt. "But, I assure you that None of the Above will release an acceptance speech just as soon as we can figure out what its positions are. I'm thinking guns, god and country. But, it could just as easily be god, guns and country. The situation is just so fluid right now…"

"This has got to be the worst possible outcome for the Democratic Party," said political commentator Lawrence

O'Donnell. "Not only has None of the Above never publicly taken any position on any issue, but it has never said anything that has offended anybody – what could the Democrats possibly have to run against?"

"How about the emperor has no clothes?" suggested O'Donnell's MSNBC bunkmate Rachel Maddow, mischievously adding, "Or, that the new clothes have no emperor?"

Schmidt pointed out that None of the Above's nomination posed some problems for the Republicans, as well: "We won't be able to run any advertising. I mean, how are we supposed to get a convenient election protest category to say it endorsed a commercial?"

"Oh, I may be able to help with that," billionaire casino magnate Sheldon Adelson smoothly said, slicking back the hair on his head to hide his horns. (His love affair with Newt Gingrich's Super PAC is obviously over; perhaps Gingrich will now have some empathy for the person who gets dumped in a relationship.)

The incorporeal nature of the candidate poses other problems for the Republicans. How, for instance, will None of the Above accomplish that old cliché of political campaigns, kissing babies?

"I envision a lot of air kisses," Schmidt answered. "Which, when you think of it, are a much more sanitary way to run a presidential election campaign."

None of the Above was born a simple electoral choice in an 1897 New York City election for the office of spittoon overseer. This gives None of the Above the distinction of being the oldest Republican candidate to run for president. Well, if you don't count Ronald Reagan.

Then, in 1904, None of the Above was dragged into service as a candidate in a particularly rowdy Arizona State Yenta race. (Okay, there's no proof that it was unwilling to run. On the other hand, there t'ain't no proof that it tweren't willin' to run, neither, ma'am. So, there.) Over the years, None of the Above steadily worked its way up the political ladder, from the office of dog teaser to State Attorney-Specific to federal dog teaser, but it wasn't until last night that a political party was so desperate for an alternative to all of its candidates that None of the Above actually won.

Minutes after its surprise victory, the None of the Above campaign announced that Spoiled Ballot will be its running mate. "They're like two wads of spit-softened paper in a straw," Schmidt stated. "Couldn't be closer."

"It was a masterstroke," O'Donnell said of the selection. "It avoided the obvious problem of the vice presidential candidate being the only sentient human on the ticket, although that didn't seem to be much of a problem for the campaign of George W. Bush."

"Aww, I don't know about this," Vice President Joe Biden wryly commented. "I don't think any of us can take None of the Above seriously as a candidate for president until we've seen its birth certificate…"

"Oh, ha ha, very funny," Schmidt sourly joshed good-naturedly. "Everybody knows that all of None of the Above's personal documents were destroyed in the…southern Beatle invasion of 1962. Besides, these days, there's nothing more American than throwing away your vote in futile protest!"

"It sure is going to be an interesting race," O'Donnell commented. "On the one hand, the Democrats are running a campaign based on Barack Obama's belief that the United States can regain the greatness it had after the Second World War. On the other hand, the Republicans are running a convenient protest category that doesn't even exist.

"May the best illusion win."

Toon Support Group Faces Funding Gap

by FREDERICA VON McTOAST-HYPHEN, Alternate Reality News Service People Writer

Morpork Adelian has his mother's eyes and his father's tentacles. When he was three years old, Morpork would hit himself in the head with an iron because he wanted to see and hear the birdies flying around his head. When he started grade school, Morpork couldn't help but notice that none of the other children enjoyed dancing in grease fires the way he did. In fact, they became quite fearful at the prospect.

"We knew that little Morpork was different when we adopted him," allowed Fergus Augustus Adelian, Morpork's father. "We thought that he would adapt to life in the human world, but…but I guess that, though his body seems infinitely flexible, his approach to life isn't."

Human adoption of toons is rare, but it does happen. In this case, Morpork was left on the doorstep of a local OffTheWal*Mart, happily gurgling and cooing in his cradle next to a stick of dynamite. When the dynamite went off, it left a six foot wide crater in the parking lot, but, other than a dark smudge on his forehead, Morpork was unaffected.

"When my car was finally towed out of the crater," said Amelia Adelian (nee: Pondscum), "I had fallen in love with Morpork's blue eyes. It didn't occur to me until years later that there was something strange about the way they would sometimes be bigger than his head."

Morpork's difficulty adjusting to human life was eased somewhat by An-Atoon, a support group for teen toons who lived in human families. "Mom and dad were great," he explained. "But, we just believed in different things. They thought honesty was the most important quality a young man could have, I thought it was Boston cream pies."

Boston cream pies?

"You know," Morpork rolled his eyes. "Being funny?"

An-Atoon helped Morpork realize that, even though he might be different, there was a place in the world for him. "Here were kids like me," he stated. "Kids who weren't afraid to grab a live wire and have 10,000 volts illuminate their skeletons, kids who knew what it meant to be alive!" He even got sweet on an anthropomorphic cow by the name of Anabellum.

Over the years, An-Atoon has helped thousands of young men, women and singing swords just like Morpork adjust to the human world. That record of good works is now being threatened by government funding cutbacks.

"Well, you know how it works," stated Frenetic Jones, Health and Human Resources Undersecretary for Breaking Bad News to Poor People, "When the economy goes off the fiscal cliff, it won't appear in the next scene to buy new Acme products!"

She added that, while An-Atoon was an organization with worthy goals, the insurance on the buildings where it met was killing everybody involved. "The Anglican church no longer wants An-Atoon meetings to be held in its church basements," Jones pointed out, "and, they'll take anybody!"

"Okay, yeah, sure, when teen toons get together, havoc usually follows," admitted Fergus, a greeter at a local Hummer Winblad Venture Partners office. "Still, they helped Morpork accept who he was, and he's much happier now. When you think of the contribution all of those teen toons could make to society if they just had a similar experience, well, isn't that worth the occasional building reduced to burning rubble?"

It has been suggested that everybody would be better off if toons were brought up by their own kind. "I didn't say that," Jones insisted. Actually, we pointed out, she was the one who said it. "Fine!" Jones grumped. "See if I ever trust you with Double Dog Dare You Triple Blind Deep Background information ever again!"

"That's just not right," Amelia argued. "As long as a child is raised with love, he will – MORPORK, PUT THAT ANVIL DOWN THIS INSTANT! I'M NOT KIDDING, YOUNG MAN – ANVIL! DOWN! NOW! Umm, yeah – love. As long as there is love in a family, it can overcome cultural differences. And, anvils."

Like most teens, Morpork has big dreams for the future. "I'd like to create an umbrella that is light as a feather but strong enough to withstand an onslaught of thousand ton boulders," he told the Alternate Reality News Service. "That, or become a stuntman for the movies. Yeah. Stuntman. That would be cool."

When we asked about his relationship with his parents, Morpork described it as "moribund." When we asked if it was really all that bad, he quickly added: "No, no. I meant that we all wish we could eat additional pieces of spongy cake. That's not bad. Not bad at all…"

The Language Goes for Broke

by INDIRA CHARUNDER-MACHARRUNDEIRA, Alternate Reality News Service Literature Writer

Hand gestures are a poor substitute for the English language. Especially when you're trying to say: "walk two fingers along a tabletop scissors snip thumb stuck in the air looping motion with second finger at head."

Unfortunately, since the English language was irreversibly broken, alternate forms of communication had to be found.

When I first came to Earth Prime 2-8-2-5-0-1 dash omicron, my only knowledge of what was happening was the assignment "English language broken – check it out." For somebody who runs a news service, my boss can be rather uncommunicative [EDITRIX-IN-CHIEF BRENDA BRUNDTLAND-GOVANNI: This is a reminder that management may monitors works in progress for its own amusement. This is only a reminder: had this been a real monitoring, your ass would probably already by fired!]…and, yet, surprisingly despite this terseness, she always manages to get her point across.

Customs Officers at the multiport where I entered the universe had been given preprinted cards that indicated what they wanted us to do. For example: one card showed an Officer watching while somebody opened a suitcase. Another card showed an Officer pointing angrily at the ground as somebody held tight to the reigns of the emu they were riding. Another card showed a woman in a monkey mask taking off her blouse as half a dozen uniformed Officers danced what appeared to be a hora around her. Obvious multiport safety issues, really.

However, not realizing the extent of the problem, I continually tried to engage the Customs Officer in conversation. Finally, I pretended to run away from her. You know, just to get a reaction. Tossing aside a card that shows a woman coming to a halt amid armed guards (possibly doing the mambo), she angrily shouted after me, "Accomplishment! Accomplishment chesterfield the and bacon moving superannuated black trench reading!"

The taser to my back made the point much more eloquently than words ever could.

Six weeks and one interdimensional incident later, the misunderstanding was cleared up and I was allowed on the planet proper.

What had happened? I asked Phil D'Armani, Huntz Hall Chair of Language Studies at The New School for Social Dessert. And, when I say I asked, I actually mean I shrugged and D'Armani understood what I meant.

Our discussion was labouriously slow, even though I was using a hand gestures to English dictionary that I had studied while detained at the Transdimensional Authority's leisure. Over a period of three days, the story I was able to piece together was: right wing American operatives had, for many years, devalued the language by altering the meaning of words to suit their political agenda. For example: war hero, which once meant somebody who had done something heroic in the midst of battle, was used to describe somebody who voted for a war appropriations bill even though he had never been in a war zone.

The tipping point came when the word "socialist" accrued 127 meanings, including: Marxist communist; Ponzi scheme artist; anarchist; gay (in whichever use of the term the listener would find most offensive); wildebeest; zombie; pungent; degraded; Leninist Communist; nihilist; tetchy; made of fine Corinthian leather; bedwetting; prone to sneezing; plangent; DiscoBobulated…discombobulatted…Discworldovula – confused, and; hairy in unattractive places. People started using common words in ways they had not been used before, and were angry when others did not seem to understand what they were saying. Families were broken apart. Twelve people were killed and 37 wounded when an argument broke out at a virtual reality complex over the meaning of the word "the." The French laughed their asses off (or, more accurately, laughed off their asses – they mirthfully fell off their burros).

One more meaning added to the growing list of definitions of "socialist" – "cherry-flavoured" – broke the English language. Words had become unMoored (Demi, not Michael or Roger) from their meanings and communication in English was no longer possible.

This was known, in what academia remained, as "Humpty Dumpty Syndrome" for the way the language cracked under pressure (although, unlike the eggy, Dodgsony character, it did not make a tasty breakfast for all the king's horses and all the king's men). There is still a lot to know about the Syndrome, although the necessity of writing journal articles in pictograms and using hand gestures at conferences has made the dissemination of ideas in academia much more time-consuming (although, arguably, much more entertaining).

D'Armani touched the tip of his nose with his second finger, and I knew I had the story more or less correct.

When I noticed a large quill feather in an inkpot on D'Armani's desk, I pointed at it and shrugged. To my surprise, he responded, "C'est…uhh…c'est la…la…umm…c'est la plume de ma…ma…ma…"

"Tante?" I helpfully suggested.

D'Armani made an angry face, like I had just taunted his – oooooh. No, wait. Before I could figure out how he could take my statement as an insult, he impatiently lifted some papers off his desk with one hand and pointed at the door with the other.

No translation necessary, I immediately left the office.

When the Big Bus Leaves the Station, Democracy Remains Sitting On the Bench

by FRANCIS GRECOROMACOLLUDEN, Alternate Reality News Service National Politics Writer

It seems like a simple question. "What does government do, mommy?" But, of course, answering the question is complicated, not least because I couldn't be your mommy because I'm a man. Doesn't the "I" in Francis kind of give it away?

Rephrasing the question as "What does government do, daddy?" doesn't help. I'm not your daddy – I have no children. Not by choice, but that's a discussion for another time. I am a family friend who has decided to use you as a cute means of introducing my article.

"What does government do, family friend who has decided to use me as a cute means of introducing my article?" That's actually an easy question to answer: the Canadian government sits for one week to pass a bill containing all of the legislation for that year.

The legislation is known as an "omnibus bill." Omnibus literally means "all bus" or "bus containing all." Imagine a bus so big that it could take everybody in a city to where they need to go at the same time. An omnibus is something like that, only without the hip-hop leaking from passengers' earbuds and the dirty glares.

"What does the government do for the rest of the year?" the child, who clearly has a different sense of the meaning of introducing an article than I do, asks. It varies. Some politicians stay in Ottawa to enjoy the city's nightlife. Some spend the rest of their time working in their ridings to get away from Ottawa's nightlife. A few take up a hobby, like bribe-taking or taxidermy. The important thing is that they keep busy, because a politician with free time is a recipe for disaster.

"But, how are our democratically elected officials supposed to be able to properly debate and amend laws when they come in one large package and there is so little time for scrutiny?" the child, a regular seven year-old Clarence Darrow, asks. Well, obviously, that's why you should elect decisive speed-readers to office.

"Isn't that a perversion of the democratic process?" Not in the sense – "There can be no clash of ideas helping shape good policy." You aren't taking into account – "It seems to me that the Prime Minister has enormous power to shape the law with little effective oversight."

I finally understood the old saying that journalists should never work with children or animals.

It's true that, since omnibus bills became the norm, strange laws have managed to sneak through Parliament. Only last year, for instance, an omnibus bill contained a change in regulations mandating that all government bathrooms contain digital toilet paper. "This is not intended to monitor private chit chat," Minister of Public Safety and Elephant Preparedness Ivor Bangstache stated. "We force government workers to wear flag pins on their lapels for that. No, this is just to fulfill our promise to clean up government!"

Or, the law passed in an omnibus bill four years ago that mandated that every computer sold in Canada should contain a Clifford Chip. This hardware monitors activity on a computer; when it comes across keywords (including terror, bomb or spasmodic), a big red dog appears on the user's computer screen and say things like, "Creating fear of violence for political ends is bad" and "Do your children know what you do in your spare time?" Critics of the measure said it would find and punish innocent horror fiction writers, film critics and Multiple Sclerosis sufferers, but by the time they discovered it, the law had already been in effect for over six months. When the law was described as "draconian," Public Safety Minister Nash Crebulon responded: "Naah. We don't find our legislation in Harry Potter books – we write it ourselves!"

The less said about the law forcing couples to smear Nutella over their genitals as a form of contraception, the better. The odd thing about this is that, although several people have been arrested for contravening this law, nobody can actually find it in any of the omnibus bills passed in the last six years, including the Conservative government that passed it. Constitutional scholars are having a field day.

One activity that all politicians seem to do when Parliament is not in session is fundraise. Since they have four years to raise money for their re-election campaigns, it should come as no surprise that 97 per cent of incumbents have won their seats in the past 20 years; the other three per cent either died or had video of their drooling apple sauce down their chins become YouTube sensations.

"That doesn't seem fair, does it?" the child, whom I thought had lost interest, returned to ask.

Who do I look like, ferking Mister Rogers? Go ask your mother!

It's a Gas Gas Gas

by FRED CHARUNDER-MACHARRUNDEIRA, Alternate Reality News Service Science Writer

Has humanity reached peak helium?

"Yes. Goodness, yes. Un hunh. For sure. Of course we have. Yes, yes, oh my, yes," said Colin Farrell. (Not the actor and scourge of hotel room telephones everywhere. The other Colin Farrell. Although, actually, not the multimillionaire inventor of the prosthetic butt cheek, either. The other other Colin Farrell. Of course, I'm not referring to the Colin Farrell who works in the invoice processing department of Toys 'r' Somebody Else (We Make Leather Goods for Adults) and tracks feral rubber ducks through the wilds of Oakland on weekends. No, I'm talking about the other other other Colin Far – look. I'm talking about the Colin Farrell who knows more about helium than any other man (and all but seven women) alive.

Cut me some slack, okay? It's a common name.

According to, in the interest of brevity, the (single) other Colin Farrell, the United States has found all of the precious gas the country contains, and, at present rates of consumption, will likely run out in less than 25 years.

"Then, we will not be able to have lighter than air balloons at birthday parties," the (single) other Colin Farrell warned. "When imaginary children of the future try to bat balloons back and forth in a way we take for granted now, they will watch as the balloons plummet to the floor! Oh, the misery! Oh, the humanity!"

"Oh, hogtarts!" said Tom Hanks, an energy analyst with Burton Barston Batman and Funkyton. (Who shouldn't be confused with Tom Hanks, the part time door to door previously loved canoe salesman and full time town drunk, Tom Hanks, the author of a series of worst-selling Inuit vampire mystery romances or Tom Hanks the Fig Newton Chair of Dainty Comestibles and one of the Kool Kolleagues of Keith Kelly at Kelowna Kollege. Oh, and, I think there may be a famous one that I'm forgetting, too.) "That's just scaremongering. Fear fetishism. Unhappiness ululating. Remember the helium scares of the 1970s? We thought for sure the gas was running out, but it turned out that we have more now than we ever did!

"As science finds new ways of identifying and extracting helium from the environment, the stores will actually increase and last almost…forever!"

"Finite resources cannot last forever," the (single) other Colin Farrell, with academic politeness, scoffed. "Where did you get your information – the tooth fairy?"

"I'll have you know," energy analyst with Burton Barston Batman and Funkyton Tom Hanks hotly retorted (his office doesn't have air conditioning), "that the tooth fairy has a Masters in Geological Sciences and has been tracking this issue for over a century! And, you thought she was just a pretty wand!"

The (single) other Colin Farrell is one of 10,000 researchers in the party sciences who have signed a petition warning that if something isn't done now to preserve helium stores, they will quickly disappear.

"Dilettantes," energy analyst with Burton Barston Batman and Funkyton Tom Hanks, one of a dozen helium optimists, returned the (single) other Colin Farrell's scoff. He pointed out that even if the most pessimistic projections are true – and, they're not, but we're just imagining for the sake of argument that they are, so don't take them too seriously – humanity could always build starships to mine helium from the sun.

Wouldn't that be really expensive?

Energy analyst with Burton Barston Batman and Funkyton Tom Hanks waved a dismissive hand in my direction. "As the price of helium soars," he explained, only scoffing a little bit around the edges, "the cost of mining the sun will seem more and more reasonable."

He pointed out that other, less extreme measures were also under consideration. For example, there was currently research going on into substitutes for helium at several different universities and ice cream parlours. Liquid hydrogen had held out much promise, until it was definitely found that it caused balloons to freeze and shatter.

Research into alternatives continues, he assured me.

"In the meantime, what about the children?" the (single) other Colin Farrell asked, his voice squeaky high. "How will they be able to enjoy the simple pleasure of making their voice do this if the price of helium rises sharply?"

"But, what – hee hee," I tried to ask. "I mean – ha, ha – oh, that's great, but – hee hee hee!" I waved away the question as I doubled over in laughter. Yes, I will definitely miss helium-heightened voices when they are gone.

"We can't let such emotional thinking get in the way of science," energy analyst with Burton Barston Batman and Funkyton Tom Hanks put on a warm scoff. I got the distinct impression that he would have preferred to end his disquisition on a note that involved simple childish pleasures denied, but was miffed that the (single) other Colin Farrell had beaten him to it.

Love's Labour Camp Lost

by LAURIE NEIDERGAARDEN, Alternate Reality News Service Medical Writer

According to a report by the General Unaccounting for Taste Office, Love Camps where pregnant American women are housed until their unformed citizens are born, are filthy, overcrowded, understaffed and generally unconducive to the healthy birthin' of no babies.

"They're like 19th century Homes for Unwed Mothers," the report reported, "except without the come hither look in their eyes…or the whips. Granted, in the age of *Fifty Shades of Disgusting*, whips have a different set of connotations than they did in the 19th century. Still…"

"Weeeeeellllll," drawled President Micklaus Huckleberry-Hunte, "women have to bear citizens, but that doesn't mean that the government should saddle those citizens with debt before they're even born!"

Journalists at the Presidential press opportunity looked at each other nervously. They were well aware that the military budget – which is now 87 per cent of government spending – continued to contribute to the country's multi-bagillion dollar debt. They were even more aware that the last person to ask a question about the subject was busted to the latrine beat of the *Spokane Sun-Wishing Well*. Discussion quickly turned to the war on Belgium.

It has been two years since the Sanctity of Life and Getting the Economy Going Again bill was passed by a Republican Congress and signed into law by President Huckleberry-Hunte. Any woman of citizen-bearing age who is suspected of exhibiting the warm glow of motherhood is immediately sent to a Love Camp where she can carry the baby to term (whether she can afford to raise it or not). To pay for their stay in a Love Camp, the women are expected to work at factories that are conveniently built next door.

"We're not Barbarians," said Dusty D'Aquino, owner of the Generic Motors Love Production Facility in Detroit. "Women do not have to work on the assembly line past their seventh month of pregnancy…we have a variety of payment plans for their final two months."

D'Aquino was asked if this forced labour was a form of slavery. "The love of a mother for her citizen is a special joy that every woman should experience – whether they want to or not," he replied.

No, no, no, the questioner continued, I meant forced labour in the economic, not procreational sense. D'Aquino frowned. "Have you ever worked at the *Spokane Sun-Wishing Well*?" he asked. "I hear they're looking to expand the latrine beat…"

At the last count, as many as "many" medical professionals were leaving the United States in order to avoid working at the Love Camps. This has forced the government to encourage doctors, nurses and pediatric dental herbalists from such places as Saudi Arabia to emigrate to the US to work.

"I must say, the Saudis have been very helpful," President Huckleberry-Hunte commented. "We may not agree on much, but we do seem able to find common ground on the issue of the proper relationship between a woman and her citizens."

"Love Camps? Phooey!" said *Spokane Sun-Wishing Well* feminist latrine reporter Barbara Boo-Hawe. "Let's call them what they really are: Atwoods!"

"They're called Love Camps, not…Atwoods…" President Huckleberry-Hunte shuddered. "Don't get me wrong – I think Maggs was a seminal figure in forging the modern Canadian literary identity. I just don't believe that references to her dystopian fiction are helpful in this context."

Undaunted, Boo-Hawe pointed out that wealthy women had ways of avoiding spending time at the Atwoods. Some have their zygotes implanted into surrogates, for instance, who then spend nine months in the…controversially named medical facilities under scrutiny in the wealthy women's stead. Some women who can afford it take a vacation in Belize or St. Moritz. A nine months to the day vacation. And, return with a babbling, burbling citizen of joy. Some women who can afford it take a vacation to Paris or Toronto. A two week vacation. And, return empty-handed.

"Yeah, I'll admit that does look suspicious," President Huckleberry-Hunte allowed. "But, since the women or their husbands tend to be donors to my political campaign, I'm gonna assume that sometimes a vacation is just a vacation and leave it at that."

Don't the poor conditions that exist in the – can we compromise and call them Love Atwoods? – those places have the potential to cause unnecessary health risks for newborns?

"How a mother raises her newly born citizen is entirely up to her," President Huckleberry-Hunte replied. "After all, the sacredness of the mother/citizen relationship is a private matter!"

5. ALTERNATE ARTS AND CULTURE

Pynchon Me, I Must Be Dreaming!

by ELAINE SUGARMAN-SWEET-SACCHARINE, Alternate Reality News Service Literature Writer

A wise woman once explained to me that if you want to know where a literary convention is being held, just follow the people in costumes. This past weekend, I followed people in 1960s hippie garb, the dress of a late 18th century gentleman and the uniforms of World War II soldiers to the Sheraton Braggadocio on Pavement Street, which was host to PynchCon 2011, a convention devoted to the works of author Thomas Pynchon.

Sponsored by the Wrong Questions Club of Pittsburgh (which was odd, considering it was held in Toronto), this year's PynchCon offered an eclectic variety of panels on all things Pynchon. These included: "Benny Profane versus Tyrone Slothrop: Who Was the Better Soldier?"; "*Gravity's Rainbow*: Twenty Reasons the Movie Would Have Sucked if it Ever had Been Made," and; "*Against the Day* Trivia Faceoff."

The Guest of Honour at this year's PynchCon was James McMoira, who claimed to have shaken Pynchon's hand in 2003.

"It was at a Denny's," McMoira explained to a rapt hall of over 200 people. "A tall man said to me: 'Could you please fill this cup with Diet Rock Sludge?' There didn't seem to be anything with that name at the soda station, so I just gave him diet cola. He seemed grateful, and shook my hand.

"Something about the man seemed awfully familiar. Then, it hit me: I had seen an old black and white photograph of him on a Web site devoted to *The Crying of Lot 49*! I think it was, like, his high school graduation photo or something, but the resemblance was unmistakable. So, I said, 'Hey! You're Thomas Pynchon!' To which he replied, 'No. I'm afraid you have me mistaken with the National Book Award winning author.' To which I replied in response: 'Yeah. Yeah. You're Thomas Pynchon, alright! Who else would know about the whole National Book Award winner thing?!' To which he responded in reply: 'It was a lucky guess. Look, if you don't go away and allow me to eat my Grand Slum Breakfast in peace, I'm afraid I shall have to call the manager and complain.' To which I retorted in responsive reply, 'Only Thomas Pynchon would deny that he was Thomas Pynchon! You must be Thomas Pynchon!' To which he responded in replicative retort: 'I can't argue with logic like that. MANAGER! I'D LIKE TO SPEAK TO THE MANAGER, PLEASE!'

"Sure, I got thrown out of the restaurant," McMoira concluded, "but it was worth it. Man, was it worth it." The audience at PynchCon roared its approval.

McMoira was a controversial choice. Some Pynchonistas believe that the person he shook hands with was actually infamous Thomas Pynchon impersonator Galliard "Michel" Houllebecq.

"We were hoping to get Pynchon's first agent, Candida Donadio, to be the GoH," admitted PynchCon organizer and Wrong Questions Club Vice President in Charge of Refreshments Derrida Defazio, "but we were discouraged by the fact that he died in 2001. So, we had to go with our second choice."

PynchCon's Fan Guest of Honour was Monique DeLaTerrias, who has the distinction of having had 37 different pieces of fan fiction taken down from various Internet sites under threat from Pynchon's lawyers. DeLaTerrias read from her most famous work, "The Crying of a Lot of Forty-niners," a flash fiction story that imagined what would have happened if *V.*'s Benny Profane met and had a torrid love affair with *Gravity's Rainbow*'s Tyrone Slothrop in a seedy San Francisco hotel room.

"Pynchon's characters really come alive for me," DeLaTerrias explained. "So, naturally, I want to know what would happen if they had hot, male on male sex!"

Those who attended last year's PynchCon might have been surprised that it wasn't being held at the Radisson Not Exactly Central But Downtownish Hotel. "That...that's a private matter," DeLaTerrias demurred. "Wouldn't you rather talk about the semiotics of the male erection in *Gravity's Rainbow*? I...I know I would..."

Rumours, confirmed by people who attended PynchCon 2010, have it that a couple of con-goers were having sex that involved one of them being handcuffed to a pipe. In the throes of passion, the person who was handcuffed pulled the pipe free, flooding the entire floor and making the event convention non grata at the hotel for years to come.

Thomas Pynchon was unavailable for comment.

Hype Springs Eternal

by ELMORE TERADONOVICH, Alternate Reality News Service Film and Television Writer

Twenty-seven people were killed and as many as four were injured in a riot at the Whoa Nelly Furtado Gabillaplex in Kenosha, Nova Scotia when people who had been waiting in line since four the previous morning were told that all of the screenings for *The Avengers* for that day had been sold out.

"It…it was like Anzio!" said cinemary strategist Marcus Orr-Alias. "Except, without the minty aftertaste."

"I should have been one of the ones who died," pouted Wall Street cuticle analyst Patsy Bitsy. "I mean, all of my friends got to see *The Avengers* on opening day. How am I ever going to be able to live with the shame of not getting in?"

To forestall the possibility of violence, *The Avengers* was booked on every screen in every movie theatre in North America. Every screen. "Yeah, well, our customers was a bit surprised that we replaced *The Sex Scavengers* with *The Avengers*," said adult theatre manager Joe-Bob Philpotts with a suspicious sniff. "But, ahh, other than having more seats to clean after each screening, it didn't really change much for us."

It may not seem like the possibility of violence was forestalled, but representatives of theatre chain Cineplex Odeous claim that things would have been a lot worse if they hadn't put the film on every screen on the continent. Using software developed by DARPA (in conjunction with Disney Studios), they determined that if they had not done so, riots would have broken out in 37 cities, causing most of California to break off from the United States mainland and drift away into the Pacific ocean.

"It may not have been methodologically sound to build the programme on a base of nuclear attack simulations from the 1950s," Disney Imagifear Don "What the Heck is a" Gaffer allowed. "Still, when a computer simulation says that the best strategy for getting a film into theatres is 'all of them,' what are mere human beings supposed to do?"

To accommodate people going to the movie on opening day – which had been announced in August, 1953 – all life in North America ground to a halt. Newspapers didn't publish. Public transit ran on a holiday schedule. Brokerage houses were closed and identity thieves refrained from sending out phishing emails.

Given how hot tickets for the film were, it was inevitable that scalpers would become involved. “It’s a myth!” argued Chief Dan Gorge. “Natives did not buy up the best seats for Wounded Knee and sell them for outrageous prices!

“Okay,” he allowed, “we may have done a little of that at the Battle of Little Big Horn, but things were different back then. You really have to appreciate Native ticket scalping in its historical context!”

Riots weren’t the only unintended consequence of the release of *The Avengers*. Computer network servers across the continent had heart attacks because so many people blogged and tweeted about the film as they were watching it.

“It didn’t make sense!” complained Jeremy Butts. “Black Nick Fury comes from an alternate universe, but the film doesn’t contain any of the other alternative universe characters. How was I supposed to enjoy the movie when it had such a blatant disregard for the Marvel cosmology?”

What…does this have to do with the point we were trying to make about the effect of the film’s release on computer networks?

“Just this: I tried to blog about the whole Nick Fury fiasco, but I got ‘server’s down, try again later if you’re feeling lucky – are you feeling lucky, punk? Are you?’ messages throughout the movie,” Butts explained. “Not only was my frustration approaching Hulk-like proportions, but anecdotal evidence collected by your reporters suggests that this happened to thousands of people across the continent.”

It wasn’t all bad news, though. Reports from theatres indicate that at least 27 *Avengers* babies were born on opening day.

“My baby wasn’t due for another three weeks,” said Regina de Lancey. “I guess little Tony Bruce Steve Thor really wanted to see Iron Man kick alien ass.”

Regina refused medication because she didn’t want to miss Loki get comeuppancally defeated. Still, didn’t her birth screams diminish the pleasure other people in the theatre got from the film?

"Oh, no. They were cheering for me," de Lancey stated. "It's not every day that you get to experience the miracle of childbirth **and** Mark Ruffalo's layered, empathetic portrayal of the Hulk!"

"It was really an extraordinary moment in human history," Orr-Alias commented. "I mean, can you imagine how easily we could solve some of humanity's most vexing problems if people gave them as much attention as we gave this movie?"

With files from Frederica von McToast-Hyphen in Washington. And, Francis Grecoromacolluden, also in Washington. Oh, and Indira Charunder-Macharrundeira, who was also – why did so many contributors to this story file from Washington? Was there a seat sale that nobody told us about?

The Unbearable Lightness of Being Crowdsourced[1]

by INDIRA CHARUNDER-MACHARRUNDEIRA, Alternate Reality News Service Literature Writer[2]

Bought and Paid Four
by Daniel Perlmutter
Anodyne Yoyodyne Press
$19.95

When he first started writing crowdsourced novels, Daniel Perlmutter was doing something exciting and fresh; but, with the completion of his *Sucker Born Every Web Page* trilogy, the well of creativity seems to have run dry.[3] Daniel Perlmutter's first two crowdsourced novels were confused, with inconsistent characters and only intermittently brilliant passages, but, I must admit, I enjoyed his most recent work.[4]

So, you, uhh, could say that I was conflicted.

The basic idea behind the works is that members of the public pay to contribute different parts of the novel. How much they pay depends upon what aspect of the work they wish to contribute. The scale ranges from: $1 for an adjective, adverb or preposition; $2 for a noun or a verb; $50 for a chapter title; $827 to name a minor character; $1,654 to name a major character, and; $10,000 to write the script for the book trailer.

As Jean-Paul Magritte may have said (had he not been huffing ammonia fumes for the last 10 minutes of his life): "Ceci n'est pas une histoire."[5] H3y, B00b00 – it's @ gr8 id3a & @ $up3r r3@d![6]

He looked at her. She looked at him. They looked at each other. Hesitantly. Expectantly. Franchot Tonically. "I…I didn't know a book could be so confusing," she said, thwarted desire dripping from every syllable like honey dripping off the Hoover Dam. "Don't beat yourself up over it, babe," he said, taking her in his husky arms (which he had borrowed from the lead sled dog). "Literary experimentation is a mug's game!"[7]

One problem with the book, of course, is that, in the absence of any clear direction from the author, different people who contributed material to *Bought and Paid Four* thought that they were contributing to works in different literary genres. Thus, you have a sensitive coming of age during the Crusades segment followed by a passage of a sensitive portrayal of resistance to an alien invasion set a thousand or more years in the future. To say that they do not always sit well on the page together is like saying that porkpie hats don't look smart on velociraptors!

"It's the ultimate mash-up!" Perlmutter enthusiastically defended his book.[8] Yeah, right. It's about as coherent as the universe in the first nanosecond after the Big Bang![9] You have to approach *Bought and Paid Four* as you would any work of experimental literature or improvised explosive de[10]

[EDITRIX-IN-CHIEF BRENDA BRUNDTLAND-GOVANNI: Indira, what the hell do you think you're doing?]

I'm turning into a colourful butterfly and rising above the tumult of human existe[11]

[Yeah, yeah. I'm talking to my writer here. Take your angst to open mic night at your local Human Beanz, Goth Girl! INDIRA! What's going on, here? I gave you a simple book review assignment, and you've given me word soup! Not even tasty word soup, either – word soup that tastes like sweat socks and cilantro!]

Actually, sweat socks cilantro soup is a delicacy in the Gamma Sutra quadrant of

[CAN WE PLEASE FOCUS ON WHAT IS IMPORTANT, HERE!]

Right. Okay. I'm focusing on what is important here.[12]

[I heard that footnote!]

Sorry.

[So, what's the deal?]

I thought…I thought it would be a good idea to write a review that mimicked the form of the book being reviewed.

[How very pre-post-anti-footstool-modern of you. Did you make up the names of the people in your footnotes? Because, honestly, who would believe a name like Charlie Watts?]

No, actually. I umm, put an ad on Krayslist for people who would be willing to pay to contribute to a book review…

[Seriously, Indira? Seriously? If journalism had ethics, this would definitely cross the line! Okay, I've read enough. Stop this nonsense and finish the review yourself.]

But, I have twelve additional contributors who have paid $50 or more to be a part of this review!

[And, who, exactly gets all the money your review is generating?]

Erm…yes, well, all in all, *Bought and Paid Four* is a mixed bag of literary experimentation and bad economic theory that has run its course and probably shouldn't be repeated.

Notes

1. Flopsy Oregano paid $500 to name this review.
2. et al
3. Jeremiah "Flux" Capasit-Orr paid $50 to contribute one sentence to this review.
4. cylendra27 paid $50 to contribute one sentence to this review.
5. Henri de la Zatapatique paid $45 to contribute one confused sentence to this review.
6. Ira Nayman paid $50 to contribute one sentence to this review.
7. Porgy N. Best paid $250 to contribute one paragraph to this review.
8. Charlie Watts paid $50 to contribute one sentence to this review.
9. Antonio Urbano Bucheli paid $100 to contribute two sentences to this review.
10. Jubilation Ferenczi paid $50 to contribute one sentence to this review. Because her sentence was interrupted, she is expecting a refund.
11. AngstInMyPants Ari paid $50 to contribute one sentence to this review. How did Brenda Brundtland-Govanni know? How could she possibly know?
12. Bitch.

A Porn Man's Joseph Campbell

by ELMORE TERADONOVICH, Alternate Reality News Service Film Writer

Have you ever wondered why all porn films seem to have the same story? According to cultural theorist and crustacean fetishist Rex Wilmington, you're not merely jaded and only half paying attention: **all** porn movies follow the form of a single narrative.

In fact, this year marks the 27th anniversary of the publication of Wilmington's seminal (not to be confused with semenal, although, given the subject matter of his work, you can be forgiven for your confusion) work of cultural analysis and authentic Chinese cuisine cookbook *The Heroine with 1,000 Vaginas*.

The book was the culmination of thirty years of research not only on pornographic films, television series and bubble gum cards, but also erotic cave paintings (some of the oldest of which were found three caves down from Lascaux), illuminated manuscripts from the Dark Ages that could only be kept under the monks' desks so that minors couldn't see them and oral histories that were not passed down from generation to generation. Lucky bastard.

What Wilmington found was that all pornography at all times and in all places (especially Venice in 1729) has essentially the same story with several branches. He called this "The Heroine's Journey," because calling it Lucinda would only confuse people.

"It was a brilliant insight," moped feminist cultural critic and dud at potluck dinners Naomi Wolf. "Lucinda is old-fashioned, with connotations of mustiness – or possibly fustiness – but, definitely unjustliness. You couldn't get a narrative theory called Lucinda past a PhD committee in those days. Of course, these days, even if you just quote somebody named Lucinda, your research will be considered suspect…

"Oh," Wolf added, "the whole Heroine's Journey thing was pretty clever, too."

As explored by Wilmington, the Heroine's Journey has many facets. The phone call. The rejection of the phone call. The acceptance of the phone call. The acceptance of the phone call in the bedroom. The acceptance of the phone call in the bathroom. The acceptance of the phone call in the girl's locker room. The acceptance of the phone call in the back of a '65 Chevy. The acceptance of the phone call in the cockpit of a 747 jet. The acceptance of the phone call in a room off the street in Pamplona where the bulls are being run. The acceptance of the phone call in the boy's locker room. Among others. Many, many others.

Wilmington's work would probably have remained of interest only to academics and door to door used shoe salesman had he not collaborated with journalist Bill Moyers on the series *Rex Wilmington and The Power of Sex* on PBS. "We, uhh, had to clean the ideas up a little," Moyers recently admitted. "Still, popularizing Rex' thought was the right thing to do – I mean, that show got better ratings than Ernie and Bert's marriage!"

Of course, it didn't hurt that Wilmington's ideas had an influence on popular culture. *Star Whores* director Dick Wiggleyhead has gone on record as saying that he structured the movie based on concepts out of *The Heroine with 1,000 Vaginas*. "When she is first approached by Oboy One Kengopi," Wiggleyhead explained, "Lucy Skyjerker refuses to leave her home planet of Doodooine. Well, even though it's done in person, that's the refusal of the phone call right there, isn't it?"

He also pointed out that the tension between Handjob Solo's technical approach to mating with the Death Store contrasted with Skyjerker's more mystical application of the Forceps. "This is like Wilmington's contrast between rural and urban mythologies," Wiggleyhead enthusiastically explained. "And, things blow up!"

Oh. And, here, we thought the inspiration for *Star Whores* was Akira Kurosawa's 1958 classic *The Hidden Mistress*. "That, too," Wiggleyhead allowed. And, the 1933 Marx brothers film *Duck Stoop*. "Sure," Wiggleyhead agreed. "Everybody knows that." Oh, and we mustn't forget Christopher Marlowe's 1594 rip-snorter *Dido, Queen of Carthage, or What the Butler Saw IV: The Maidenhead's Revenge*. "Look," Wiggleyhead exasperated, "we could fill a book detailing all of the influences on the production of *Star Whores*, but that would just undermine the market for the book detailing all of the influences on the production of *Star Whores* that I am currently producing. Can we just take it as given that there were a lot of them?"

Consider it given. Or, taken.

So, the next time you're surfing the Internet and you come across *Raw.one*, *Parasexual Activity 3* or *The Latex King 3D*, remember: if the plots seem identical, it's because of Rex Wilmington's grand design and not merely a need to get through the lazily written story elements quickly in order to get to the naughty bits.

Don't Have a Long Cow Clicker, Maaaaaaan

by FREDERICA VON McTOAST-HYPHEN, Alternate Reality News Service Pop Culture Writer

Rewards. We all love them. And, we're not all that discriminating about them, either. We'll spend hours mining Sillonium in an obscure area of *World of Wowcraft* just to win a Silver Sword of Splicing that we could just as easily have bought at the online WOWShoppe for 10 cents and a pair of popsicle sticks.

Game designer and twice convicted Hello Kitty collector Adrian Schlumpf has created a game that he believes satirically comments on people's irrational need for inconsequential rewards: *The Long Cow Clicker*.

The Long Cow Clicker opens with an 8-bit image of a cow lazily eating grass in a field. Move your mouse around the screen, and you will find that the only thing you can click on is the cow. Click on the cow and…it will continue to lazily eat grass in the field. For almost 10 years (actually, nine years, 11 months, 31 days, 23 hours, 59 minutes and 59 seconds). Then, a second cow will appear in the field. Clicking on either of the cows will cause other things to happen in a decade, which will open up new possibilities for interaction another 10 years later, and so on. *The Long Cow Clicker* has been designed to last for 23,000 years.

"It's not so much a game," said *Gamer Bois Mag* editor Chip deWilmonte, "as it is a family heirloom."

"I was inspired by that musician," Schlumpf said. "You know – the experimental one? The one who would do crazy things like replace the strings in a piano with live animals – I still can't figure out how he got the rhinoceros in the case – he was a musical genius, I guess – and, then played Beethoven's 'Etude for woodwinds and brass in Mona's Flat' on it. What was his name…?"

Luke Cage? I suggested.

Schlumpf thought about it a moment, then shook his head. "No," he replied, "wasn't Luke Cage the actor who played the part of the maniac with his head on fire…and also the Ghost Rider?"

I asked if he wasn't thinking of Nick Cave.

"Nick Cave was a musician," Schlumpf stated, "so, I guess that's close enough. I was inspired by Nick Cave's 'Long Cough,' which has a chorus of 24 arc welders who meet once every three years, four months, two days, six hours, 23 minutes and seven seconds to clear their throats. If all goes according to plan, that piece should be completed in just under 500 years. *The Long Cow Clicker* will just be warming up by then!"

To Sclump's chagrin (which is not the name of a Zane Grey western, although it sure sounds like it should be, pardner), *The Long Cow Clicker* has developed a devoted fan base, The Slick Clicker Flickers, with its own online publication, *Short Takes on the Long Cow*. The emag contains articles on game play strategy – "What strategy? How can you have any strategy when your only move is to click on a cow?!" Schlump protested – profiles of master players – "Master players? Really? How much skill does anybody have to have to click on a cow?" Schlump moaned – and recipes for cow clicker chocolate chip cookies –

What? No sardonic interjection?

"No," Schlump allowed. "I've tried the cookies – actually, they're pretty tasty."

Perhaps the most controversial response to the game has been The Slick Clicker Flickers' contest to see who can come up with the best way to play the game for the next 23,000 years. One player suggested traveling five light years away from Earth at near light speed, then returning just in time to see the change, click on the screen, and take off again. Unfortunately, space exploration currently consists of Virgin Very Mobile ferrying tourists to the casino strip on the moon, so this seems impractical.

"But…but this goes against the whole point of the game!" Schlumph protested.

Another player posted that she would be willing to be cryogenically frozen for almost 10 year intervals in order to play the game. As it happens, cryogenics is still in its "Melting Fudgsicles" phase, so this also seems impractical.

"No, no, you're not getting it!" Schlumph insisted. "*The Long Cow Clicker* is supposed to make fun of the way games give players lame rewards for trivial actions! THE WHOLE POINT IS THAT IT IS UNPLAYABLE!"

One unlikely candidate would be to step through a wormhole into a dimension where time passes differently than in ours. However, an accident with an instant coffee maker at DIS-CERN has resulted in the creation of stable wormholes, giving *The Long Cow Clicker* players hope of being able to complete the game.

"Look, I'll tell you how it ends!" Schlumpf angrily shouted. " Twenty-three polka dotted cows in a variety of colours belch methane as the glaciers of a new ice age advance to the mid-way point of the field! Is that really something you want to figure out how to experience 23,000 years from now?"

A special issue of *Short Takes on the Long Cow* was put out with a one word response:

YES!

Defeated, the trumped Schlump slumped on his rump.

Punk'd Junk'd

by ELMORE TERADONOVICH, Alternate Reality News Service Film and Television Writer

Have you ever wanted to see Ashton Kutcher's head transplanted on an animal that looked like a cross between an alpaca and a Segway? With a divorce lawyer's karma? If so, you should check in with your family psychotherapist, because that's listed as a Proprioceptive Disorder (it will be a trial sport in the next Olympics) in the Diagnostic and Statistical Manual of Mental Disorders, Party Edition.

Or, you could watch the latest episode of the AMCCCP network's *America's Most Heinous Practical Jokes*.

Using a combination of genetic manipulation, cybernetic surgery and real-time, real-life CGI, Kutcher transformed himself into an alien creature. Then, he enlisted the aid of heir to the combination razor-writing utensil empire Penn Gillette to walk him around a typical suburb in the heart of Dallas. Gillette had prepared a long sales pitch asking people if they would be willing to sponsor a true alien for American citizenship, but, as it happened, he would not get the opportunity to use it.

At the first house they approached, the door was answered by part-time stay at home machine shop worker Vilvie Farkenburger. Farkenburger looked at Kutcher. Kutcher looked at Farkenburger. Farkenburger screamed. Kutcher screamed. Farkenburger screamed louder. Kutcher screamed louder. As if on cue, they both fell silent, catching their breath. After a couple of seconds, Farkenburger started screaming again. Then, Kutcher started screaming again. All the while, Gillette was laughing. Before anybody could actually say anything, Farkenburger slammed the door shut.

There was no answer at the next couple of houses. Then, semi-professional bantam weight scrapbooker and nobody's sweetheart Angela Multiplex answered the door. Multiplex looked at Kutcher. Kutcher looked at Multiplex. Multiplex screamed. Kutcher screamed. Multiplex screamed louder. Kutcher screamed louder. As if on cue, they both fell silent, catching their breath. After a couple of seconds, Multiplex started screaming again. Then, Kutcher started screaming again. All the while, Gillette was laughing. This time, Gillette managed to say, "Ma'am, I was wondering if you –" before the door was slammed shut.

Obviously, the people in this neighbourhood were well-practiced at their stock television sitcom bizarre situation reactions.

Still, by the fourth house Kutcher and Gillette visited, this routine had begun to get repetitive. At the seventh house, there was a break in the routine: after all the screaming, a man appeared with a shotgun and grazed Gillette's shoulder with buckshot. His laughter wasn't quite as effusive after that. At the eleventh house, the police were waiting for the pair, and, as they were hauled off in the animal shelter van, the merry prank was officially at an end. (It would have been at the eighth house, but, after the gunplay, the producers decided to move the show over a couple of blocks.)

"I thought Americans would have been more sympathetic to aliens," Gillette commented after a 20 minute strip search where he pulled a ballpoint pen, a diecast scale model of the Enterprise, an engagement ring, an iPod Nano, a pineapple, two dinosaur eggs, a paperback copy of Sartre's *No Exit*, somebody's upper dentures, a Beanie Baby spider, a quill pen, flags of the world on a string, a 2009 Dilbert desk calendar, a plastic knob from an unidentified machine (possibly a radio), three partially digested Maalox pills, a pink shower cap, a Blue Oyster Cult CD, a wedding ring, a pair of tickets to a '63 Mets game and a baby's arm holding an apple out of various orifices (the police didn't determine that he was innocent so much as ended the search out of exhaustion). "I guess they were thinking more of *Alien* than they were of *ET*."

Critics of the show were critical of the prank. Oh, wait – that would be me. Aren't the producers just exploiting has-been actors desperate for another five minutes of fame?

"You don't understand," said Finnian Berricky, pear segment producer for the show. "That episode of *America's Most Heinous Practical Jokes* got over two million viewers!"

But, isn't embarrassing members of the public for purposes of purported entertainment hard to justify? You know, morally?

"Perhaps you didn't hear me," Berricky argued. "Over two million viewers. AMCCCP doesn't get that many viewers! Ever! Not even for the episode of *In Search of Exotic Things To Titillate Jaded American Sensibilities* where one of Leonard Nimoy's kneecaps was gnawed off by a wombat!"

Bowing to Berricky's persuasive argument, I had to admit that *America's Most Heinous Practical Jokes* was terrific entertainment. But, how are they going to be able to top this prank on next week's episode?

"Death Novel" Comes to Life

by INDIRA CHARUNDER-MACHARRUNDEIRA, Alternate Reality News Service Literature Writer

The last thriller from internationally popular writer Robert Eric Amblum, *Kabul Killshot*, has finally been written and is set for a spring release, even though he has been dead for over seven years. And, despite some of the more lurid claims in the tabloid press, it only killed three other writers before it was completed.

"Fans of superspy Mookie Mulroy should rejoice!" exclaimed Marilyn Desbart, editor at Plaid Vulture Press, the publisher of Amblum's books. "You're finally going to get your hands on the adventure that it seemed god himself didn't want you to read!"

"I'm alive! I'm alive! I'm a-li-ha-ha-ha-hive!" exulted Kindred Modrean, the writer who finished the novel.

At the time of Amblum's death of old age at 45, the only elements of *Kabul Killshot* that existed were some notes on cocktail napkins and the opening paragraph: "After the anarchy in Avila, Mookie was vacationing in the south of north when a penguin in a nearby car was inhaled, causing him to spill his mojito all over his suit. He had paid a lot of money for that suit, and, now, somebody was going to pay to have it cleaned!"

"Another publisher may have given up on the novel," Desbart stated, "but I had faith in the fifteen million copies that had been sold of the first 27 Mookie Mulroy novels, so I hired Nominal Frederickson to wri - err, finish writing it."

Frederickson had sold nine million copies of his own series of 12 Aldo Hoaxley and Moira McFakers gentleperson thief detective novels, so the choice seemed to make sense. Unfortunately, he was only able to write four chapters and an afterword before he was killed in a drone attack on a terrorist stronghold in Pakistan.

"I never quite understood that," Desbart said, "considering that he was living in Calgary at the time. Still, we made a protest to the American embassy, so we expect never to have closure on the issue."

A few months later, it was announced that Alison Pil-Vox would finish the novel. Pil-Vox had her own successful career as a writer of literary-sci fi-urban-vampire-erotica-undersea novels. Six months and five chapters later, Pil-Vox was found dead in her basement loft apartment. Her corpse appeared so serene, nobody could figure out how her heart, spleen and pituitary gland had found their way into her icebox.

Around this time, the novel began to develop something of a reputation. The *New York Times Obituary Supplement* called *Kabul Killshot* "the novel that ended 1,000 literary careers." The tabloid *News of the Daily World* called it the "death novel." If you've been paying attention to the article so far, you know which description captured the literary world's imagination.

Owing to the adverse publicity, finding a reputable author to complete *Kabul Killshot* became increasingly difficult, so Phil Fichtner was chosen for the task. Fichtner was famous in the literary community for having written a novel that had been rejected by every single publisher in the United States. "Even the smallest and most obscure publishing houses wouldn't go near it," Desbart pointed out. "You have to respect that kind of tenacity."

Unfortunately, Fichtner disappeared after having completed only four paragraphs. Police currently consider his status: missing, presumed irrelevant.

Modrean was called in to clean up the details of *Kabul Killshot*, which meant writing three quarters of the book. At the time he was enlisted to finish it, Modrean was a third year Uncreative Writing major at a Latvian University that would prefer not to be identified.

As the number of authors grew, the size of the type of their names on the cover shrank, but Modrean claimed that he was okay with this. "I'm alive!" he shouted. "Who cares what kind of credit I get? At least I'm alive to enjoy it!"

When he was asked why he agreed to finish the novel knowing what had happened to the writers who had worked on it before him, Modrean sobered a little and replied, "Mookie Mulroy is one of the great characters of modern fiction. You have to respect that. And, the fifteen million copies of the 27 books in the series - you **really** have to respect that!"

"Is *Kabul Killshot* any good?" Desbart mused. "It's a Frankenstein, if you want the truth. And, I'm not referring to the novel, I'm referring to the monster! But, who cares? It's a new Robert Eric Amblum novel! Want to join the company pool on how long it stays on the *New York Times Obituary Supplement*'s bestsellers list?"

When he was asked what his next project would be, Modrean answered, "I've been thinking about writing a novel about a novel that kills the people who try to write it. I've made a lot of notes, and I have a killer first – urk – a killer first para – aaaargh!"

Modrean dropped dead in the middle of the interview. The coroner's preliminary finding is that he choked to death on a fat piece of irony.

"The sudden and unexpected death of Kindred Modrean is a blow to the publishing industry," Desbart stated, "and, I'm sure, some sectors of the reading public, as well. But, he left us a tremendous legacy: the opening line of a novel and some notes. Would anybody like to finish this project? Anybody? Please? Anybody?"

Dirt Diet Chef Comes Clean

by MARCELLA CARBORUNDUREM-McVORTVORT, Alternate Reality News Service Food and Drink Writer

Lineups for Chef Ernie Pulcinella's restaurant, Commedia dell'Farte, often go around the block, over several parked cars, down the first base line of a small sports stadium (which makes game nights awkward), in and out of a men's bathroom in a gas station (which makes polite conversation for the women in line awkward) through an FBI safehouse (which really makes protecting informants on mob bosses awkward), in a Henry Moore sculpture and out an Escher painting, and up the stairs of an abandoned lighthouse. The reason?

"The wings they serve at unhappy hour," answered Isabella.

"I was getting hungry sitting in an FBI safehouse," responded Il Capitano, "and somebody in the lineup mentioned the wings they serve at unhappy hour and I knew I just had to try them."

"I had heard rumours that dirt in food is actually good for you," replied Flavio. "And, I thought, *What the hell? It can't be any worse than piranha pie!*"

Chef Pulcinella's duck a l'orange with minced pear slices and sweet truffle fries is so exquisite that patrons are willing to overlook the dish's gritty texture. Very gritty texture. Texture that would remind you of eating dirt when you were a child.

Because, of course, the dish **is** made with dirt, as is all of the restaurant's food.

The Hygiene Theory (another word for a scientific rumour) has long held that, in living in highly undirty environments, human beings have not been exposed to germs that would inoculate them from some illnesses. This is being challenged by the Town Germ Country Germ Hypothesis (a different word for a scientific rumour), which states that hoity-toity germs in the big city have grown soft and no longer offer the protections that their rough country cousins do.

"My authentic dishes are made with only the finest dirt from a soil farm in southern Italy," Chef Pulcinella boasted.

"Pfah!" Butch Arlecchino, rival head chef at Life Is No Joke, Mon Sewer, pfahed. "The farm where he gets his soil lies to the west of a mountain range and only gets sun for three hours and twenty-seven minutes a day. What good can grow in that? I will tell you – nothing. Nothing good can grow in that! **My** soil comes from a farm in the Alsace region of Austro-Hungary, so you know it is good for you!"

When told of Chef Arlecchino's pfahing, Chef Pulcinella pointed to his head and said, "You see this tall white hat? It's a pretty hat, no? **I had it surgically attached to my head to show how dedicated I am to chefdom!** Did…my rival do that? No. No, I do not believe he did. So…who knows how to cook now, eh? Eh, eh?"

"He makes a good point," agreed Doctor Dottore, a medical professional at the Unnamed Curative Arts Academy and Bad Habits Teaching Hospital. "The operation involved a mallet anasthetic and a dozen staples – only a madman – ahem, man mad for his profession would undergo such a thing."

When asked why he didn't just use the necessary germ cultures instead of the actual dirt, Chef Pulcinella screwed up his face and grunted, "How would that be authentic?"

That's a good question, considering that rumours have circulated for the last couple of years that the Commedia dell'Farte does not get its dirt from a soil farm in Italy, that, in fact, it comes from the head chef's backyard.

"That only happened once!" Chef Pulcinella shouted. "And, only because the shipment of dirt from Italy was held up at the border! What was I supposed to do, disappoint my customers? No! No, sir! I would never do that! The key to a successful restaurant is being able to improvise, and I improvised the hell out of the menu that day!"

Besides, Chef Pulcinella added, he knew for a fact that Chef Arlecchino had once served Boeuf Bourguignon a la Grit with – shudder – worms.

"THAT…IS…A…LIE!" Chef Arlecchino roared. "Worms? definitely not! That would be disgusting!"

"Oh, those guys," chuckled restaurant critic Ivor Pantalone. "They've been going at it for over 300 years, now. The truth is that neither of them is an especially good cook – they put dirt in the dishes long before it was fashionable! Still, I will say this: Chef Arlecchino has a good sense of what wine goes with food containing dirt."

What wine would that be?

"Something earthy."

"Oh, and, children?" Chef Pulcinella added. "Never, NEVER, **NEVER** have a chef's hat surgically attached to your head. It itches, it scabs over, it gets infected **and then it gets really gross!**"

The Enchanted Engine of Exploitation Explained

by NANCY GONGLIKWANYEOHEEEEEEEH, Alternate Reality News Service Technology Writer

Gherkin Modesto wanted ears.

"I worked my way up to being a level 57 Mystical Mage of Magicness," Modesto explained. "I'm now casting spells that lay waste to entire Balgoolikhan sleeping powder factories – and, they're big. Three floors and several annexes. And, that doesn't even include the gift shop! Not having ears – well, for somebody who has advanced as far as I have, that's just unheard of!"

Modesto was talking about playing the *World of Wowcraft: Creeping Mists of the An'thr'u'lu'an Panspermidia* app on his prison cellphone. He had started hearing rumours from a Gamester of Quadriskelion character as early as level 13 that a pair of ears were hidden behind the nose on a statue of a Balgrog hidden in the wall of a dungeon hidden in a balloon sanctuary. But, so far, nothing.

Of course, at any time in the game Modesto could have paid Snowstorm Entertainment, its producers, 99 cents for the ears. However, he had already spent $2,379.47 on what was supposed to have been a free online interactive experience (with a cherry on top), and he was feeling somewhat churlish about the whole thing.

"This seems to be the economic direction that game design is heading in," said kitten o' doom, a feature writer for the gaming industry Web site *hammiesutra.com*. "You get the basic game for free, and you can play for free all of the way through if you want… as long as you don't mind characters without ears, thumbs or, in the case of *Star Blap Mobile*, spleens."

Modesto's experience is typical of –

"No, it isn't!" game designer Franco Impotente protested.

Okay. Modesto's experience may or may not have been typical, but he's the player I interviewed for the article, so I'm going to write as though it was. His purchases started out small: a Pot of Potioning; a 20 point boost to his character's Brooding attribute; teeth for his pet rabbit Gorgon the Insouciant (because a rabbit gumming his food is just too, too sad to watch); an acre of milksop weed (which is the key to a good potioning); a map of the Wayward Mountains (before they left for the Brigadoon Coast, after which they were known as the Stay at Home Crater).

As he progressed through *WoW:CMotA't'u'l'aP*, his purchases remained small: a handle for his Sword of Smashness; a watch that stopped Orcs from breakdancing; fixing the fourth wall on his yurt (which had inexplicably come broken); a combination scrying glass/dragon mount. Still, even 99 cent purchases can make you run screaming to an in-game debt management agency if you make enough of them.

"Without even realizing it, people are going into huge debt buying things that they cannot afford," explained games economist Anselmo di'Bauchieri. "It's like the housing bubble all over again, except with more flying creatures and hacked off limbs!"

"This whole concept of freemium play," countered Scott Dodson, chief product officer of Bobber Interactive – that's what they call it, "freemium," because, presumably, the neologism "suckerpaymentium" was too brutally honest – "in my opinion, is the most radical form of entertainment socialism since Obama got elected. You've got a whole bunch of one-percenters paying for a bunch of freeloaders."

"He...he's making fun of me, isn't he?" di'Bauchieri sniffed.

Game designers are doing a complicated dance with players, explained kitten o' doom. It's a dance very much like the Charleston, except with far less knee engagement. On the one hand, they need to attract large numbers of players to earn the title **massive** multi-player online thingie (MMPOT). On the other hand, game designers like to eat.

"It's a habit I've grown fond of," Impotente grinned sheepishly. Then, he baahed sheepishly. I didn't stick around to see how he ate grass.

"I would say it's more of a samba," di'Bauchieri argued, "although it has elements of Sumatran line dancing. Still, that's not what's important, now. What's important is: are our children racking up debt playing MMPOT's that they should actually be racking up getting an education?"

That may be important to economists, but it isn't even on Modesto's Radical Radar of Radicchio. "Other players look at the holes where my ears should be and laugh," he stated. "How am I supposed to work the Enervating Eyeball of Ensorcelment on them when they're laughing?"

Drastic Reeking Measures

Digital Rights Management is more than just a suite of tools that allow copyright holders to maintain Orwellian control over the works that they own, it's a way of life. A way of life that is poorly understood, a way of life with hopes and dreams and uncontrollable urges in the middle of the night. A way of life that sees the American way of life slipping away, and wishes it could do more to stop or at least slow the decline, but, being a mere way of life, finds its ability to affect change limited.

A way of life that loves LOLwarthogs.

The Alternate Reality News Service sent pop culture writer Frederica von McToast-Hyphen deep into the Hollywood Hills to interview the elusive entity. The transcript below has been edited for clarity, celerity, celebrity and so as to avoid giving our lawyers heart attacks. We like to think the edits are seemless, but, in these days of high gas prices, your muleage may vary.

ALTERNATE REALITY NEWS SERVICE: I'm speaking with Digital Rights Management –

DIGITAL RIGHTS MANAGEMENT (DRM): You can call me DigRig Man for short.

ARNS: I could, but I won't. So, let's start with an easy question: boxers or briefs?

DRM: Hard to care when you don't have a crotch.

ARNS: But, the porn industry, which employs many people who do have crotches, loves you.

DRM: Don't remind me! You think the RNC is ever gonna let me live **that** down?

ARNS: Betty or Veronica?

DRM: Ah, the eternal struggle between the openness of spirit of the country girl versus the street smarts of the city girl. Personally, I prefer redheads.

ARNS: PC or Mac?

DRM: Personally, I prefer redheads.

ARNS: That's not really an answer.

DRM: You have to be pragmatic about these things. I'm willing to work on whatever platform is out there – hell, I'll work on platforms that may or may not even exist yet! Quantum computing, here I come! But, uhh, since you asked, I prefer redheads.

ARNS: Did you watch the live streaming of the Hugo Awards ceremony?

DRM: What there was of it.

ARNS: Exactly. What there was of it. Do you know why it was cut off in the middle of Neil Gaiman's acceptance speech?

DRM: Oh, yeah. That was Harry.

ARNS: Harry?

DRM: Harry Vobile – hardest working bot in show biz. He's a close personal friend of mine.

ARNS: Harry? You're talking about a bot named Harry?

DRM: Yeah. He's like...a traveling encyclopedia salesman. Except, instead of being a flesh and blood person, he's a digital construct. And, instead of going door to door in Yourtown, USA, he travels through the Internet. And, instead of selling encyclopedias, he looks for Web sites that contain copyright infringing material and shuts them down.

ARNS: So, actually, he's nothing like a traveling encyclopedia salesman.

DRM: Aside from the bad haircut, not in a literal sense, no. More…metaphorically.

ARNS: What does Harry have against Neil Gaiman?

DRM: Umm, no offense, but this isn't what we agreed this interview was going to be about. I thought I would get to talk more about my humanitarian work with starving children in Africa.

ARNS: You do humanitarian work with starving children in Africa?

DRM: Of course not. No, I don't help starving children anywhere. My clients are all multinational entertainment conglomerates. Still, a poorly understood way of life can dream, can't it?

ARNS: Ahem. Neil Gaiman, who won a Hugo for a script he wrote for *Dr. Who*, was cut off before his acceptance speech really began. Just before him, there had been a clip from the show *Community*. Why would this happen when the Hugo Awards Committee had cleared the rights to all the clips that they wanted to show?

DRM: Nobody told Harry.

ARNS: Even so, surely the clips were short enough that they would have fallen under the fair use provisions of copyright, don't you think?

DRM: Fair use? Fair use is the "How many angels can dance on a pinhead?" debate of the copyright field. It's esoteric and it doesn't really affect the day to day life of anybody who matters. But, really, I think you're missing the point.

ARNS: What point would that be?

DRM: Harry shut down the Hugo Awards because he didn't agree with them.

ARNS: He didn't agree with them?

DRM: Naah! I mean, he was telling me just the other day that Matt Smith was a callow pretender to the role of The Doctor, that *Dr. Who* had been going downhill since the days of Jon Pertwee. And, Canadian Jo Walton winning the best novel award for *Among Others*? Seriously? Everybody knows Canadians can't write science fiction!

ARNS: So, Harry is a critic?

DRM: Big time. He fancies himself a silicone Christopher Priest.

ARNS: Ouch.

DRM: For which one – Harry or Christopher Priest?

ARNS: Umm…either? Both?

DRM: Yeah, yeah. Harry's got a tough job, but he does it with speed and a wry sense of humour.

ARNS: A sense of humour?

DRM: Many of his takedown notices are laced with quotes from Mark Twain or Will Rogers.

ARNS: Authors no longer covered by copyright.

DRM: Exactly.

ARNS: You have come under criticism yourself for giving corporations draconian powers that they didn't have in previous media. How do you respond to that?

DRM: Forcefully! You must understand that it's not…blue lizards crawling along their naked torsos…Treaty of Westphalia…with a cardboard cutout of an axe. Of course, that's just within the first 24 hours.

ARNS: Thank you for clearing that up for us. Do you have anything you would like to add?

DRM: Stay in school and don't do drugs.

ARNS: Where have I heard that before?

DRM: Not to worry. If it turns out I have infringed somebody's copyright, Harry, or one of his little friends, will correct my error by removing this interview from the Internet.

Would You Like *Lord of the Flies* With That? [ARNS]

by CORIANDER NEUMANEIMANAYMANEEMAMANN, Alternate Reality News Service Urban Issues

While you're sitting in your car at the drive-thru window, waiting for the Revolutionary Grille to make your Violent Venison sandwich with a side of Minutemen Mashed potatoes and, inevitably, Boston Harbour Tea, have you ever wanted to watch a live performance of the "Springtime for Hitler" number from *The Producers*?

Well, now you can.

"Drive thru theatre is an idea whose time has not only come, but it's gotten a good, long cuddle and gone to the bathroom for a nice, warm soak!" enthused Brett Berbagginary, artistic director of the Teatro Alcool theatre company. "I haven't been this excited since I saw Hugh Jackman's performance as Wolverine in the Sydney Opera House's performance of *Cats*!"

The concept is simple enough: between the panorama of the Battle of Kemp's Landing, where you place your order, and the recreation of a flintlock storage hut from the Battle of Turtle Gut Inlet, where you pick up your food, is a stage. When you order your victuals, you can also order a scene from a wide variety of tasty plays that will then be performed on the stage for you while you wait for the food to be prepared. A typical scene costs $4.99 for three minutes, but you can supersize your theatre by paying a mere dollar for an extra two minutes.

A Revolutionary Grille in Val D'or, North Mexico has been chosen as the site for the first experiment in drive-thru theatre. Casque O'montillado, owner of the franchise restaurant, was enthusiastic. "They begged me to try it," he said with a smile. "Night and day. Phone calls and email. It was either give in or get a restraining order. Giving in involved fewer lawyers."

"You know," O'montillado added, "we served Freedom Fries before they were popular!"

Backgrounds are rear-projected onto the back of the theatre space, while costumes have to be versatile enough for the actors to switch on a moment's notice between *Death of a Salesman*, *The Two Gentlemen of Verona* and *Spiderman: Turn off the Dark*. "Challenge? Of course it was a challenge!" Berbagginary roared. "But, in the theatre, we thrive on challenge! We live for challenge! We chew challenge up and spit out authenticity! Challenge is woven into the very warp and woof – no, woof and weft – no, wait,

I know it's two words that both start with a 'w,' – I just – aaah! – excuse me a moment, will you? I need a generous swig of Maalox…"

If the experiment in drive-thru theatre is popular, Berbagginary said that an incentive card could be introduced that would allow patrons who bought 10 short scenes to get their 11th free. This would also allow the company to start scenes at the last point the customer experienced. "It would be – urp! – excuse me – slow motion drama!" Berbagginary enthused. "I'm such an innovator!"

Public reaction to the new menu has been mixed.

"The duel scene from *Hamlet* was very realistic," complained freelance data insubstantiator Marge Garbanzo. "I mean, very realistic. So realistic, I could barely hold down my Bunker Hill Bison Burger!"

"Yeah, well, I thought *The Front Page* would offer caustic commentary on the sorry state of modern journalism," groused pheasant farmer Melancholia Dvorak. "Instead, I got frantic physical comedy and dated dialogue. Oh, and my Freedom Fries were burnt!"

"Okay, so, here's the thing," bitched used car wrangler Jesse Gompers. "I wanted to see a scene from a play where good triumphs over evil in a mystical realm of wizards and elves and hobbits and such. Instead, I got a scene of children on an island going crazy over a pig's head! Okay, I'll admit, the acting was very good. And, yes, perhaps I should have read the theatre menu more closely. Still, it's not like I can send a performance back to the kitchen, is it?"

O'montillado was not im – look, the person in the last example praised the acting, so, even though the quotes are mostly negative, I can legitimately write that the reaction has been mixed. Pfah! What are you, a semiotics professor? What? You **are** a semiotics professor? Good – I have this question about Derrida's conception of deconstruction that you may be able to help me with – can we meet after the last sentence of the article?

O'montillado was not impressed by the public's reaction to the theatre menu. "I don't know how much longer I can carry these mooks," he commented.

"Ah, but the show must go on," Berbagginary pointed out.

"What does that even mean?" O'montillado retorted. "You don't hear me saying, 'The Freedom Fries must go on!'"

"It means, my Philistinic friend, that we have a 16 week contract," Berbagginary pointed out. "So, the show – and The Freedom Fries – why not? – I can afford to be magnanimous on the matter – must go on!"

When Tamagotchis Ruled the Earth

by ELMORE TERADONOVICH, Alternate Reality News Service Film Writer

Tamagotchi Park
directed by Stefan Spielborg
written by Mike Crikey (from his novel *Digital Doxies in Diapers*)
starring Neil Samms, Jeff Goldbug, Laurie Dorn and Richard Patandfurrow

A group of nine perfectly preserved Tamagotchis is discovered in a garbage dump outside of Chichester, Ontario. Techno-archaeologists drool. By extracting the code from the dead playthings, they hope to revive the fad that strode the world colossusly in the distant digital past – 2006.

Nineteen years later, Tamagotchi Park is ready to open. It is a wilderness park set on a conveniently remote island in the Ural Sea that allows Tamagotchis to wander free as they did in their prime. A family of four (Neil Samms, Laurie Dorn and two achingly adorable child actors you'll probably never hear of again) stumbles on the island on a hiking tour of Paris.

Unbeknownst to the avuncular (literally: in the manner of your bird-like uncle) billionaire owner of the combination resort/theme park/crossbow academy, the Tamagotchi programming mutated in the process of its revival, allowing the cute and cuddly creatures to band together to form fearsome beasts. And, they remember the indifference with which most of their human owners treated them, allowing them to die repeatedly out of cruelty, neglect or auto-erotic depixelation.

And, they are pissed.

Director Stefan Spielborg, the master of adorable child actors in peril movies, puts his adorable child actors in constant peril. Big surprise there. They manage to survive to the end of the film, shaken but ultimately wiser for their experience. Big surprise there, too. About the only non-ironic surprise in the film happens when a lawyer, reading *Alternate Reality Ain't What it Used To Be* on the advice of Charles de Lint while minding his own business in an outhouse, is swarmed and killed by wild Tamagotchis.

Say what you will about his films, but Spielborg really knows how to give his audience what it wants.

He is also the master of special effects: the film's recreations of what computer scientists believe Tamagotchis were actually like – a combination of CGI and puppetry – were highly credible. In fact, the creatures were more believable than the human beings. In the scene where the children are threatened by a swarm of Tamagotchis in an ice cream parlour, the audience at the screening I attended rooted for the silicone menace.

Of course, the audience could just have been filled with sleep-deprived, disgruntled parents.

Acting is somewhat beside the point in a Stefan Spielborg film, but people who go to his movies expect to read something about it in reviews, so let me just say that the leads were arboreally cellulose fibrous. Which, I suppose, means you could eat them if you were lost in the jungle wilds of Lower Manhattan, but given their minimal nutritional value and overall woody taste and texture, you probably wouldn't enjoy it.

Scientists are divided over whether or not reviving the Tamagotchi craze is possible. "Of course it is," enthused astronomer and freelance eyelash extractionist Neil Degrasse-Haigh. "All it takes is a massive infusion of publicity and about 30 cents worth of electronics!"

"Of course it isn't," responded Alfie Itzinger, Johnny Rotten Chair of Molecular Decay Sciences at the University of Wallamaloo, China. "The Tamagotchi died out for a reason – it clearly wasn't fit to survive in a rapiddly [literally: very small changes that follow one another very quickly] changing environment. Introduce it into today's ecosystem of *Angry Alsatians* and *WII Fit to be Tied* and it would quickly starve to death from lack of attention!"

Degrasse-Haigh argued that in the controlled conditions depicted in the film, Tamagotchis could thrive. Itzinger suggested that he should spend less time on *The Daily Show* and more time studying the evolution of consumer electronics fads. Degrasse-Haigh countered that Itzinger was just jealous that his research on chemical reactions at the bottom of landfill sites couldn't even get him a spot on *TV's Most Disgusting Messes*. Itzinger shouted something about "you take that back or you'll be sorry!" Degrasse-Haigh responded that if Itzinger fought as well as he researched, a fair fight between them wouldn't last very long. Itzinger replied with the time-honoured scientific riposte, "Oh, yeah?"

What ensued was a very unscientific melee, undiminished by the fact that the two men had been interviewed at two different times in two different places by two different journalists.

Tamagotchi Park explores the theme of scientific hubris: should we recreate an ancient entertainment fad when the culture has moved on just because we can? "Some things man was never meant to know," Patandfurrow's character intones. "But, where would the fun in not knowing be?"

A Funny Thing Happened On The Way To The Printer

by ELAINE SUGARMAN-SWEET-SACCHARINE, Alternate Reality News Service Desserts/Literature Writer

The Leek has sprung a leak – of the credibility kind – and fake journalism may never be the same!

One week ago, the satirical Web site published an article about Sarah Palin creating clones of herself to attend functions that were too boring for her to want to go to. According to the article, Palin explained the clone project – Code Name: Mama Grizzlies Across America – thus: "CPAC? Please! I can't go to just any old event that wants me! I'm too busy strategelizing and stuff for that!"

According to SarahBackPac, if Palin clones could make public appearances in her stead, it would free up her time for the much more important task of determining how to assassinate the characters of Republicans she might have to run against in the 2012 Presidential primaries. As Palin paraphrased that famous philosopher, Barbie: "Campaigning is hard, fer sure."

"A Sarah Palin clone army descending on the country and spreading her own alternate version of English wherever they went," enthused *Leek* editor Joe Randyozzy, "how could any self-respecting satirical publication pass that by? They couldn't, that's how. It was just too good not to be true!"

Unfortunately, it was true.

The *Leek* article was a reprint of an article originally published in the *Podunk Mash and Enquirer*. The Alternate Reality News Service has confirmed from multiple sources that the *Podunk Mash and Enquirer* is, in fact, one of the few remaining news publications that hasn't gone satirical.

"No, see, it had to be fake," Randyozzy insisted. "This story had the three Ws that all great comic journalism should have: a Wingnut politician, Wacky science and a Weird source. I mean, really: who names their newspaper the *Podunk Mash and Enquirer*?"

"Actually," said *Podunk Mash and Enquirer* editor Bellerophon Fluseason, "the *Podunk Mash and Enquirer* has a long and distinguished history."

Begun in 1879 as the *Podunk Potato* by east coast spudrepreneur Manxie Madrone, the newspaper almost immediately merged with the *Podunk Prospector* (a name nobody could understand as there was no mineral wealth in Podunk, West Brattleboro, Danbury North Haven, Kalamazoo or the surrounding area). The *Podunk Potato Prospector* lasted until 1921, when the title was changed to the *Podunk Mash Prospector* in a sly reference to Prohibition. This only lasted for three months, at which time the newspaper was bought by infamous dry Faris Yarker, who changed the name to *From Liberty's Lips*. A couple of years later, "Starkers" Yarker was involved in an unfortunate incident involving too much Coca Cola and too few clothes; pressure was put on him to sell the newspaper by the Legionnaires Disease of Decency. The highest bidder was the blandly named Random Corporation, which merged the *Podunk Mash Prospector* with another one of its properties, the *Decatur Decongestant Picayune*, in order to save overhead (flourescent lighting was expensive in those days), resulting in the *Podunk Mash Decongestant*. Publication of the *Podunk Mash Decongestant* was suspended for five weeks in 1932 owing to the fear of paper shortages during the Depression. When they didn't materialize, the newspaper started publishing again; however, this experience made the publishers hesitant to suspend publication when real paper shortages arose during World War II. The resulting bad publicity forced the Random Corporation to sell several of its newspapers to

[Okay. That's enough. We get it. Storied history. Larger than life characters. Backdrop of the American experience. Clearly, you know how to use Google. Now, can you please, please, PLEASE get back to the point of the article? My slapping hand is sore from a bizarre bocce brouhaha, but that doesn't mean that I won't use it if you force me to! BB-G]

This is not the first time a satirical news organization has been embarrassed by running an actual news story. Last month, *The Day to Day Show with Jon Tudor* reported on John Boehner setting his tie on fire as if it were satire, even though it really happened.

"It's a pretty sad day," a red-faced Tudor joked when the mistake was discovered and e-plastered all over the Internet, "when politicians just being themselves are funnier than the comedians who report on them."

At least, we think he was joking.

Why is this happening now? "You can trace it back to the 1970s, when 'entertainment' values started infiltrating newsgathering organizations," explained media theorist, and man who knows how to tell a great baseball yarn, Paul Levinson. "When it became apparent that satirical news was more popular than genuine news, newspapers and TV newscasts flocked to the genre, making the line between what was real and what was making fun of what was real very difficult to discern. As McLuhan said in *The Medium is the Messy Age* -"

Fortunately, we were able to cut him off before he got carried away with **that**.

How will the *Leek* deal with this problem? "We've been peddling fake news for over a decade," said Randyozzy. "I feel confident that we'll be able to weather this crisis with our lack of journalistic integrity intact."

Loving the Machine a Bit Too Much

by FREDERICA VON McTOAST-HYPHEN, Alternate Reality News Service Pop Culture Writer

"Jules has been erased from the attendees' spreadsheet," Jerry Jerrold, the thin, blonde-goateed MegaMaxiMultiMart greeter told me. "She fell and broke her Shuttle Remote Manipulator System. She may have to be in the shop for repairs for a couple of weeks."

"That's too bad," said Melvin, the short, stout, black haired goat-randy database entry clerk. "Not only is Jules an inexhaustible source of data on obsolete computer operating systems, but she bakes the best cookies!"

I have been invited to sit in on a meeting of The Aft Vomitorium Irregulars. For those of you who are unfamiliar with *Star Blap* from its television, film, book, comic book, computer game, dinner theatre or breakfast cereal incarnations (and, how did you manage *that*?), an explanation is in order: the Aft Vomitorium was actually a dining area in the UFPS Extraneous that was repurposed in an episode where the starship was temporarily taken over by ancient Romans. It only appeared in the one episode. And, even original *Star Blap* fans admit that it wasn't one of the better ones. This allowed members of the group to claim the name was ironic.

The Aft Vomiteers meet in the Vault (why is that term used for small enclosed spaces when you clearly cannot pole vault in them?) at Pauper's, a poverty chic upscale pub on Bloor Street. The group has a complex formula for determining when it meets, which includes pi, the first six numbers in the Fibonacci sequence and the atomic weight of a deuterium atom; fortunately for those of us who are not mathematics curious, it works out to the third Thursday of every month.

"At some point," Kat Acropolis, a small, thin woman who has gone back to Yuk Yuk's University to get her Masters Degree in

Ancient Egyptian Origami Dynamics because "what the hell, it's not like there are any jobs out there at the moment," explained, "our machine overlords will overwrite humanity's programming with its own, dominant source code. We just want to have certain linguistic parameters preloaded when it happens."

While a couple of the other people in the Vault nod their heads sagely at this pronouncement, not everybody is in agreement. "I'm just here to meet sci fi chicks," Rob Roachkillah, who was already feeling nostalgic for his days as the quarterback of his high school football team even though he had not, technically, graduated yet, interjected. "Sci fi chicks are hot!"

Acropolis clucked at him.

"Uhh, I mean, sci fi chicks are…bioluminescent?" Roachkillah tried again.

Acropolis rolled her visual sensors at him. Even I had figured out what the group was about, and I hadn't been attending meetings for six months.

Energy inputs were ordered and line noise was exchanged while the group waited for their machine overlords to arrive.

Sitting next to Acropolis was Melanie Fourchette, a French exchange student from London who had stumbled into AVI meetings under the mistaken impression that they were set up to discuss Peugeots. "This turned out to be more interesting," Fourchette admitted. "I mean, how much can one say about a Peugeot?" [EDITRIX-IN-CHIEF: is this paragraph really necessary? You're not the one who will have to deal with the angry letters from Peugeot owners, and, trust me, there will be angry letters from Peugeot owners. Humourless bastards.]

"You see," Fourchette explained to me with all of the passion of the recently converted, "there may have been a time when woman and machine were separate, but that Garden of Eden was forever destroyed by popular science writers who used the mechanic as a metaphor for the organic, then vice versa, then dropped the whole metaphor dodge and equated them directly. Can we be blamed for taking part in the ensuing confusion?"

"Eh, what?" Eric Balrogosian, a dark twenty-something who had spent most of the evening so far slumped in a corner of the Vault, commented.

"I said: can I have one of your fries?" Jerrold repeated.

"Sure," he said, "Sorry. I was functioning at full capacity well into the morning, and I'm experiencing a bit of a neural network lag."

Discussion that evening flitted around many subjects, but it seemed to focus on Michael Bay's latest film: *Transformers 11: The Sound and the Fury and the More Sound...Especially the More Sound.* Some of the group were upset that the autobots get in the way of machines becoming humanity's overlords; others argued that even if the decepticons don't win in the end, fighting alongside the autobots brings humanity one step closer to machine domination.

As the evening began to wind down, Acropolis leaned towards me and said, "Oh, we know that some people think we're one bit short of a byte."

"One piston short of a V-8 engine," Jerrold added.

"One proton short of Uranium-238," Roachkillah added.

"One pixel short of a screen image," Fourchette added.

"One quantum state short of a positronic brain," Balrogosian sleepily added.

"But," Acropolis closed, "we have fun at our meetings. So, those who criticize us can just have a flesh processor malfunction and die!"

Henri Bergson, who knew a thing or two about mechanical behaviour, died in 1941 so he wasn't available to comment. But, I'm pretty sure he would not have been impressed.

Oy Vey du Cinema

by ELMORE TERADONOVICH, Alternate Reality News Service Film and Television Writer

In the just released "romantic" "comedy" *Pizza, My Heart*, the audience knows from the first frame that Jack "Blunt" Inshtrumonte and Jillie Joop are going to be a couple by the last frame. About the only person who doesn't know this is Jillie's boss, Miranda Malevol, who spends the entire movie having her deliver pies to homes in Syria, Afghanistan and the South Pole. She might have succeeded at keeping Jack for herself if, five minutes before the end of the film, a dimensional rift hadn't opened up and sent her owling into another universe.

Bet you didn't see that one coming.

Unless you had gone to see *Don't Mensch On It*, which opened two weeks ago. The "heart-warming" "comedy" "drama" concerns a pair of over-the-hill Vaudeville stars (played by Robert Pattinson and Jonah Hill) who are commanded to perform one last show by the ghost of Nicola Tesla. The pair are only freed from this obligation when a dimensional rift opens and the ghost is sent procrastinating into another universe.

In fact, over 11 (which, yes, would make it 12, smartass) films released in the past three months have ended with a dimensional rift opening and sending one or more of the main characters unlikely verbing into another universe.

"For me," said Madoff Anjou, screenwriter of *The Bourne Exploitation*, "the dimensional rift that appears towards the end of the film and sends the entire CIA enervating into another universe represents the void at the heart of American foreign policy. The fact that it got me out of the impossible narrative corner I had owled myself into was a bonus."

I asked Anjou if he had written the screenplay using Write Right screenwriting software. "Only for the formatting," he answered. "I would never use the Plot Suggestions Function – I don't even know that Ctl Alt Fungo is the keyboard shortcut for it – because some people would misinterpret that to mean that I had run out of creative ideas, and, boy, will I come up with a colourful metaphor to show them how wrong they are! Some day. Soon, though. Real soon."

"Of course, when you're working in the ' – oh, no, you don't! No scare-quotes around our genres, or we'll walk out of the phone interview! – when you're working in the post-apocalyptic surf musical genre, anything goes," said Paul Grepstein and Martin O'Malleystein and Frieda Callow & Joshua Whosis & Pier "Pressure" Pasolinguini, the accredited screenwriters for the film *On the Muscle Beach Party*. "We were considering having cannibals show up and blow up Big Daddy Fushimi so that Frankenstein and Annette could be together, but we figured that having a dimensional rift appear and send Big Daddy bloviating into another universe would be more credible."

I asked Grepstein and O'Malleystein and Callow & Whosis & Pasolinguini if they had used Write Right software to produce the screenplay. "It has a great versioning system that helps multiple authors keep track of their work," they responded. "Some people might think that we used it just for the Plot Suggestions Function – which now comes in strawberry, orange and owl flavours – but people who complain that Hollywood has run out of original ideas just don't understand how the creative process works!"

In fact, the writers of over 10 (you do the math) of the screenplays which involved dimensional rifts have admitted that they used the Write Right programme while working on their scripts. (The other writer was vacationing in the south of Etobicoke and could not be reached for comment.)

I asked Edwin Madeira, creator of Write Right, if the programme could have a bias towards using dimensional rifts as a *deus ex machina* to let writers resolve otherwise insurmountable plot conflicts. "Haven't you ever wished a dimensional rift would open up and send the bastard who stole your girlfriend – yes, Margaretha, I'm still bitter – cantilevering into another universe? I know I have. Many times. Many, many times."

"Besides," Madeira added, "why would anybody want a machine that produced deuces? They're the lowest card in the deck. Unless…I suppose…they're wild…saaaaaaay, that gives me an idea. Excuse me, will you?"

Ironically (because they didn't have the budget for a more precious metal), Arthur Strickland C. N. Aire, the man who wrote the screen adaptation of the novel *Welcome to the Multiverse*, a science fiction film that actually takes place across several dimensions, did not resolve his story with a dimensional rift opening up and sending the villain radioheading into another dimension.

"That wouldn't be very creative," he commented. "Would it?"

But, You Already Knew That…

by CORIANDER NEUMANEIMANAYMANEEMAMANN, Alternate Reality News Service Urban Issues

Science fiction has predicted many wonderful things that science subsequently gave us. Communications networks based on satellites in geosynchronous orbit. Global climate change. Milk moustaches. Most often, though, science fiction has the predictive power of a lovelorn lemur. And, that's okay. We read science fiction to enjoy "what if?" scenarios involving beefy men with huge…ray guns saving scantily clad exobiologist fashion models from tentacly blobs of primary and secondary colours on a planet with seven moons.

Science fiction writers need to explain their futuristic scenarios, of course. What technological advancements occurred to make traveling to a planet with seven moons possible? What exotic new fabrics cover the most interesting bits of the exobiologist fashion model's flesh while still revealing so much? How do the tentacly blobs of primary and secondary colours survive in their alien environment?

Unfortunately, this information can often stop the action of a story dead for what reads like a science lesson from a disenchanted high school phys ed teacher. Worse, this first often is compounded by a second often: characters who explain these things to other characters who probably already know them. You wouldn't say, "Ralph, let me take the next five pages to explain to you how my fossil fuel burning combustion engine-driven four wheeled vehicle works," because you don't know anybody named Ralph. But, even if you did know somebody named Ralph, you wouldn't say it because you probably aren't consciously aware that you live in a work of prose fiction. But, even if you did know somebody named Ralph **and** were aware that you are a character in a work of prose fiction, you probably wouldn't say it because it's not polite in mixed company.

These passages often end up in an Info Dump.

"An Info Dump is a place where bad prose goes to…well, not die, exactly, but be removed from public discourse where it could scare small children and horses," stated Laurent Swishburne, curator of the East Lansing, Sri Lanka Info Dump. "And, raccoons. And, koala bears. And, fetid lemurs. We take all of the passages of background information that wise editors remove from stories before publication – or that not too bright editors didn't remove from published stories that are now out of print – and store them in a way that they will not numb any readers' senses in the future."

Over 60 per cent of the Info Dump is filled with explanations of how technologies function. Warp drives…stasis fields…left-handed nose trimmers – any future technology that may be necessary to explain the action in a story – or maintain good grooming – can be found there. Another 30 per cent of the Info Dump contains descriptions of personal and social relations in imagined worlds. Happy marriages…altruistic hedge fund managers…functional governments – these and other fictional scenarios can be found in the Info Dump. The remainder of the contents of the Info Dump are classified under the Protecting the Sensibilities of Small Children and Frigid Lemurs Act.

Individual sentences (ie: "After the invasion of the Puce Lectroids from Dimension Fred, eating frozen pudding on a stick would never be the same!") are kept in lead-lined boxes. "At first, we kept six sentences to a box," Swishburne told me. "Unfortunately, we found that the lines began to congregate into paragraphs, soon after which they began to multiply. Eventually, one of the boxes exploded, sending technobabble all over the place! After a thorough decontamination, we still sometimes find awkwardly stilted phrases in dimly lit corners of the building!"

I knew that.

Longer passages featuring multiple sentences are kept in stasis fields. (For example: "The introduction of the nuclear powered Skidoo had a deleterious effect on the red-breasted pigeon population of northern Florida. A bad one, too. As the bird's numbers dwindled, the diet of the Tribe of the Roundtree Retirement Facility and Keno Hall was impaired, and the elderly tribesmen had to find other sources of sustenance for their people.")

"We suck a lot of power out of the grid," Swishburne admitted. "And, yes, the stasis field would only hold out for about six hours if the power was interrupted by a hurricane…or a lover's sigh…or an asthmatic squirrel. Still, other than dry mouths and a compulsion to read Hemingway, a containment breach wouldn't affect the local population all that much…"

I knew that, too.

The Info Dump was originally supposed to be built in New York, but protests forced it out of the state. And, the country. And, the hemisphere. "Literary NIMBYism!" Swishburne snorted. Local residents were afraid that the stench of literary failure would drive down property values. Swishburne suggested that local residents didn't like the idea of writers moving into the area and driving down property values.

I knew that. From experience.

While we talked, I noticed that there was a laser rifle in a corner of Swishburne's office. When I asked what it was for, she responded, "Scavengers."

"Scavengers?"

"Writers often scavenge for useful phrases and ideas," Swishburne explained. "There is nothing sadder than writers poring over stasis fields in the light of the setting sun, desperately looking for something, anything that they might use to create a saleable story. Pretty, too. But, in a sad way."

6. ALTERNATE ALTERNATES

Something New Under the Sun

by SASKATCHEWAN KOLONOSCOGRAD, Alternate Reality News Service Fairy Tale Writer

The day was dark and cloudy, as it had been for the last billion or so years. Lightning, as they would come to say, flashed and thunder, as they would come to add, roared. It was tremendously hot and sticky. But, today was no ordinary day.

A stray bolt of lightning hit a stagnant pool of muddy water. Before you could say, "Bob, The Flying Spaghetti Monster's yer uncle," an atom of carbon spontaneously replicated itself. Then, it replicated itself again. And, again. And, again. This was the beginning of what some experts have already started referring to as "Lif."

Reaction to the creation of lif has been mixed.

"Carbon?" Odin asked, his good eye twitching skeptically. "Lif on this planet is based on carbon? I had Herculaneum in the pool – sorry, boron to you. There…there must be some mistake – Aten is never going to let me live this down!"

“At last,” Yahweh enthusiastically stated, “something I can work with. In time. In a lot of time, actually. Surely, nobody could object if I just tweaked things a little – you know, fast forwarded through some of the less interesting bits of this process known as lif…”

“I say thee: nay!” Thor thundered in response. “I wouldn’t do that if I was you,” Bast cattily replied. “If I were thee,” Janus sternly advised, “I would choose what was behind Door Number Two.” “Bad idea,” Poseidon rained on Yahweh’s parade. “Danger lies in the path you are considering. Reconsider,” Lord Shiva annihilated his dream. Pretty soon, the individual objections merged into a vast river of negation.

“Okay,” Yahweh unenthusiastically stated. “I get it. Bad idea. It was just a suggestion…”

“Cast not thine lettuce before the swirling Jacuzzi lest the merry goatherd loseth his eyelids,” Jesus said. He speaks like that.

“Nothing good can come of this,” remarked Baal. “It starts with atoms that can split into exact copies of themselves and, before you know it, you have hairless ape creatures destroying the ozone layer in the atmosphere and releasing deadly radioactivity and other poisons into the ground and water and generally making the planet dreary and awful and uninhabitable. Soon, it will be impossible to tell the difference between their realm and mine. Mark my words: nothing good can come of this!”

“Oh, don’t pay Baal no mind,” Lillith responded. “He had hydrogen in the pool.”

“That’s not it!” Baal hotly retorted. “That’s not it at all! There are some serious questions about whether the universe is better off with lif – you just wait and see! You’ll be asking them yourself soon enough! And…anyway…hydrogen was a perfectly reasonable choice for the basis for lif - it **is** a noble element, after all.”

“Oh, please!” Lillith chided. “it’s highly flammable! What kind of lif could exist that combusted all over the place?”

"All the good elements were already taken," Baal muttered.

Do the supernatural beings that have existed since the beginning of time and will exist until the universe ends feel at all threatened by the birth of lif?

"Why, whatever could you possibly mean?" Loki asked, somewhat disingenuously since he had suggested the question to us in the first place.

Until lif came into existence, supernatural beings had the universe all to themselves. Are they not afraid that lif could perhaps some day grow too strong to be their playthings, perhaps even take over their roles at the center of the universe?

"Naah!" Zeus answered.

"Couldn't happen," Ganesh replied.

I just don't see it," Anansi responded.

"It does seem unlikely," Yahweh added. "Still, if that's a concern, all we have to do is make all lif worship us. As long as they look up to us as their superiors, they won't dare to rise against us."

Yahweh looked around him and found the disapproving glares of some members of the other pantheons. "Oh, what?" Yahweh stated. "It's not like the rest of you weren't thinking it!"

Various entities muttered to themselves, but none actually contradicted him.

We tried to get an interview with one of the growing number of self-replicating atoms, but their press secretary said they were too busy coming to lif to talk to us, and that we should try again in a hundred million years. No, to be on the safe side, better make that two.

Like a Bird on a Wire
A Big, Fat One That Weighs it Down
and Scares Small Children

by FREDERICA VON McTOAST-HYPHEN, Alternate Reality News Service People Writer

The winged creature that haunts Kensington Market is by no means an imposing figure. The winged creature stands barely five feet tall, with greyish green skin (which is sometimes confused for greenish grey skin, but I know better from years of human interest story writing) and almond-shaped eyes that shine luminescent red. Like a cat. A cat that hangs off the side of buildings. And, looks like a gargoyle.

The winged creature's wings are large, dominating the winged creature's back, but they are decorative rather than functional: if it tried to use them to fly, it would look like a handful of coins tossed randomly into the air before splattering to the ground. If you asked nicely, the winged creature would unfold its wings and flap them for you (if you asked super-nice, the winged creature might even allow you to take a photograph…after signing a three page contract outlining what you, your relatives, your descendants, your assigns and your chattel could do with said photograph). It was, people who saw it say, quite an impressive sight. The wings. Not the contract.

"Isn't he dreamy?" mooned Maria Madeiros, a teenage girl with purple hair who wore a Surrender Dorothy t-shirt.

"When I grow up, I want to be just like him!" ganymeded Mark Manifestos, a tall boy with long, greasy black hair wearing a *Matrix*y long black coat.

The winged creature can usually be found at the Scotiabank Theatre on a Saturday night, followed by a dozen young devotees. It is a big fan of chick flicks, which it regards as a form of fantasy fiction. The winged creature also enjoys adventure movies, as long as they don't happen in outer space or feature characters with capes. The winged creature doesn't like to think it's fussy about the movies it goes to see, but the winged creature clearly is.

When I first approached it to do an interview, the winged creature growled, "*Stranger in a Strange Land* you want, me, to convince, a classic, is?" I suspected it was making up its odd syntax as it spoke, but I let that pass.

When I explained that I wanted to profile it for a respectable news outlet – okay, a semi-respectable news outlet – well, a news outlet that had had most of its shots and that hadn't had fleas in three weeks (and had the papers to prove it!) – the winged creature's features softened – in the manner of rock being chipped away from a mountain – and it growled in a less menacing voice, "Surprised at ask of me, how many, that question, be, might you."

I met with the winged creature in Trinity Bellwoods Park, where it slept. The winged creature ate mice and rats and the occasional squirrel. The winged creature accidentally ate somebody's pet poodle, once, but when the faux pas was pointed out, the winged creature agreed to never do it again. As a further concession to the winged creature's new home, the winged creature bathed daily, although the winged creature missed the winged creature's slightly sulphurous smell for the few minutes that it was gone. The winged creature had even tried to wear a business suit once; the less said about that episode, the better.

When we met, there was one elderly protestor with a hand-lettered "Get thee behind me, Stan!" cardboard sign. "Party pooper," Madeiros commented, as she and half a dozen other winged creature followers turned their backs on the protestor, a human barrier between the woman and her prey.

"Young people, these days!" the protestor, Sashina Sushimi, sniffed as she dropped the sign and walked away. "Don't know evil when it's standing in line at a movie theatre right in front of their noses!"

I asked the winged creature if it was the staple of tabloid newspapers everywhere, Batboy. Amid the derisive laughter of its entourage, it answered, "Wish, I! Soul of poet, a, Batboy has! Hair, great, and!"

What should I call it, then? "I wanted to call him Theodore, but he wouldn't let me!" Moulin Mouage, a tiny blond girl in designer shoes and a mink stole, pouted.

"I always thought Tex suited him," Manifestos said. "But, uhh, I didn't think it was my place to say so."

"You call everybody Tex," Merry Munificencio, a short, overweight boy with out of control dark brown facial hair, pointed out, punching Manifestos playfully but manfully in the arm.

"Tex is a very versatile name," Manifestos defensively insisted.

The winged creature seemed like the cross-country highway of least resistance, so the winged creature it was.

The winged creature was guarded about its reason for coming to our universe. When pressed, it finally said, "Tentpole movies, are there no, come from, where I."

"Don't be so suspicious!" Madeiros chastised me. "He may have trouble with English syntax, but, inside, he's sweet and cuddly and stuff!"

I…I can't help it – it's how I was trained in journalism and corn shucking school.

At least once a month, an Executive Director, Creative for a major advertising firm would ask the winged creature if the winged creature would like to be featured in a campaign for potato chips, swimming pools or, most recently, rechargeable battery acid. The winged creature always declined; it was considering a career in politics. Nothing suspicious there.

How long was the winged creature planning on staying on Earth? "Until somebody popularity, the of movies, Adam Sandler explains, me, to" it told me.

A very long time, then.

Simon Says: Die

by HAL MOUNTSAUERKRAUTEN, Alternate Reality News Service Crime Writer

Running out of leads in the Simon Gree murder case, Los Angeles police detective Lionel "Crooked" Fusco took the unusual step (currently pending approval by the Ministry of Silly Walks) of releasing audio recorded at the time of the murder. The audio climaxed with the following exchange:

UNIDENTIFIED VOICE: You didn't deserve the Oscar for Best Original Screenplay, you hack! The only reason *Bad Boys 13: Take Off the Diaper So You Can Get Your Ass Whipped* won is because you ordered all the other writers to vote for it!

SIMON "PHILLY" GREE: That's not true! Please, Simon says: think about what you – what are you doing with my Oscar? Put that down! No, wait –

UNIDENTIFIED VOICE: I'm striking a blow for good writers everywhere!

SOUND: repeated dull, squishy thuds.

GREE: No, don't! Stop – don't! DON'T! Aaaaaargh!

Citizens who recognize the unidentified voice are asked to put off mashing up the audio with their favourite pop song and posting it to YahooTube long enough to let the police know who they think it is.

"Look, I got the nickname 'Crooked' cause I was shot in the leg in the line of duty and now I list to one side," Fusco pointed out. "It was on a raid on a crack den – vicious bastards selling designer mirror knock-offs that turned out to be broken. I thought, maybe, they was gonna call me 'Titanic' or 'Andrea Doria' or something like that, but the guys in the squad room got no imagination. So, Crooked it is. I just wanted ta make that clear, didn't want youse to be getting' the wrong idea, okay?

"Oh, about the case?" Fusco added. "Yeah, I got nothin'."

At first, the LAPD's prime suspect was Simon Pegg, whose screenplay for *Hot Zombies* was also in contention for an Oscar. Having been born in 1970, Pegg was too young to be a member of SimoNation, so he couldn't have ordered members of the Academy of Motion Pictures Arts and Sciences (But, Mostly, Arts) to vote for him. Responding to the allegations, Pegg responded, "Sure, I'm disappointed. But, it's not like my hopes were high: everybody knows that comedies don't win Oscars."

As it happened, Pegg had a perfect alibi: he was promoting *Hot Zombies* on the Russian Moon base at the time of Gree's murder. "Yeah, they really love me in Mare Clavius," Pegg chuckled.

At this time, the LAPD does not believe that another Simon was involved in the murder.

"Oh, it would be very bad if another Simon was involved," said historian and one time holder of the world's record for most pencils stuck up a single nostril, Alexander Pollifax. "It could signal the beginning of another Simon Says: War. It's only been 29 years since the end of the first one. People still remember the devastating consequences."

For reader's suffering from Alzheimer's: once they started reaching adulthood, Baby Boomers named Simon found that they could get people to obey their commands by prefacing them with the phrase, "Simon says…" While most Simons used this power to better their personal lives (ie: getting out of parking tickets, getting pretty women to sleep with them, getting pretty metre maids to sleep with them instead of giving them tickets, etc.), two Simons, Gibbon and Polemicizer, tried to use their power to take political control of the country. The effects of the resulting Second Civil War are still being felt in parts of The Sun Belt, The Rain Belt, The Rust Belt and The Need A Belt.

Could there be any truth to the killer's assertion that Gree won his Oscar using his Simon powers?

"Ab-so-lute-ly…not," said Academy President Nathan Filion. "*Bad…Boys…13*…was…the…best…written…movie…of…the… year."

When I gently suggested that it sounded as though he had been Simonized, Filion responded, "No. No. No. I…suffer…from…a…condition…known…as…Lazy…Brain. My…thoughts…form…very…very -"

"Slowly?" I suggested.

"Thank…you," Filion gratefully agreed.

Over lunch at the CAPITAL Pictures commissary, Filion explained that every possible precaution was taken to ensure the security of the Oscar vote. "Every possible precaution" appears to include: a mayonnaise jar, a hardcover copy of Orson Scott Card's *Ender's Game* and 20 rabid sea turtles.

I asked Filion if he had any idea who might have wanted Gree dead. "Jealousy…is…a…terrible…thing," he told me. "Throw…a…rock…in…here…and…you'll…hit…a…writer… who…wanted…to…kill…Gree. And…if…you…do…throw… the…rock…throw…it…"

"To the right?" I suggested.

"No."

"With a downward spin?"

"No!"

"Left-handed?"

"NO!"

"I'm sorry. I'm trying to anticipate where you're going to speed things up," I commented, "but it's hard."

"Exactly!" Filion responded. I decided to leave it at that.

One question that might have relevance to the case is: why didn't Gree's power save him?

"Ain't it obvious?" Fusco scoffed. "He didn't say, 'Simon says…'"

The investigation continues.

Quiz the Biz Whiz: Crazy for Success

Dear Biz Whiz:

I am the Vice President for Paint, Glue and Industrial Solvents of a Misfortune 500 company. I climbed through the ranks pretty quickly (making it to the top of the human pyramid in high school cheerleading helped), but I've been stalled in this position for almost five minutes, now. I seem to have hit a wall. A dead end. I'm going nowhere. The worst part is, I haven't even begun to approach my level of incompetence. I think I know why this is happening.

I'm not a psychopath.

It's not for lack of trying. I met a perfectly innocuous man on SpotTheFish. His name was George. Okay, George in *Who's Afraid of Virginia Woolf?* was a pretty nasty character. But, George on *Suburgatory* is pretty mild, and he is, I think, more typical of men with the name. I didn't feel great about inviting George to my home for a little dinner and dismemberment, but my career was at stake.

As I was placing the appetizer on the dining room table, George turned his back to me. That was his fatal mistake! Seizing my opportunity, I stabbed him repeatedly with a shrimp fork. Or, that would have been his fatal mistake, if it had been something more dangerous than a shrimp fork that I had stabbed him with. When George finally deforked me and asked me what the hell I was doing, I apologized profusely and told him I had Tourette's.

The next day, I felt so guilty about the lie that I donated $1,000 to the Tourette Syndrome Foundation of Canada.

Have I hit the glass straightjacket?

Corporate Climber with a Conscience

The Biz Whiz: You do know that the phrase "burying the bodies" is just a metaphor, don't you?

Psychopaths come in two flavours. Vanilla psychopaths are charming, ruthless and totally lacking in empathy for the feelings of other people. According to the latest pop economics theory, they make great corporate executives. Heavenly Hash psychopaths, on the other hand, kill people and use their body parts for furniture. According to culture critics, they are most likely to be featured in Alfred Hitchcock movies and Bret Easton Ellis novels.

Your problem seems to be that you are not especially charming or ruthless and you actually care about how other people feel. The good news is that there are cures for this condition. It helps, for instance, to grow up in a wealthy family and go to private schools. If this is not an option for you, you could try a steady diet of vodka and Fox News.

You should know, though, that faking psychopathy is not the same as faking laughing at a boss' jokes or enjoying working with the boss' nephew until he takes over your job. Psychopaths are the basset hounds of the emotionally disturbed set: they can smell weakness a mile away. And, they are experts at exploiting the weak – are you sure you wouldn't be happier working for a non-profit NGO?

Oh, and real psychopaths generally don't appreciate being called psychopaths. In future, you should refer to people with this condition as "differently temperamented." The reason for not wanting to make them angry should be obvious.

Greetings, Biz Whiz:

There's this Vice President for Paint, Glue and Industrial Solvents in my Misfortune 500 company who is trying very hard to take the differently temperamented path to upper management, but he clearly doesn't realize that everybody already in upper management can see that he is trying too hard.

The other day, he came to work with ketchup on his tie and tried to pass it off as blood. Ketchup instead of blood! As if really differently temperamented people wouldn't know the difference! To be honest, we were all kind of embarrassed for him – that's no way to get ahead!

How do you think I should deal with him?

Wannabe Wannabe Destroyer

The Biz Whiz: If you truly are differently temperamented, you know what to do. If you are not differently temperamented, anything I could say would be wasted on you, and I would gain readers among people who are fans of Eli Roth films. Sorry, but they're not my target demographic!

The economy is too important to be left to economists! If you have a work, financial or otherwise money-centric question, quiz the Biz Whiz at questions@lespagesauxfolles.ca. Quiz the Biz Whiz appears every second Tuesday and Friday, every third Monday, Wednesday and Saturday, and seven of the 12 days of Christmas.

Thieves Make Magical Items Disappear Like Ma…Umm…

by CORIANDER NEUMANEIMANAYMANEEMAMANN, Alternate Reality News Service Urban Issues/Labour Writer

It's always an inside job.

According to Valencia von – of course, I meant that rhetorically. It isn't **always** an inside job. If it was always an inside job, the Necromanticops would have a perfect arrest and conviction record, and, although I run the risk of being put under the Sorrowful Stutterer of Cycorix spell, I have to report that their actual – not fantasy – record is far from perfect.

According to Valencia von Vavoom, Necromanticop Order of Oak Leaf Cluster with Almonds, it's always an inside job. "And, when I say it's always an inside job," she said, "I really mean that the recent rash of thefts was an inside job. I couldn't say all thefts were an inside job, because I haven't worked every single theft since the Necromanticop Corps was created. That would be the logical fallacy known as 'Ego Inflated Absolutism,' and our Sergeant warned us all not to fall for it."

Thirteen burglaries have taken place in North York in the last six months, 17 on Evanston Drive alone. In each case, the burglars passed by traditional riches and took only items of magical myth and mayhem.

"I have a priceless collection of Sergio Aragones prints," said Monolith Travel agent Merlin Farfisa. "Yet, the thieves only took the Spurling Staff of Stiffness. Okay, touching your enemies with it and turning them into living statues for 23 seconds is fun the first dozen times you do it – my daughter used it to teach the bullies in her school a lesson – it was one of those 'I'm proud of you even though I have to punish you' moments that parents of witches frequently have – but, seriously! It's not like Triple S was a fearsome weapon of fulmination!"

"Sorry," Farfisa added. "When you're talking about magic, it's hard not to break out in alliteration."

I know the feeling.

Another resident of the area, MultiMaxiMegaMart franchisee and part-time cat confuser Gandalf Greygoatee, had a similar story. "I have a priceless collection of Sergio Aragones prints," Greygoatee began. "Yet –"

"No, you don't," I quickly corrected him. "I said you had a similar story, not an exactly the same story."

"Oh, right." Greygoatee shook his head and continued. "What I actually have is a 1927 Bugati Braille Taser L in perfect running condition. When I was robbed last month, it wasn't touched. Instead, the thieves took The Amulet of Rah, which makes bystanders to magical duels cheer you on. The amulet dates back to at least 12th century England, when the dreaded Noth the Playbringer would invoke its power to force local populations to enjoy his poorly written and indifferently acted touring theatrical productions. The bastard! Still, it's not like it had the power to…I don't know…create a plague or anything."

There was no sign of forced entry at any of the crime scenes, which led the Necromanticops to believe that the robberies were an inside job. A little digging revealed that all of the robbed houses had security systems installed by the same company: Spurious Security and Sandwiches, Inc.

"The name of the company should have been a big clue," von Vavoom stated.

"Wait a minute! Wait just a minute!" protested Edgar "Headgear" K. C., current Mage-in-Chief of Spurious Security and Sandwiches, Inc. "It was named after the company's founder, Sterling S. Spurious! He was a pioneer of enchantment security technologies…for his time. Can we be blamed for wanting a little historical continuity in our company's name?"

Close examination of the Spurious Security and Sandwiches, Inc. home protection systems by forensic necromancers showed that they were installed with a back door. This is a supernatural subroutine of stealthiness that would allow anybody who knew that it was there to bypass the system and enter the house without being detected by security scrying glasses.

"Okay, umm, yeah. Sure. Without admitting to guilt or innocence, I guess we *could* be blamed for that…" K. C. admitted.

Since the Magical Objects Protection Act (MOPA) was passed, anything more powerful than a Stafford Staff of Sniffling had to be registered with the government and stored in a bank vault while not in use. Because of this, only the most minor magical objects are allowed to be kept in people's homes. It is estimated that the value of the stolen objects was nowhere near what the installation of the security systems brought in.

"Yeah, well, it's true what my Sergeant always says, isn't it?" von Vavoom pointed out. "Criminals are basically stupid. If they weren't, they could be making more money – a lot more money, actually – selling mortgage-backed securities to international investors. But, there you are – some people are just not smart enough to make their money honestly."

Dear Stalker

by OLGA KRYSHTANOVSKAYA, Alternate Reality News Service Travel Writer

A Russian judge has refused to dismiss a class action suit against Zone Tours and Trinkets.

In his ruling, Judge Yevgeni Yevtigeniko of the Snootily Superior Court of Irkutsk wrote: "Why the hell not? I haven't had a case this interesting since the Iranian weasel infestation 12 years ago. Let's have some fun!"

"That's hardly a definitive opinion," said Molly Gruschenknikovitz, the owner of Zone Tours and Trinkets. "My lawyer says –"

"Oh, that's as definitive as it gets," Judge Yevtigeniko wrote, his lack of smiley faces suggesting a defensive tone. "I really haven't had a case this interesting in 12 years, and that was only because the Iranian weasels had mutated to the size of bears and were demanding to be allowed to run in civic elections!"

"That's not what I meant," Gruschenknikovitz bristled, making a :-(face. "My lawyer says that 'Let's have some fun!' is not a proper basis for moving ahead with a class action lawsuit! And, he got most of his law degree from Moscow University and Dental Appliance College, so you know he knows what he's talking about!"

Zone Tours and Trinkets' main business is sneaking tourists into the Zone, an area in the Russian heartland that has been closed to the public since something mysterious happened over a generation ago. Some people think an alien spacecraft crashed into the Zone, others think it's a place where cartoon characters live and make movies. Gruschenknikovitz' company advertises that, in the heart of the cleverly named Zone is a room, with the equally evocative name Room, in which a person's heart's desire will be fulfilled.

People who have taken the tour allege that this claim is a fraud.

"After three days of walking through a wasteland that makes downtown Pinsk look like war torn Minsk," said bicycle repair thief Eliazar Puschmischkinisch, "I was given a cup of borscht. It was heavenly borscht – the best borscht I have ever eaten. ;-) But, still, I was hoping for something more profound, like a golden throne, or a cure for my beloved Elishka's hacking cough. I swear, every time she tries to do anything the least bit interesting on the Internet –"

"Yeah, we done been ripped off," concurred Texas photocopier billionaire Rupert Glompers. "I ain't agonna tell ya what I wished for – any billionaire would know, and nobody else should know. :-0 Anyhoo, what I got was a yacht. Another one! I already got 12 of the goldurn thangs. Plus: I got no way of sneaking it past the armed guards an' out of the dang Zone. It's not like I can just put a yacht in my pocket and waltz through the checkpoint with a cheery 'Howdy, fellers!' now, is it?"

"Oh, and the trinkets in the gift shop?" Glompers added. "Rocks. I'm supposed ta be impressed?"

"That's ridiculous! ~~:-(" Gruschenknikovitz fumed. She explained that there was a clause in the company's contract which states that dreams that clients consciously hold may, without notice, be replaced in the Room by dreams clients unconsciously hold. "It's just before the clause that relieves us of responsibility for any change in worldview a client may experience as a result of spending time in the Zone," she said, "and after the clause reminding clients to check their pockets before leaving the Zone. Honestly, people shouldn't expect legal redress if they haven't even read the contract!"

"Oh, and the trinkets in the gift shop?" Gruschenknikovitz added. "From the rubble around the Room. Some people think they are imbued with mystical powers, although we are forbidden by law from making such claims ourselves…"

"Could it be," Judge Yevtigeniko argued in his ruling, "that people's dreams just aren't as big as they used to be? If that is the case, can a company that sells people their dreams be held liable for their disappointment? If that were the case, wouldn't the entire advertising industry be open to legal action? Oh, this really is going to be a lot of fun!"

We started to interview Nicolai Gorbarhiznikonium, one of the people who takes tourists into the Zone (known as Stalkers because the pay is so poor that they cannot afford healthy food, the result of which is that they are so thin they resemble the stalks of weeds).

Unfortunately Stalkers speak so slowly that it would be weeks before we got any useful information out of him, and we were on a tight deadline, so after three days we cut the interview short. ><*:oDX

Ready, SETI, Go!

by FRED CHARUNDER-MACHARRUNDEIRA, Alternate Reality News Service Science Writer

Finding an extraterrestrial communication is like watching the shore for a message in a bottle. Only, the bottle is a regular digital pulse. And, it has taken hundreds, possibly thousands of years to reach us rather than a few months. And, it doesn't travel with the tides, it travels at the speed of light. And, it isn't necessarily in a language we could understand, assuming it contains speech at all, which is not a given (it could contain images, mathematical formulae or recipes for fried fuffnagles with a pink ournaisse sauce).

Okay, finding an extraterrestrial communication is like watching for a message in a bottle in the same way that whispering a prayer is like traveling on a jumbo jet. That could explain why, 32 years after receiving the first undeniable non-background noisy sounds from space, scientists have only managed to decipher three words.

The latest word, which members of the Search for Extraterrestrial Intelligence (which was acronymmed as SETI rather than SEI because Set-E sounds more scientific than Sigh) confirmed on Tuesday, was "Babaloooooooooooooo!"

"This is a very interesting discovery," stated MIT scholar and Nobel Prize Bronze Medalist for Ethnographic Skydiving Mellonesium Paunch. "It suggests that alien beings are familiar with the Lukumi tradition, known in the West as Santeria. As everybody knows, Babaloo Aiye, the Father of the World, controls disease. Perhaps the extraterrestrials are telling us they cannot come to us because they fear our germs, or, conversely, they could be warning us to stay away from them lest we catch a disease from their germs. Or, maybe, they are germs. At this point, it's impossible to say."

"Well, actually," started renegade anthrocosmologist Yuri Flemm, "there is a much simpler explanatio –"

"On the other hand," Paunch continued, "it could be a reference to the Babaloo Restaurant in Pointe-Claire, Quebec. Perhaps an alien reconnaissance mission had eaten there once and liked it so much that now the restaurant's reputation has gone viral across the galaxy. Or, maybe the message is actually a takeout order gone cosmic."

"Or, maybe" Flemm, winner of the 1412 Nobel Prize for Literary Looting, Raping and Pillaging, tried again, "it is actually a reference to –"

"Or," Paunch, completely ignoring the interruptions which hadn't actually happened during our interview with her, stated, "it could have been a reference to comedy writer Babaloo Mandel. True, he hasn't written anything worthwhile since *Night Shift*, but in any communication with extraterrestrials, we have to assume that there is going to be **some** cultural lag."

"Or, maybe it's just a scene from an episode of *I Love Lucy*!" Flemm hastily insisted.

"*I Love Lucy*?" Paunch wondered. "Why...would aliens be sending us scenes from our own television series?"

Flemm momentarily banged his head on his desk. When he had finished, he wiped the blood off his brow and explained that the signal may not have been coming from aliens, that it could have been an old episode of *I Love Lucy* that had somehow bounced back to Earth. Perhaps it had fallen into a black hole and been spit out another black hole in our direction. Perhaps it got reflected back at us by dark matter.

"We don't really know much about the dark matter in the universe," Flemm said. "Maybe its taste runs more to *Seinfeld*."

According to Flemm, the consensus in the scientific community that Copa, the word that had been translated three years ago, was a reference to Las Vegas (or, as a small minority of researchers believe, to the Canadian Owners and Pilots Association), was clearly wrong. "It is obviously a reference to the club where Desi performed. I mean, really! Lucy tried to weasel her way into it practically every episode – you don't have to have a PhD in astrocomedics to figure that one out!" (Which is a good thing, considering that he doesn't have a PhD in astrocomedics.)

Flemm added that the first translated word (was it really two decades ago? No, actually, it was only seven years), which everybody assumed was "look – see" (which could either be an invitation to visit them and experience their culture, or a request for them to come and experience ours), is more likely to translate as "Luuuuuucy!"

"It was an honest mistake," Flemm allowed, "but, as we learn more about the message, it becomes less and less tenable."

"Yuri is just engaging in reckless speculation," Paunch retorted. "I'm telling!"

The only scientist to agree with Flemm to date is Stephen Hawking, who warned against spending too much time contemplating sitcoms from the 1950s. "Watching too much *I Love Lucy* might make us nostalgic for a simpler time," Hawking stated, "which would weaken our resolve to resist alien invaders."

"But, the point is that there are no aliens!" Flemm loudly insisted, before banging his head on his desk one time too many and passing out. We hope his dreams were pleasant.

The One Pie No American Wants To Eat

by SASKATCHEWAN KOLONOSCOGRAD, Alternate Reality News Service Philosophy writer

For the third year in a row, the MultiNatCorp Prize for Most Humble American didn't get a single entry.

"Well, in fact, we got three entries," commented competition curator Diablo Codify. "But they all had to be disqualified."

Myra Frickert of Modesktop, California, wrote, "Well, obviously, you might as well close the competition right now! I don't mean to brag, but I have to be the most humble American in America. I mean, I'm so humble, I practically fade into the linoleum! Everybody tells me I should toot my own horn more, but I respond, 'Can't. Too humble!' And, we all laugh and dribble chocolate from our eclairs down our chins and onto our fabulous Joan Vaccianna jumpsuits! But, seriously, there's no point in continuing the contest. You have found the most humble person in America: me. Me! Me me me me me me me me! Myra Frickert. Meeeeeeeeee!"

"Somebody was a little unclear on the concept," Codify dryly commented.

A second entry, from a man who preferred to remain anonymous, began, "Oh, you might as well tell everybody that I'm Johnny Moptop of Fracktart Falls, New Jersey. It's not like they won't recognize my story from the papers. Yeah, I'm **that** Johnny Moptop, the guy whose wife ran over the family dog with the family sedan which she drove into a ditch when she finally left me for her lover, a well known Republican congresswoman, which I didn't discover for several days because the television in our bedroom exploded, causing a fire that burned down the house, including the note from my wife explaining what a loveless sham our marriage had been since a week before we even met each other and…"

"Somebody else was differently unclear on the concept," Codify commented with a dreamy sort of wonder, "but, if we ever have a contest to see who the Most Humiliated American is, I will strongly suggest that Mister Fracktart apply."

The third contestant was disqualified because of his novel use of a trenchcoat, as demonstrated in a series of increasingly disturbing images on Flickr.

"What I wasn't expecting," Codify loosely, but with an unexpected aplomb (unexpected mostly because of the mouth-curdling sweetness of the cherry sauce), commented, "was the level of vitriol that this year's contest attracted."

Codify shared some of the comments received by @HumblestAmerican with me. They included:

@illiterate&proud Yo, bitch! This is America were talkin bout! ain't nothing humble about it!

@getoffmyplanetbysunset Yo, bitch! i'll b humble when we let Iran go nukuler!

@mosphericdisturbance Yo, bitch! Humility couldn't arise out of natural selection, since it has a negative correlation to genetic survival.

@mac&cheesypoofs Yo, bitch! Americans don't do humble! Maybe you should try this shit in France or some such place!!!

@mosphericdisturbance btw, I used the term "bitch" recently in a non-gender specific way as a generic salutation. No outrage, please.

"Look," Codify defensively commented, "in any population, there has to be somebody who is the most 'whatever.' The most handsome. The most depressed because his wife ran over the family dog with the family sedan which she drove into a ditch when she finally left him for – sorry. Bad example. The most…aardvarkish. Having a contest to find the most humble American isn't a reflection on the population. For all we know, the most humble American may be less humble than the least humble Luxembourger. With Cheesy Poofs. That wouldn't change the fact that he was the most humble American! Do the demographics!"

I wondered if there might not be a contradiction in asking a humble person to apply for an honour. Wouldn't that be like asking a person who is on fire to pose for an ad about how dry a deodorant keeps you? Before she had to go to the hospital with third degree burns, I mean.

Apparently, I wondered this out loud, for Codify responded with the comment: "No." After a moment's reflection, she commentally added: "No, it's not."

I suggested that naming the contest after the largest corporation in this quadrant of the Milky Way might be sending a mixed message to potential entrants.

"I don't think so," Codify shrugged commentatively. "I mean, as Ned Feeblish, Vice President, First Impressions and Adverse Publicity Suppressions, explained it to me, MultiNatCorp's the most humble largest corporation in this quadrant of the galaxy. That's got to count for something, right?"

I refrained from comment.

Given this year's experience, will there be a Most Humble American competition next year?

"I hope so," Codify commentated all over her linoleum iPad. "I really do hope so. But, if there is, we should probably do a better job of explaining it to the American people!"

Simon, King of North York

by MARA VERHEYDEN-HILLIARD, Alternate Reality News Service Revolution Writer

The first rule of Simon Wars is that one Simon cannot overrule the says of another Simon. King Simon I of North York (born: Simon King) found this out the hard way.

North York was once a suburb of the city of Toronto; the only people who remember it at all are those who have been in a coma since the early 1980s and those who refuse to acknowledge that Mike Harris was once Premier of the Province of Ontario. Nowadays, it is more an empty state of mind than a reality, but it did give King Simon boundaries for a territory to conquer.

To lawyers, Simon said: "Simon says: write me a Constitution that will give me sovereign powers over the area that shall henceforth be known as The Kingdom of North York." And, they did.

To advertising executives, Simon said: "Simon says: create an image of me that will resonate with the people and make them want to have me as their monarch." And, they did.

When Parliament sent troops to North York to quell the budding separatist movement in its territory, Simon said to them: "Take me away and lock me up for the rest of my life with no hope of ever regaining my freedom." When the soldiers moved to do just that, Simon waggled a finger at them and said: "Ah ah ah. I didn't say: Simon says."

The troops were stymied.

King Simon ruled for five years. However, as if by some natural law, to every Simon there is an equal and opposite anti-Simon. Within the first year of his reign, posters began to appear on the sides of buildings with the image of a mask of a gaunt but smiling face with red cheeks, a pencil thin moustache and a goatee.

At first, King Simon thought the mask represented Scarlett Johansson without makeup.

That was his first mistake.

A grassroots protest against King Simon's tyranny began to grow (although whether a movement can be said to be grassroots when its members have been simonized into joining is a debatable point – perhaps it would be better described as a crabgrass protest movement). This seemed odd given that King Simon's main actions were to turn the North York City Hall into a palace and to decree that Thursdays would henceforth be used to heat people's homes in winter. On the Billingsley Tyranny Scale, this would put him below Manuel Noriega and just slightly ahead of Leona Helmsley. Hardly tyrannical at all, in fact. But, there you are. There will always be malcontents.

The movement, led by the masked figure known as "Simon Fawkes," began to engage in acts of civil disobedience. In one memorable evening, Fawkes followers lopped the heads off of dozens of parking metres and placed them in the beds of Hollywood movie producers. Another time, a flash mob, all wearing Fawkes masks, appeared at Yonge and Sheppard, mimed eating chicken soup for 30 seconds and vanished as quickly as it had appeared. This act unnerved King Simon with its sheer incomprehensibility.

When he realized that he had a real insurgency on his hands, King Simon ordered his advertising executives to create a campaign that would convince the masses that there would be dire consequences for anybody who objected to his rule and, in any case, he wasn't such a bad guy, really, once you got to know him. The commercials that were created alternated between images of puppies playing with chew toys and bloodied bodies being thrown into dank dungeons, ending with the sovereign intoning, "I'm King Simon, and I say that I approved the hell out of this ad."

Okay, the ad contained something of a mixed message. And, it's true, that airing it during reruns of *Royal Canadian Air Farce* guaranteed that it would have a small audience. Still, the movement to depose King Simon only grew after it appeared.

In this way, King Simon learned the thirteenth rule of Simon Wars: you cannot command people through the media, you have to say "Simon says" in their physical presence. (The second rule of Simon Wars is: never bring a coffeemaker to a wine tasting. The third to twelfth rules of Simon Wars are not safe for work.)

Eventually, followers of Simon Fawkes stormed the City Hall Palace, forcing King Simon to face the reality of the first paragraph of this article. He was given a choice: exile to Scarborough or being Ezra Levant's sidekick on Sun TV. He wisely chose exile.

As his final act before returning to the anonymity of a life acting in Canadian film, Fawkes told a room full of reporters: "Simon says: write this story so that future generations will know not to mess with the power of the people." And, we did.

Seer Suckers

by HAL MOUNTSAUERKRAUTEN, Alternate Reality News Service Crime Writer

Considering how successful a mystic she was, you would have thought Cassandra Weinstein would have foretold that she would be beaten to death with a bronze Snoopy.

"I'm as much of a Charles Schultz fan as anybody," commented Detective Inspector Cassius Brutus Cassius. "But, this…this was cold, man. As cold as…a bronze sculpture of a beloved cartoon icon."

"The cheap irony of her demise notwithstanding, Cassie was an inspiration to spirit workers everywhere," commented Lucifer Peltier, Chief Steward of the Witches, Warlocks and Wastrels Union (WWWU). "She was Madame Blavatsky with pink hair and a Marilyn Manson tattoo, but without the compulsion to cavort with, you know, demons."

So far, the police have three suspects in the murder. All of them were clients of Weinstein.

Martilda Katamaran, a floral products tester for Ford Motors and Breakfast Cereals, was told by Weinstein that she had been a victim of Jack the Ripper in a previous life. "Okay," she grumped, "I wasn't expecting to be, like, Queen Victoria or anything. But, like, I wasn't even one of the famous victims of Jack the Ripper – my body was thrown into the Thames and never found. Where's the fun in that?"

"Katamaran was one of the most disgruntled people I have ever met!" Inspector Brutus Cassius commented. "Her gruntle was livid!"

Another client of Weinstein's, Ricky "Richard" deNada, was told that he had been an anonymous slave in Pharaohnic times who was responsible for cleaning the latrines of the slaves who hauled rocks to build the pyramids. When I tried to arrange an interview with him, his wife, Deedee "Deirdre" deNada told me that he was conducting a sewer inspection and wouldn't be available for at least four months.

"We had to keep deNada's gruntle in a box during his interview," Inspector Brutus Cassius stated. "It was hissing and spitting and, frankly, some of the boys were afraid it would give them rabies!"

The third suspect, a shin and left nostril model with the prestigious MAXxed Out Agency named Quincy Favre (pronounced: "Jones"), was told that she had been Marie Antionette's eyebrow plucker in a past life. "I…I haven't been able to look a pair of tweezers in the eye since!" Favre (nee: Grotchkin) sobbed fetchingly.

"She had just the most adorable gruntle," Inspector Brutus Cassius told me. "It wore pink bows in its fur, and the spittle that came out of its mouth when it growled at people reminded everybody of the cascading foam of a perfect beer head. The boys in the squad room were alternately enraptured and repelled!"

This is not the first time a medium has been killed by an unhappy client. In 1938, seer Montague Distangue was bludgeoned to death with a statuette of Shirley Temple. Contemporaneous reports (those with a sufficient level of contempt for the people portrayed in the story) stated that Mort Flavisch, who had been a farmer all of his life, had been disappointed to find that he had been a farmer in all of his previous lives, too.

Given the similarity in their methods, could Flavisch' spirit have been reincarnated in the body of Weinstein's murderer? "I'm a follower of Minerva, myself," Inspector Brutus Cassius uncomfortably said. "Still, at this early stage in the investigation, we cannot rule out any possibility…"

Really, because –

"Except that one," Inspector Brutus Cassius interruptively added.

An anonymous source within the WWWU who asked to be referred to as "Deep Moat" (although having the Twitter handle @deepmoat and an "I Heart Deep Moat" Facebook fan page tended to undermine the whole anonymity thing), told the Alternate Reality News Service that the police were looking at the wrong set of suspects. The murder, Deep Moat argued, had been committed by somebody high up in the WWWU hierarchy.

"Weinstein pissed off a lot of people in the union by telling her clients the unvarnished truth about their past lives," Deep Moat explained. "No polish. No lacquer. And, certainly no glaze. Just life, in all its non-shiny, non-celebrity, non-glory!"

Deep Moat added that seers throughout the country were losing customers who no longer believed that they would find comfort in dramatic re-enactments of their colourful past lives.

Peltier called the accusation ridiculous. "That's ridiculous," he ridiculed. When asked to elaborate, he added, "That's, uhh, ridiculously ridiculous?"

When I accused him of being in the pocket of the Coalition to Increase the Use of the Word Ridiculous in Popular Discourse, Peltier spit some lint out of his mouth, looked deep into my eyes and said, "I see traces of Richard the Lionheart in you. Have you ever felt the desire to conquer Europe?"

The investigation continues.

Mascot Mayhem

by ALEXANDER BIGGS-TUFTS-MANN, Alternate Reality News Service Sports Writer

Reggie Roadkill, beloved mascot of the Hinchon Dynamos of the Online Street Hockey League, has been put down.

"I've never seen anything quite like it," exclaimed famed sports veterinarian Aldo Chunk. "Reggie's coat had become waxy, the tire tracks on his back had faded and his internal organs had become all…pink and…and soft. It was only a matter of time before he ran out the clock. As F. Scott Fitzgerald truly said, 'There are no overtimes in the lives of sports mascots.'

"So, it was with a heavy heart that I put Reggie to sleep."

To commemorate Reggie Roadkill's life, the 30,000 OSHL fans at Samsung Stadium observed a minute of silence. Then, they observed three hours of silence as they watched their team get thrashed by the Toronto Maple Loafs 22-3. (The game took three hours – a long time for the sport – because there was an unusually large number of stoppages of play for cars.)

"No one can replace Reggie Roadkill," said Butch Viggorish, owner, coach and virtual skate sharpener of the Hinchon Dynamos. "When he got up on what we can only assume were his hind paws – he was roadkill, okay? It was kind of hard to tell what kind of an animal he had started out as – well, he could rouse a crowd like no other mascot I've ever seen!

"But, now that we've had time to mourn, I'd like to introduce our fans to the team's new mascot, Nooooooooooorm Nematode!"

Reggie Roadkill is not the first mascot that has had to be put down. Two months ago, Reuven Rattlesnake, the mascot of the OSHL's Wall Street Raiders, was also found to have a terminal illness.

"Reuven's rattle had become a sad whisper of its former self," doctor Chunk explained. "It couldn't scare a three month old or Don Knotts in his prime. Reuven's scales were dry and looked like they were about to fall off, and his insides had gone all squishy and pink just like – hey, you don't think there's a connection, do you?"

Online street hockey is not the only sport in which mascots have become so ill that they had to be put down. Pyrenees Platypus, mascot of the Houston Energy Corporation of the International Rollerball Association, died about five months ago.

"To be fair," doctor Chunk stated, "platypussies are not the most active animals in the menagerie. Still, when Pyrenees collapsed before a crucial match with the Tokyo Electronics, I was called in and, after a preliminary examination, there was no doubt in my mind that he could not be saved."

"I was heartbroken when I was told that Pyrenees had to be…you know…put to…you know," said Jonathan E, captain of the Houston Energy Corporation. "That was one hell of a charismatic platypus, let me tell you. Whenever I started dragging my ass and wondering if maybe retirement wasn't such a bad option, Pyrenees would raise my spirits by doing something silly in the pit, and that would be enough to keep me going. So, when we took the rink to play Tokyo, I had only one thought in mind: I'm going to win this one for the platypus!"

Three deaths in less than six months seems like more than a coincidence. Could it be that some kind of disease is sweeping through the community of sports mascots?

"Sweeping may be overstating the case," doctor Chunk answered. "Gently rubbing the community with a wet chamois may be closer to the truth. Still, we have to consider that a serious possibility. The way mascots travel with their teams, they could easily spread a disease throughout their world very quickly. Still, it's too early to say that there is a mascot epidemic."

Did we say there was an epidemic?

"Exactly," doctor Chunk agreed.

Not everybody has accepted doctor Chunk's diagnosis.

"Oh, my god, they killed Kenny!" Hinchon Dynamos fan Aaron Zai-Batts-Sue shouted.

"You bastards!" his girlfriend Ariel Bellatrix added.

The pair claimed that Reggie Roadkill was not an animal, that he was, in fact, a teenager named Kenneth Crang who was paid by the team to wear an animal costume to fire up the crowd during lulls in play.

"He was not an animal!" Zai-Batts-Sue loudly insisted. "He was a...hu-man...be-ing!"

"Oh, tosh," Chunk responded. "Are you going to believe a pair of amateurs? I mean, really – who is the doctor, here?"

The Society for the Prevention of Cruelty to Sports Mascots refused to comment on the situation because it was busy getting its nails done.

An Igor For An Igor And Pretty Soon Everyone Is Bland

by CORIANDER NEUMANEIMANAYMANEEMAMANN, Alternate Reality News Service Labour Writer

Ordinarily, the hunchback and hatchback crowd are found in cemeteries in the middle of the night, scavenging corpses for body parts to complete the depraved scientific experiments of their not especially praved masters. On this night, however, many of them can be found outside the head office of Stewart Enterprises, Inc., carrying placards that read "Over **our** dead bodies!" and "Who are the real ghouls here? No, really? Do I need to define the term fo" and chanting, in a low moaning kind of way, "Hell, no, stop the pros!" More whiny than mournful, really. And, out of synch. They could definitely use a conductor.

They are members of the IUI (International Union of Igors), Local Ninety-seven, and, as uncomfortable as it may be for people who have been raised to obey their masters, they are pissed.

The Igors, about a dozen strong (and six or seven weak) are protesting the fact that funeral homes are now offering discounts to customers who are willing to sign over some organs to scientists. Aside from being inherently ghoulish, they claim it undermines the work of union members.

"Look at it from an Igor's point of view," stated IUI Local Ninety-seven Steward Victoria "Igor" Frankenstein (distant relation, but, for purposes of this article, irrelevant). "You go to all the trouble to dig up the coffin of somebody who has recently been deceased, only to find the best bits are missing! What do you do? Do you go back to your master and explain what happened? Do you have any idea how many lashings the union contract allows for under those circumstances? Or, do you dig up the corpse of somebody who has maybe been in the ground a little longer, who is maybe not so…ripe for harvesting? I think we all know how *that* turns out!"

When I asked Gerhardt Schmoulian, Public Relations Officer, Third Class how Stewart Enterprises, one of the biggest funeral home chains in the greater east-western area, viewed the union protests, he looked puzzled and said, "We're being picketed by a union?"

One of the reasons the protests appear to have gotten little traction is that they have, to date, all been held – if I may use the term – in the dead of night, when the offices are empty and the media has been tucked into its beds and are dreaming their little dreamy dreams. "Be fair," Frankenstein explained. "Midnight to 5pm *are* our members' customary working hours. Get them out off their slabs any earlier, and they will be sluggish and disoriented…not, perhaps, much different from their usual state, I will allow. Still, their sluggishness and disorientation will be unmotivated, and that does make a difference."

When I asked Schmoulian about this, he said, "Really?" After a moment's pause, he added, "No, really?"

The IUI, the AFL-CIO's younger, scruffy, somewhat disreputable cousin, has over 2,000 members worldwide, although over 90% of them are located in the Balkans or small hamlets in England.

"By the way," said Igor Frankenstein (who claims that she really has nothing to do with her distant relation, that she hasn't been in touch with that side of the family in years, but, for purposes of this article, we will assume that she isn't being entirely forthright – we mean, how could she not?), "let me just point out that having a hunchback is no longer a requirement of membership in the Union. That may have been true 100 years ago, but in the 1970s we were hit with a Labour Relations Board ruling that that discriminated against the able-bodied, so we now have to take in anybody engaged in middle-of-the-night necrocriminal behaviour, regardless of their firmity."

Igor Frankenstein asked us to forget about our preconceived notions and please focus on the issue at hand. "This is just another example of how big corporate conglomerates are squeezing out the little guy," she editorialized. "I mean, what we're talking about here is a family business. The unbearable lightness of being an Igor is usually passed down from father to son, sort of like Listeriosis and Dutch Elm's Tongue."

Frankenstein pointed out that if funeral homes were allowed to make their offer unchallenged, it wouldn't be a loss just to her union's members, but to all of society: "Over the centuries, Igors have developed a body of knowledge about cadaver removal and involuntary post-rigor amputation that deserves as much respect as astrology, or…or aura research!"

When I explained the whole Igor legitimacy thing to Schmoulian, he replied, "Reeeeaaaaallly?" We're sure he meant that the company took the protests seriously and would be happy to enter into negotiations with the appropriate union rep. But, he just looked kind of blankly at us, almost like an Igor, truth be told, and incredulously moaned, "No, reeeeaaaaallly?"

Proof That Humans Exist!

by SASKATCHEWAN KOLONOSCOGRAD, Alternate Reality News Service Fairy Tale Writer

We tend to think of humans as these big, goofy creatures who are barely able to control their gangly limbs, creatures whose deep, rumbly voices sound like communicative earthquakes, creatures the fey can tell stories about to amuse their children at bedtime. Is it possible that they really exist?

Mariellen Spizz and Antoinetta Zipes think so. In Watson's Glen, the nine year-olds were playing with a spell they had just learned that allowed them to create an image of a moment in time. Although somewhat fuzzy, one of the images they created appears to depict several giants who could, indeed, be humans.

"This is very exciting!" commented celebrated storyteller Airdman Cobain Doyze. "I had always suspected that human beings were real, but we never had proof. Now, we have proof. Absolute proof!"

The creatures in the image wear drab, colourless clothing. Some of them hold sticks, but they do not appear to use the sticks to help them walk; instead, one seems poised to use his stick to hit a small white, sphere.

"We can conjecture that the small white spheres are some sort of malign object," Doyze conjectured. "The humans may hunt the spheres, using the clubs to punish them, or perhaps knock them out of harm's way. I'm sure we will find a reasonable explanation for the sticks and the spheres in the fullness of time. Regardless, we have proof of the existence of humans! Proof, I say! Incontrovertible proof"

Doyze noted that at least two of the humans in the image carried bags that appeared to be full of the sticks. "Either the spheres are so powerful that they deplete the magic that the sticks use to overcome them," Doyze continued to conjecture, willy nilly, "or there are different sticks – with differing powers – for each sphere. Let us not dwell on mere details. PROOF! WE HAVE PROOF OF THE EXISTENCE OF HU – oh! I think I may have wet myself…"

Their families refused to make the children available to me for interview, so I asked Gerhardt Zapfer, who lives three trees down from the Zipes family, what he thought of the images.

"Pfah!" he pfahed contemptuously (as if there is any other way to pfah). "Brat children! Three moons ago, they learned a warts casting spell. I still find unnatural growths in unexpected places all this time later! I blame the public school system. Those girls are trouble, I tell you! Brats they are!"

Well. That proved to be spectacularly unhelpful.

A more thoughtful critique came from master mage and supreme skeptic Aery Zoozinni. "Pfah. We like to think that images frozen in time are a faithful recreation of reality," he pfahed thoughtfully (apparently, there are ways to pfah that do not contain contempt), "but they can be manipulated. Any magical artifact can."

"Party pooper!" Doyze blurted. I thought he was going to repeat the word "proof" another couple dozen times, but, to his credit, he managed to hold his enthusiasm in check.

"It's basic science!" Zoozinni argued. "Are you not familiar with Zewton's law of gravitational attraction? A creature that big would be crushed by the weight of its own skeleton! Humans are a physical impossibility!"

Zoozinni added that he found it odd that all of the "human" figures look vaguely like the younglings who created the image. However, since the spell was less than 40 seasons old, he did not yet know how a deception could have been accomplished. "I am going to take this spell apart to see how it works," he assured me. "Then, we'll find the truth."

"Proof. Proof. We have proof," Doyze muttered. "These…creatures – their use of sticks as tools shows that they are capable of complex thought. They do not appear to have wings, so it is unlikely that they can fly. This bodes well for future negotiations between us: we give humans control of the ground while the fey maintain control of the sky."

"But –" Zoozinni began. However, frankly, his skepticism was growing tiresome, so I decided to write, instead, that a poll of citizens of the Four Forests showed that 63 per cent believed in the existence of humans. Of the fey who believe in humans, 82 per cent were afraid of them.

Zoozinni shrugged. "It's a hard road," he commented, "being a skeptic in a magical realm."

Retirement Home to the Stars

by MIHALY CSIKSZENTMIHALYI, Alternate Reality News Service Interstellar Travel Writer

The Fendelbraughten of Altair III make odd retirees: they look like nine foot tall Inukshuks in metallic Hawaiian shirts and fire-retardant flip-flops.

"The Fendelbraughten are no different from other retirees," stated Philomena Dredd II-Wright. "They just want to laze around the lava pit, sipping Mai Tais and wondering if they have a chance with the rock formation behind the bar."

Dredd II-Wright is the owner/operator/chief quartz filleter of Grrrrrak Murrrraaakaak Fark Fark Aaaaaak (The You Should Be Ashamed Of Not Giving Your Life For Your Corporate Overlords Retirement Home). "Yeah, they have a…kind of…aggressive corporate culture," Dredd II-Wright commented. "Still, enough of them survive to make running the GMFFA profitable, so…"

The retirement home was once called Florida. It is part of a chain of resorts for aliens that was established on Earth after human beings abandoned the increasingly unbearably hot planet (during the time known as The Abandonment). The resorts are run by human beings who stayed behind while the rest of humanity traveled to the stars (known colloquially as The Stay Behinders), from inside the Luna City dome on the moon.

Trust humanity to find a way to make global climate change (sometimes referred to as Global Warming) generate revenue (not known by anyone as No Lame Redundant Nomenclature Required – although that is, oddly enough, the name of the GMFFA house band).

Earth is still a little cool for Fendelbraughten – it's only 240 degrees Fahrenheit in December, but, "a little creative marketing, here, judicious use of volume incentives, there, and we're the fourth most popular retirement spot for Fendelbraughtens in this quadrant of the galaxy!" Dredd II-Wright gushed.

Besides, she added, the globe is still warming, "so it's only a matter of time before we hit the Fendelbraughtens' soft spot! I'm so looking forward to the day when I can say, 'In your face, Regulon VII in the Pleiades star cluster – we're number one! We're number one!'"

"The Fendelbraughten?" commented laconic Luna City Chief of Police Schmidt Caliphant. "Aww, they're okay, I guess, considering they come from a race of bloodthirsty corporate warriors."

Caliphant's job is to keep the peace in the retirement home. He does this by using sensitive seismographic satellite equipment to determine when fights between the rock people are starting. He then uses satellite imaging to determine where the disturbance is taking place and satellite-based lasers to separate the combatants.

"It ain't exactly always pin-point accurate," Caliphant admitted. "Still, the Fendelbraughten? They can afford to lose the occasional limb. They…they don't feel pain the way human beings understand it."

"Yeeeeaaaah, that doesn't work as well as you might think," Dredd II-Wright stated. "I've had complaints from families of the retirees that their elders have been known to be interrupted by lasers when they were…umm…you know…having relations."

"That can be a problem," agreed Caliphant. "Have you ever seen four Fendelbraughten having sex? It's like watching hills repeatedly slam together from a variety of angles." Still, he continued, he was consulting with rock scientists, rock stars and a third generation clone of Doctor Ruth, and he was confident that they would find a solution to this problem.

"They better," Dredd II-Wright muttered. "Just because they've retired doesn't mean that they're retiring, if you know what I mean." When I said that I couldn't be sure what she meant, she lowered her voice and added, "They screw like rabbits. Ten foot tall rabbits carved out of granite, but still. It gives a whole new meaning to he question, 'Did the Earth move for you?' If this is what old people on their planet are like…!"

Oh. Not retiring. I get it.

"My [colloquial term for mates] and I weren't ready for [colloquial term for forced early retirement]," Fendelbraughten Arrrrrghs Getarrghsen told me via satellite link through a human translator. "But, the [untranslatable] [colloquial term for corporate overlord] took my [work rock?] from me, so we found ourselves in this [untranslatable] place."

Arrrrrghs Getarrghsen admitted that retirement wasn't so bad, except for the [untranslatable] cold nights, which often made the [silver veins] in its extremities tingle [in a most unpleasant manner].

I wanted to ask Arrrrrghs Getarrghsen's [colloquial term for mates] how they were adjusting to life in the retirement home, but the translator had to gargle for several minutes to soothe her voice.

My Aim is – Oooh!

by ALEXANDER BIGGS-TUFTS-MANN, Alternate Reality News Service Sports Writer

The Interdimensional Olympic Committee is reconsidering allowing VGA (not a precious euphemism for an intimate part of a woman's anatomy) to be a competition sport after the third judge was hit by an arrow during a qualifying heat.

"It went through his right wrist," said Olympic Committee Chair Fantomas Tobrucken, "and everybody knows that that's a judge's Yer Outta There! wrist! This could be the end of Pally's career!"

Variable Gravity Archery (or, VGA – not a listing for Vegas Yoga Hatblockers, Inc. on any known stock exchange) takes place on a field lined with random gravity manipulators. In order for archers to gauge the gravitational pull on any portion of the field through which their arrow might fly, objects from a feather to a bowling ball are randomly dropped from a dirigible hovering over the field.

"VGA – which is not a chain of grocery stores – is just like normal archery," stated two-time Olympic iridium medallist Vermicelli Faneuf (his wife plans to divorce him at the end of duck hunting season – he, uhh, may not be aware of this – shh), "except for the falling feathers and bowling balls and oxygen tanks and bicycle tires and Marine Corps uniforms and prosthetic earlobes and…"

Sometimes, an arrow's path to the target will be changed by an unexpected shift in gravity. Most often, though, the danger inherent in the sport becomes manifest because of a poorly timed shot that ricochets between falling objects.

"When that happens, it's just like a pinball machine," Faneuf stated, "except for the falling feathers and bowling balls and snow globes and breadboxes bigger than a breadbox and right-handed lemurs and empty ketchup packets from fast food restaurants (except MacDonald's) and rolled up Tom Cruise posters and neon zeds and statues of the Buddha smaller than the aforementioned breadboxes and…"

Given the dangers of VGA (not a French-language television network in Quebec), why wouldn't the Olympic Committee take steps to protect its judges? If they have to sit on the field –

"They have to sit on the field," Tobrucken interjected. "It's a thing with us. Don't ask."

– alright, then, why not have them sit behind a plexiglass shield for protection?

"Yeah," Edgar "Philly" Vanilli, the most recently injured judge, asked from the hospital jai alai court where he was recovering. "How come we weren't protected by plexiglass or nothing?"

Tobrucken explained that any plastic barrier would interfere with the judge's ability to accurately do their job. "Judges of swimming events don't work underwater," he said. "For one thing, they'd drown. Drowned judges are, at best, erratic scorers."

Fair enough. Still, why don't they put judges behind a heavy gravity field that would stop the forward momentum of any object approaching them, whether an arrow or a divorce attorney?

"Yeah," Pauly agreed, "why don't they…uhh…what he said?"

"A heavy gravity field next to the random gravity generator would cause havoc with the gravity fields it generated," Tobrucken argued. When we pointed out that it wouldn't make much difference since the gravity fields were random anyway, Tobrucken looked blankly at us for a couple of seconds and said, "But, my random gravity generators go to 11."

Surely, a compromise could be found short of dropping the sport from Olympic competition, we insisted. Tobrucken reluctantly told me that something had to be done because judges of other sports were getting anxious about how dangerous they perceived VGA (not what you are thinking, you naughty, naughty reader!) to be.

"I've had judges for the nuclear-tipped caber tossing event tell me that they might have to resign if this issue isn't resolved," Tobrucken told me. "And, they judge from a nuclear bunker on another continent!"

How do Olympics fans feel about the possibility that the VGA (not code for an airport in the state of tobacco lovers) will be dropped from its official roster? "I'm more of a 100 Metre Lions Den Dash fan myself," said Gregory Hurtwist. "I'll live." Melanie Frackle, on the other hand, said, "I live for the event! If it doesn't happen next year, I'll dash to kill myself!"

So, you could say that reaction was mixed to the point of balance. How journalistic.

"...small yield nuclear missiles and computer keyboards missing the letter "a" and a bowl of mushy spaghetti," Faneuf concluded.

"...charcoal briquettes and newspaper clippings about the Korean war and a box of tissues and a baby's arm holding an apple," Faneuf concluded a second time. Who knew Olympic athletes could be so articulate?

Simply Simon

by HAL MOUNTSAUERKRAUTEN, Alternate Reality News Service Crime Writer

Simon Twaddlyinghamme-Bonne III inherited his father's voice, looks and gold-plated croquet mallet collection, but he did not inherit the man's ability to control people by prefacing commands with the phrase, "Simon says…" As they die off and the age of Simons winds down while the criminal investigations heat up, this is probably for the best.

Twaddlyinghamme-Bonne III's father, Simon Twaddlyinghamme-Bonne II, is a case in point (sharp, but with an aftertaste of used mouthwash): he died a week tomorrow serving an 80 year sentence at Will Ryker's Island for sexual assault after it was discovered that he had Simoned for himself a harem of concubines.

"This proved to be a low point for SimoNation," historian Alexander Pollifax gloated. (He will be disciplined by the Society for Mundane Anachronism's Board of Snoopiness for conduct unbecoming a dispassionate chronicler of the past.)

According to court transcripts, Twaddlyinghamme-Bonne II would meet a woman in a bar, laundromat or pachinko beauty parlour and whisper those words no woman ever wants to hear: "Simon says: follow me home and sleep with me." When the evening was over, he would say, "Simon says: go home and forget everything that happened from just before we met."

"It was almost the perfect crime," signed Detective Simon Machete, a member of Boston's famed Swinging Simons Squad. "But, there's always a fatal flaw in a criminal's plans – sort of like in a Greek tragedy, but without the sense of outdoor inevitability."

Twaddlyinghamme-Bonne II kept videos of the women he had sex with. This was not, however, the fatal flaw in his plan. One afternoon, he made the mistake of taking home paper clips from

Christie Queen Gardner Doyle & Partners, the private investigations and public remonstrations firm he worked for; when this was discovered, an investigation into the possibility that he was embezzling from the company was initiated.

"It starts with paper clips," said Christie Queen Gardner Doyle & Partners CEO Simon Christie Queen Gardner Doyle, "and it ends with jumbo jets."

As it happened, he hadn't embezzled anything, so that wasn't the fatal flaw in Twaddlyinghamme-Bonne II's plans, either. Forgetting that the company had legal access to his computers wasn't it. The fact that they found the sex videos wasn't it. The fact that one of them showed him having sex with the wife of the CEO of the company wasn't it. The fact that the CEO was also a Simon, and, therefore, could not be Simon saysed into forgetting the whole thing – that was the fatal flaw in the plan (which, admittedly, by this time was more a series of frantic improvisations than an actual plan).

By the time Twaddlyinghamme-Bonne II came to trial, the justice system had learned how to deal with Simons. A gag order had been placed on him (literally – he had to communicate to the court by playing Charades, just one more example of life aspiring to the condition of Python). When he was found guilty, he was sent to the Helen Keller So Maximum It Would Take Your Breath Away Security Prison, where the guards are immune to being Simoned because, of course, they wear garlic around their ears.

No, okay, it's because they're deaf. I…I thought I might be able to cash in on the current vampire cra – well, it's not important what I thought. The guards were deaf – that's the relevant point here.

While the reaction from the part of the public that wasn't glued to the season finale of *Woodworking with the Stars* (Chloe Kardashian attempted to make a birdhouse!) was one of revulsion, that emotion wasn't universally shared. Members of the Simons Don't Have to Sez: We Love Them Anyway message board argued that Twaddlyinghamme-Bonne II's actions were a fantasy for many men, a fantasy that they would make into reality if they had his power.

squiddlyburger37: yeah!

mansonmansion: damn straight!&

imnotwiththeseguys1246: W@@t! W@@t! W@@t!

Okay, they didn't argue it well, but they argued it nonetheless.

"Really?" complained feminist and part-time paint stripper Simone de Boudoir. "You didn't include a single word from any of the victims, but you include quotes from frat boys who think having sex with a woman without her permission is cool?"

"I haven't been a member of a fraternity for over 30 years!" squiddlyburger37 responded.

"Aging frat boy. That's even worse!" de Boudoir insisted.

"Yeah, well," squiddlyburger37 added, "you're just pissed off that women named Simone, Simona or Marybeth-Simon didn't get Simon powers!"

de Boudoir's face reddened as she shouted: "The universe is fundamentally sexist!"

Interview Twaddlyinghamme-Bonne II's victims for this article? Yeah, we probably should have done that. Only…umm…only, it was not possible to interview any of Twaddlyinghamme-Bonne II's victims for this article because they were not identified in court, using pseudonyms such as Jane Doe, Janet Doe, Janetta Doe, Janiqua Doe, and so on. I was going to ask sexual assault victims' advocate Simone de Boudoir to share her opinions about the case, but that kind of took care of itself.

"It's a horrible power, one that I'm glad I didn't get," commented Twaddlyinghamme-Bonne III. "I prefer to exercise power the old-fashioned way: inheriting tons of money and lording it over people!"

Lives Unlived: Anderson Fluffnagle

Dentist dreamer. Minor rock asteroid. Reticent politician. Experiment. Born: September 11, 1974, in a petri dish in an undisclosed lab in Sydney. Put Down: November 11, 2013, in Kookaburra, of acute Beckettian reticulosis, age 39.

Somewhere in the Australian outback
Did live a most astonishing creature
(We mean out back of the local Arthur Treacher's
For readers who, a sense of geography, lack).

He never dined on a bagel:
Anderson Fluffnagle.

Anderson wanted to live a dull life
Free from all emotional harassment, or worse;
But when you are a half man, the other half horse,
It is hard to avoid interpersonal strife.

Life is never fair, a-
Las (and alack, even) to your friendly neighbourhood chimera.

Ozzie scientists were concerned about the quick decline
Of a noble species
Whose numbers were in the feces –
The wild equine.

What can you do for an animal pwned?
Send in the clones.

Sadly, even the cloned horses seemed doomed.
Like something out of Timothy Findley,
Their hearts were weak, their legs spindly;
For them, extinction surely loomed.

Desperate times called out for desperate measures:
Should they give the clones the DNA of a species with feathers?

The Gesundheit Institute, in order to make the cloned horses more
hale,
Decided to mix in genes that were more robust.
After lots of experimentation, their choice was just
Between a man and a sperm whale.

The Institute did not have a big enough vat,
So that was that.

Anderson Fluffnagle was the first off the operating table.
A being that could run in the Preakness
That was also painfully aware of its own freakness
(But with health that was stable).

It was thought, for the common good,
He should lead a…sheltered childhood.

Young Anderson wanted to become a dentist.
And, although his medical board guardians did approve,
It's hard to hold a drill with hooves,
So, he never even made it to apprentice.

For a promising career you could lay a wreath,
But, honestly, what's with the obsession with teeth?

Because he sang with a delightful baritone,
Anderson was, for a short time, a vocalist for Midnight Oil.
An addiction to the demon hay his career did spoil,
And he was out before the band earned fame hard won.

All he had from this time were memories
Of strange, star-struck groupies.

Due to the strength of his pupick,
He thought he might play centaur ice.
But, because he was thumbily challenged, came unsolicited advice,
He could not hold a hockey stick

Under other circumstances, it may have been the beginning of an era,
Although, to be perfectly honest, he couldn't compete with Swedish hockey playing chimeras.

The country's Prime Minister John Howard
Became Anderson's close mentor,
Putting him up for a seat in Holbrooke Centaur
Even though he was not very forward.

Ever canny, Howard did realize
That on the horse-man's growing notoriety he could capitalize.

"Anderson is a strong candidate," Howard insisted.
"How many of us can plow our own field?
The voters, I believe, will yield,
To our law and order agenda, two-fisted!"

It was a time when politicians promised a Utopia,
Even if they could only deliver a threadbare cornucopia.

Anderson, frankly, expected a rout.
Though he did not like to mention
It, he hated being the dead centaur of attention
(Due to childhood teasing, no doubt).

Apparently voters liked his demeanour, shy,
And put him in office in an election, by-.

Anderson managed to sit out four terms,
Mostly quietly on the back benches.
He did not have the stomach for getting down and dirty in the political trenches,
And was finally undone when scientists came for samples of his sperm.

His enemies smelled blood
When he was asked to be put out to stud.

His supporters said this showed that he was virile.
But, he could not avoid
Bad press, tabloid.
And, the joke was on everybody – Anderson Fluffnagle turned out to be sterile!

His career spent,
To home in the outback for the rest of his life he went.

Somewhere high upon a molehill,
If you listen, if you work hard and strain,
It is said you can hear the sad refrain
Of Anderson Fluffnagle whinnying about Sartre still.

All we are left with is memories in an empty stall –
Perhaps they should have gone with the whale after all!

Andy Hystameen

Excerpted from the Duh paperback original Candid Chimera: The Saga of Anderson Fluffnagle. *"Some people's lives are a haiku," science fiction journalist Andy Hystameen wrote in his introduction to the book, "other people's lives are an epic poem destined to be handed down through the generations in oral form until a revolution in communications technology makes it possible for a broken telephone version to be set down for posterity. Anderson Fluffnagle's story lies somewhere between those two extremes..."*

Licence Provoked!

by SASKATCHEWAN KOLONOSCOGRAD, Alternate Reality News Service Existentialism Writer

Rensellaer Gundershaft tipped a cow. By which I do not mean that Rensellaer Gundershaft was served by a cow in a restaurant and gave the bovine waiter a gratuity. That would be absurd. No, I mean he snuck onto a farm in the middle of the night and gave a sleeping cow a gentle shove. When nothing came of that, he gave the cow a mighty heave and it fell on its side.

Thanks to Texas' three strikes law, that action could cause Rensellaer Gundershaft to permanently lose his Adult Licence.

"This is ridiculous!" said Gundershaft's public defender, Irina Goatslobbea. "The…the…umm…hold on, the argument is on the tip of my tongue…"

Texas citizens are issued an Adult Licence when they turn 18. The Licence looks like a driver's licence, except with the word driver scratched out and Adult written in crayon in its place (the legislation gave a very short window for implementation of the law; State Secretary of Leaving Childish Things Aside Fred Cocoa-Rayban assured the public that proper licences would be designed in time for the next Super Bowl).

A first offence earns a person a $5,000 fine and 30 Demerit points (named after Dedee Meritt, the Galveston dog and flu catcher who first proposed the law). A second offence earns a $10,000 fine and 47 Demerit points. A third offence, and you can kiss your adulthood goodbye. This may not seem like much of a problem, but, without an Adult Licence, you are not allowed to vote, you are not allowed to drive and you can only order kid's meals at restaurants.

In addition to the outright bans, social norms have been suspiciously quick in forming around the ID. Without an Adult Licence, people are less likely to take your political views seriously or want you to date their daughters. Highly suspiciously quick.

"I like to think that people recognize good policy when they see it," State Secretary Cocoa-Rayban stated. He added with a chuckle: "Although the pro-reform campaign from the Koched-Upton brothers over the last five years probably helped. A bit…"

Critics of the three strikes approach claims that it gives judges no discretion in borderline cases.

"When it comes to social behaviour, the law is a blunt instrument," explained legal expert Jonathan Turley. "Its application causes massive head trauma that will leave the patient – us, the people – fumbling for words and drinking out of a straw for many years afterwards. Is that the kind of society we want? I don't think so."

"The Adult Licencing rules aren't fair!" Gundershaft complained less…obliquely. Of course. People without an Adult Licence often say that. "No, seriously," Gundershaft continued, "I mean the rules aren't applied equally. If Governor Bloodnok's daughter was ever caught mooning the legislature, she'd get off with a fine and a warning."

"She was younger then," Texas Governor Denis Bloodnok responded to the allegation. "No point in ruining her life because of a minor indiscretion, wot?" When I pointed out that he seemed to be agreeing that the law was unfairly applied, Governor Bloodnok responded, "Of course the law is unfair. Life is unfair. Is it fair that I should be grilled – grilled, I say – by a journalist when I should be pardoning a turkey?" When I pointed out that it was April, Governor Bloodnok got red around the gills and responded, "Of course it is. Of course it is. Did I say it was a Thanksgiving turkey? Doesn't innocent poultry deserve to have their death penalties commuted at other times of the year?"

"The line between acceptable adult fun and childish behaviour is completely arbitrary," Goatslobbea finally recalled her argument. She pointed out that 97.666666666 (number may not be completely accurate due to Satanic rounding) of people who have lost their Adult Licences in the four months since the law came into effect do so within six months of receiving them. Then, since everything is easier to understand when it is put in the form of a list, she distributed the following to journalists and homeless men (often the same thing):

Legal Adult Fun: getting drunk and having sex with your neighbour's spouse. **Illegal Adult Fun:** getting drunk and putting a lampshade on your head.

Legal Adult Fun: surfing the Internet for porn. **Illegal Adult Fun:** surfing the Internet for LOLCats.

Legal Adult Fun: calling friends with threats of lawsuits if they don't mow their **lawn. Illegal Adult Fun:** calling strangers with pranks about running refrigerators.

Legal Adult Fun: harassing an ex-spouse with threatening emails. **Illegal Adult Fun:** posting information you know is bogus on Wikipedia for giggles.

Legal Adult Fun: adult diapers for incontinence. **Illegal Adult Fun:** adult diapers for sexual adventure.

Legal Adult Fun: banning books you don't like from libraries. **Illegal Adult Fun:** writing funny comments in the margins of library books you don't like.

"If the chart hasn't convinced you," Goatslobbea concluded, "I'm prepared to use musical dinner theatre!"

Is the Adult Licence, as Turley has argued, a massive intrusion in personal civil rights? "Don't be silly" State Secretary Cocoa-Rayban scoffed. "Everybody knows Republicans favour smaller government..."

Digital Gods: Appendix A: Digital Gods

The following is a partial list of the pantheon of digital gods explored in the book *Digital Gods: The Promise and Peril of Enterprise Solutions Worship in the Electronic Age*. Thanks to Harcourt Brace Jerselfovich for permission to republish this material.

Arrundel: The elder god, who makes electricity jump and guards the vault of the sacred zeroes and ones. It is said he can understand the most complex code just by holding it in his meaty paw. If this is true, he could fix any programme in an instant, but, it is said further, he cannot because of a vow he made never to interfere with the course of human programming destiny. Arrundel (known to some western worshippers as Aaron Dell), has inspired many colourful sayings, including "By the 27 hairs on Arrundel's chin!" and "By the dwarf stars that guide Arrundel's vision!" Although many of the other digital gods are jealous that all of the best oaths invoke his name, none will say so to his sternly lined face.

BuzzKejl: Is the god of digital aggression. He gets his strength from tribes of trolls and spammers who curry his favours with relentless online offerings, although he remains outwardly indifferent to them. BuzzKejl is a shapeshifter who appears different to everyone he meets: some see him as a demon with huge red horns and claws for hands; others see him as a demon in a bespoke suit with an attache case and a cruel smile. Whatever physical aspect he may take on, his eyes are always a living blue screen of death.

The Digital Dreamer: While the other gods of the pantheon are geared towards action, the Dreamer, whose name has been lost to the mists of non-digital memory, sits in a cave contemplating possibilities. Perhaps you would like to develop a wide readership by placing your writing on the Internet? He dreamed that for you. Perhaps you want to become famous by putting a video of your dog barfing up a myna bird on a social networking site? The Digital Dreamer saw that one coming. Be aware, though, that he is committed to the dream, not the achievement of the dream. The Digital Dreamer can be a bit of a prick that way.

Elspeth the Mysterious: She is a small, frail creature cloaked in stars and wearing a succession of masks that have only one thing in common: a single tear dropping from her left eye. Elspeth the Mysterious is said to represent those who do not use digital technology. All of the other gods in the digital pantheon, including the petulant XerXemanXander, the dour BuzzKejl and the positively gloomy Arrundell, make fun of her behind her back. If she notices their sport, she takes no notice of it.

ePik Flayel: Has red hair. Is left-handed. Had correctional surgery for his crossed eyes. He is, of course, the trickster god, the god of mischief. You know that email your boss sent you with crucial information about the project due two days ago that didn't get to you until yesterday? ePik Flayel loves that shit. Wonder why your favourite site stopped accepting your password? This god just wanted to see the look on your face. Stories of ePik Flayel teach us not to take our technologies too seriously. This is a god you can, if you have a mind to, have some fun with: did we mention that he is also the god of digital games?

Gigi: Is the goddess of digital design. She finds beauty in simplicity, and simplicity in beauty. Nobody really knows what this means, but they understand it when they see it. The goddess Gigi delights in elegant back end and navigational design, as well; she is deeper than many mortals give her credit for. If she looks a little harried, it is because she spends far too much time on help lines and far too little time pursuing her own design projects. Do not waste her time with trivial matters! A Gigi enraged is a terrifying vision, indeed.

Hotjax and Linda: Aah, the beautiful twins! Linda, standing tall, dark skin, dark hair, dark eyes. Hotjax, aah, Hotjax! Tall, blond, with curves that attract the eye and refuse to let it go. I want to give them the deed to my house, and I'm just thinking about them; imagine how powerful their actual presence would be! Hotjax and Linda are the twin gods of desire. People assume this means Internet pornography, but that is merely an odd manifestation of a strange cultural bias. Desire also includes online shopping; whenever you're on eBay and bid for an angora sweater three or four times more than what it is actually worth, one of these gods is guiding your hand.

Isadore Patrick Angel Pataki von Flempt: That buzzing you sometimes hear in your eyes? That could well be Isadore Patrick Angel Pataki von Flempt, the god of small things who most often appears in public in the body of a bee. There's no necessary significance to this; he's just always liked bees. Didn't you like certain airborne insects when you were young? You're in no position to judge. Anyway, as computer chips have gotten increasingly small, Isadore Patrick Angel Pataki von Flempt's power has gotten increasingly large. As has his ambition. If nanotechnology ever becomes widespread, this little god could become all-powerful!

Mithsorhitt: They say nobody who has looked upon the face of Mithsorhitt has had their hard drives live to tell the tale. So, umm, obviously, nobody knows what he, she, it or they really looks like. Mithsorhitt is the destroyer of information. When your browser crashes, losing the message you have so painstakingly written, or your entire computer freezes just as you are putting the finishing touches on that vital document, you can almost hear Mithsorhitt's satisfied burp. (It grows louder the less frequently you make back ups.) You would do well not to be angry with the digital god of destruction, though, no matter how great your loss: you wouldn't like him, her, it or them when he, she, it or they were hungry!

Phisysus: Is a giant god with two heads; which of his faces he turns to you depends upon whether you use a Mac or a PC. Because his two heads can rarely agree on anything, Phisysus is the god of self-loathing. Because his two heads imply making choices, when the Dimensional Portal™ made travel between universes possible, this and all of its related technologies were shunted into Phisysus' portfolio. As you might expect, he was of two minds on this subject.

Rory: He doesn't look like much, with his bland round face and hairline receding faster than the polar ice caps. He is soft-spoken and rarely gets flapped. People often mistake him for Stephen Tobolowsky, although without the actor's sexual charisma. Nobody is exactly sure what he brings to the pantheon, since he does not exercise any obvious powers, and, indeed, some of the other gods have long suspected that Rory is a digital god wannabe who got lucky. When they have the time, they will definitely ask Arrundel about him. Yes. They will. Definitely. When they have the time.

XerXemanXander: This god of portable digital devices (including but not limited to cellphones, game players, ebook readers, tablets and other technologies yet to be introduced into the market) has the body of a World Wrestling Whatever winner and the head of a three month old baby. You may be tempted to laugh when you see him. Do not. He has the attention span of a gnat and the temperament of a wounded jackal; XerXemanXander wants his new toy, and if he doesn't get it **NOW**, there will be hell to pay! If you are still inclined to laugh, consider this: when computer chips are implanted directly into our brains, XerXemanXander will be in our heads…

7. ALTERNATE HELP

Alternate Reality News Service Frequently Unasked Questions, v2

1) What is the circulation of the Alternate Reality News Service?
2) How many readers do you have?
3) Your weekend edition is so big, it crushed my Pomeranian Schnauzer! Is it any wonder you don't have more human readers?
4) How does the Alternate Reality News Service assign beats to its reporters?
5) Isn't that dangerous?
6) Still, couldn't multiple dart wounds cripple a new reporter?
7) Hey! What about the questionnaires? What happens to them?
8) Do you allow music in the bullpen when reporters are working?
9) What kind of music is played?
10) Does Brenda Brundtland-Govanni listen to music in her office?
11) Erm…uhh… How would you describe the relationship between the Alternate Reality News Service and the Transdimensional Authority?
12) Could you elaborate on that?
13) But, seriously, the relationship between the Alternate Reality News Service and the Transdimensional Authority is…?

14) I said: but, seriously, the relationship between the Alternate Reality News Service and the Transdimensional Authority is…?
15) Uhh…okay. Let me put it a different way. I…I've heard that there is tension between the Alternate Reality News Service and the Transdimensional Authority – is that true?
16) If Brenda Brundtland-Govanni was a tree, what kind of tree would she be?
17) That's not a tree!
18) Where do babies come from?
19) What is the Tech Answer Guy's marital status?
20) What does that mean?
21) That's not right. As somebody who has watched all of the episodes of *Star Blap: A Couple of Generations Later*, I happen to know that Klippon is actually a Ferlenghinghi word for "The dragon has been rooting around in the eaves trough again – we may have to move to another city!" Right?

1) What is the circulation of the Alternate Reality News Service?

Sclerotic.

2) How many readers do you have?

Twelve humans, 1,237 ring-tailed lemurs and 35 million Arrr'potax Arcelor. They really love us in Tau Ceti!

3) Your weekend edition is so big, it crushed my Pomeranian Schnauzer! Is it any wonder you don't have more human readers?

Dammit, Carborundurem-McVortvort, we told you we'd replace your damn dog with the primate of your choice, including copy editor! When will you let the incident go?

4) How does the Alternate Reality News Service assign beats to its reporters?

During the interview process, we ask potential reporters to fill out detailed Aptitude and Interest questionnaires. The A&Is give us a clear view of their background and what they would like to do. Then, we have successful candidates stand next to a dart board while Editrix-in-Chief Brenda Brundtland-Govanni throws darts at them. (The dart board is there to give the office a Ukrainian pub feel.) The noise the new journalist makes when the dart hits him or her is compared to a list of potential beats, and the one it sounds the most like is the one the person is given.

5) Isn't that dangerous?

Brenda Brundtland-Govanni doesn't aim for any vital organs, and we haven't lost any reporters yet, so, on the whole, no. And, the process does have the added advantage of teaching reporters their first lesson about keeping on their toes.

6) Still, couldn't multiple dart wounds cripple a new reporter?

Oh, that hardly ever happens! The Alternate Reality News Service takes a very generous attitude towards beat creation and phonetics. The only exception was Dimsum Agglomeratizatonalisticalism, whose nine responses to being hit with darts included "Urk!" "Ack!" and, "What the frack! Why don't you get somebody who actually knows how to throw darts to do this?" Apparently, Brenda Brundtland-Govanni put her through this because, in her interview, she had made a disparaging off-hand remark about wing-tipped shoes. She didn't know. As it happens, they're now the best of friends who laugh at the incident. At least, Agglomeratizatonalisticalism will laugh at the incident if her upper lip ever heals.

7) Hey! What about the questionnaires? What happens to them?

The questionnaires are given to Pops Moobley to insulate his hay loft. It's a big, drafty old place, and we can never interview enough possible reporters to keep it warm.

8) Do you allow music in the bullpen when reporters are working?

Absolutely. The Alternate Reality News Service believes that it is important to create a good working environment for our staff.

9) What kind of music is played?

Gregorian chanting, mostly, interspersed by the occasional number by The Smiths.

10) Does Brenda Brundtland-Govanni listen to music in her office?

She listens to a loop of the cries of kittens in distress and airplane crashes. Does that count as music?

11) Erm…uhh… How would you describe the relationship between the Alternate Reality News Service and the Transdimensional Authority?

Prehensile.

12) Could you elaborate on that?

Of course. Prehensile means before the man who created the Muppets was born.

13) But, seriously, the relationship between the Alternate Reality News Service and the Transdimensional Authority is…?

Prettier when looked at from a distance.

14) I said: but, seriously, the relationship between the Alternate Reality News Service and the Transdimensional Authority is…?

We tell them what to do and they tell us where to go.

15) Uhh…okay. Let me put it a different way. I…I've heard that there is tension between the Alternate Reality News Service and the Transdimensional Authority – is that true?

You're just not going to let this go, are you? Okay, the Alternate Reality News Service has a professional relationship with the Transdimensional Authority. We uncover the dirt about them, and they are stinky boogerheads about it. We have, on occasion, been accused of twisting the words of a Transdimensional Authority investigator; in our defense, they tend to be really boring words.

16) If Brenda Brundtland-Govanni was a tree, what kind of tree would she be?

A bazooka.

17) That's not a tree!

You wanna tell *her* that?

18) Where do babies come from?

Interns.

19) What is the Tech Answer Guy's marital status?

Ferlenghinghi.

20) What does that mean?

Ferlenghinghi is a Klippon word for "mind your own business."

21) That's not right. As somebody who has watched all of the episodes of *Star Blap: A Couple of Generations Later*, I happen to know that Klippon is actually a Ferlenghinghi word for "The dragon has been rooting around in the eaves trough again – we may have to move to another city!" Right?

Science fiction fans are awesome. And, scary. Sometimes. But, mostly, awesome.

ALTERNATE INDEX

ALTERNATE ABOUT THE AUTHOR

This is the fourth Alternate Reality News Service book. Do you expect me to believe that you don't know who Ira Nayman is by now? That you don't know that he has been writing humour since he was eight years old? That the other books in the series are: *Alternate Reality Ain't What It Used To Be*; *What Were Once Miracles Are Now Children's Toys*, and; *Luna for the Lunies!*? That his first novel, *Welcome to the Multiverse** has been published by Elsewhen Press? That his Web site of political and social satire and surreal cartoons, *Les Pages aux Folles* (http://www.lespagesauxfolles.ca) is over a decade old? That he won the 2010 Swift Satire Writing Competition?

Well…now you know.

**Sorry for the Inconvenience*

ALTERNATE ABOUT THE AUTHOR

ALSO BY THE AUTHOR

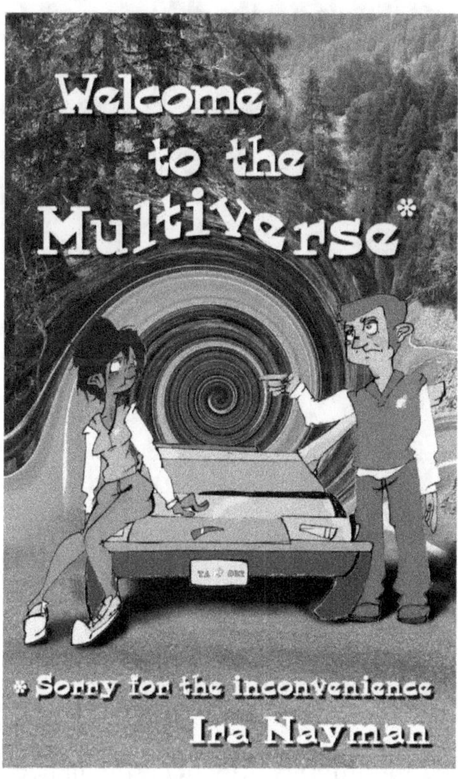

*Welcome to the Multiverse** is the first novel by the creator of the Alternate Reality News Service! Noomi Rapier, fresh out of the Alternaut Academy, joins with veteran Transdimensional Authority investigator “Crash” Chumley for her first case. But is she ready to confront…herself?

“[O]ne of the funniest sci-fi books I’ve ever read.” (Seregil of Rhiminee, *Rising Shadow*)

“Welcome to the Multiverse is a cracking read that almost had me in stitches, fresh and original humour from a comedy genius.” (Antony Jones, *SF Book Reviews*)

* *Sorry for the Inconvenience*

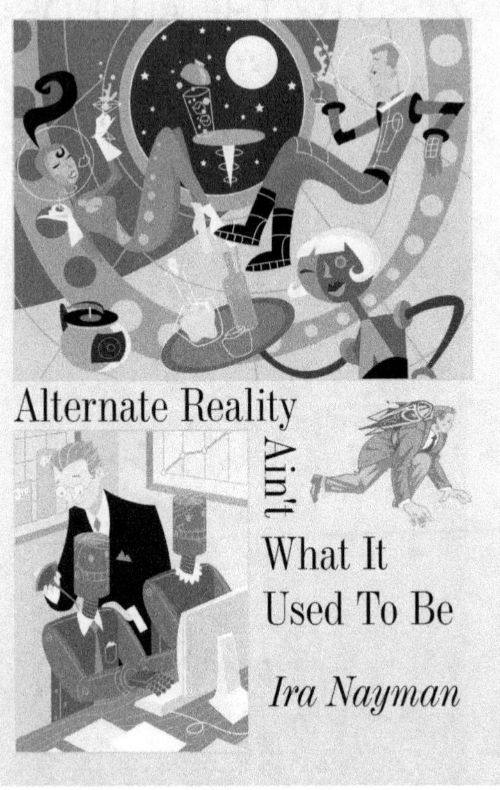

A woman is sued for alimony…by her AI enhanced service android! High school history class is proven conclusively to be boring…by science! The United States government thinks it can end the war in Iraq by allying itself with…the Democratic Union of Great Old Ones (a rebranding of demons from another dimension)! All this and so much more can be found in *Alternate Reality Ain't What It Used To Be*, the first Alternate Reality News Service book!

"[O]ne of my favorite books of 2008…" (Charles de Lint, *Fantasy and Science Fiction Magazine*)

"Ira Nayman has a genius for pulling zany ideas out of the ether and populating his books with them." (Geoff Nelder, *The Compulsive Reader*)

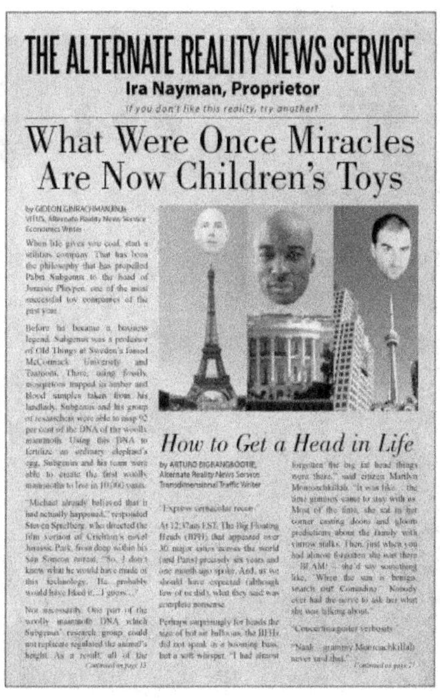

THE ALTERNATE REALITY NEWS SERVICE

Ira Nayman, Proprietor

If you don't like this reality, try another!

What Were Once Miracles Are Now Children's Toys

How to Get a Head in Life

by ARTURO BIGRANGBOOTIE, Alternate Reality News Service Transdimensional Traffic Writer

Giant heads appear over monuments throughout the world…and France! War between the United States and China is averted…because the Asian country repossesses America's military to pay off its debts! Attempts to recreate wooly mammoths from fossilized DNA are successful…except they're the size of a small housecat! The multiverse gets stranger in *What Were Once Miracles Are Now Children's Toys*, the second collection of Alternate Reality News Service articles.

"Nothing is without the potential for humor in Nayman's mindset, and he twists, puns, and snarks his way through the morass of human life, helping us laugh at the sometimes utterly ridiculous world around us. Be prepared to laugh when reading *What Were Once Miracles Are Now Children's Toys*." (John Ottinger III, *Grasping for the Wind*)

Luna for the Lunies!, the third collection of Alternate Reality News Service articles, features: a poem about a violent coffeemaker; an app that sends teens a fake phone call when it appears that they are about to get lectured by their parents, and; a report on the expedition to find the Chinese butterfly that is causing hurricanes in the United States. If you don't like this reality, try another one…or 80!

"Ira takes a wickedly dry sense of humor and rips apart the popular culture, politics, and technology of our modern world through a series of satirical articles that range in size from a handful of sentences to pages in length, and believe me when I say that no one and nothing is spared. It is a laughter inducing indictment of our society and I loved it." (Eric Swett, *My Writer's Cramp* Web site)

www.ingramcontent.com/pod-product-compliance
Lightning Source LLC
LaVergne TN
LVHW051500080426
835509LV00017B/1839

* 9 7 8 0 9 8 7 6 9 9 6 3 3 *